The Middle East

ORYX INTERNATIONAL GOVERNMENT & POLITICS SERIES

Central and Eastern Europe by John Dornberg

Western Europe by John Dornberg

The Middle East by Dilip Hiro

Africa by Edward Bever

R

The Middle East

International Government & Politics Series

by
Dilip Hiro

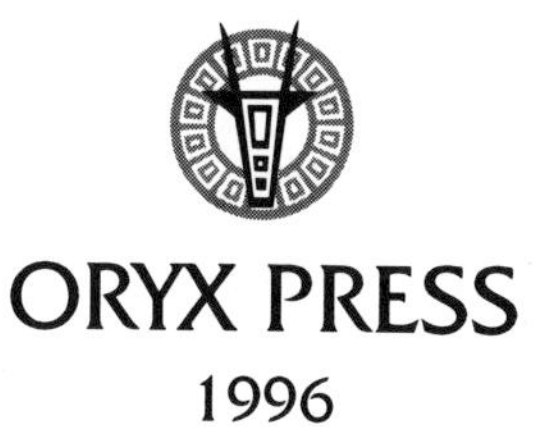

ORYX PRESS
1996

The rare Arabian Oryx is believed to have inspired the myth of the unicorn. This desert antelope became virtually extinct in the early 1960s. At that time several groups of international conservationists arranged to have 9 animals sent to the Phoenix Zoo to be the nucleus of a captive breeding herd. Today the Oryx population is over 1000, and over 500 have been returned to the Middle East.

Published by The Oryx Press
4041 North Central at Indian School Road
Phoenix, Arizona 85012-3397

Published simultaneously in Canada
Printed and Bound in the United States of America

∞ The paper used in this publication meets the minimum requirements of American National Standard for Information Science—Permanence of Paper for Printed Library Materials, ANSI Z39.48, 1984.

Library of Congress Cataloging-in-Publication Data

Hiro, Dilip.
The Middle East / by Dilip Hiro.
p. cm. — (International government & politics series)
Includes bibliographical references and index.
ISBN 0-57356-004-9 (pbk.)
1. Middle East—Politics and government. I. Title II. Series
DS63.1.H574 1996
320.956—dc20 96-12397
CIP

CONTENTS

LIST OF MAPS

Maps prepared by Suresh Vedak

PREFACE

The Middle East is a region with flexible boundaries. In its widest sense, the term applies to the area from Morocco to Pakistan, and from Turkey to Sudan. In its narrowest sense, it excludes not only the non-Arabic-speaking countries like Pakistan and Turkey, but also Arab North Africa.

One way to arrive at a working definition is to think of the Middle East as composed of a core and peripheries. The core includes Egypt, the Fertile Crescent countries (Iraq, Syria, Lebanon, Jordan, Israel, and the Palestinian-inhabited West Bank and Gaza Strip), the countries of the Arabian Peninsula (Kuwait, Bahrain, Qatar, the United Arab Emirates, Oman, Yemen, and Saudi Arabia), and Iran. To the south of this core lies Sudan; to its west the North African states of Libya, Algeria, Tunisia, and Morocco; and to its north and east Cyprus, Turkey, Armenia, Azerbaijan, Turkmenistan, Afghanistan, and Pakistan.

This book deals with the core of the Middle East and Turkey. It covers 15 states: Bahrain, Egypt, Iran, Iraq, Israel, Jordan, Kuwait, Lebanon, Oman, Qatar, Saudi Arabia, Syria, Turkey, the United Arab Emirates, and Yemen. Because Israel evolved out of Palestine in 1948, a chapter on Palestine and the Palestinians is also included.

WHY STUDY THE MIDDLE EAST?

There are compelling geographical, historical, political, economic, and cultural reasons why a study of the Middle East should matter to young Americans.

With a total area of more than 2.8 million square miles, the Middle East and Turkey are as large as the United States without Alaska. They form the central region of the Eastern Hemisphere where Africa, Asia, and Europe meet. As a crossroad between the European West and the Asian East, the region remains strategically important. This is partly why the U.S. has maintained its Sixth Fleet in the Mediterranean since the end of World War II in 1945.

The Middle East has produced the world's leading monotheistic faiths: Judaism, Christianity, and Islam. The Old Testament, the

New Testament, and the Koran are all rooted in Middle Eastern soil. Since most Americans have Christian backgrounds and grow up in a Judeo-Christian environment, a study of the Middle East and its history is a means of acquiring self-knowledge.

Two of the world's most ancient civilizations—the Egyptian and the Mesopotamian—originated in the Middle East. Egypt has one of the longest recorded histories in the world. The Mesopotamian plain, lying between the Euphrates and Tigris rivers, is the cradle of human civilization, with a history stretching back some 12,000 years. The earliest settled agrarian society evolved here.

The Middle East contains two-thirds of global petroleum reserves. At the current rate of extraction, these will last well into the late twenty-first century. Because the U.S. depends on oil imports from the Middle East, and because U.S. reserves will be depleted within a decade, what happens in the region is of vital significance to Americans. Petroleum is not only the source of gasoline for cars, but also of asphalt for road construction, fertilizers for agriculture, heating oil, jet fuel for aircraft, paints for domestic and other purposes, plastics, and synthetic rubber.

Since the end of World War II, the Middle East has been the most volatile region on the planet. It has witnessed numerous conventional wars, revolutions, and coups, and much civil unrest. Because they caused shifts in the international balance of power in a world dominated by the U.S. and the Soviet Union, these conflicts mattered to the American government and people. They also affected, directly or indirectly, oil supplies and prices. The 1979 Islamic revolution in Iran, for instance, resulted in the doubling of petroleum prices.

Middle Eastern events have twice influenced American presidential elections. One of the main reasons Democratic President Jimmy Carter (1924 –) lost his campaign for re-election in 1980 was his failure to free the American hostages held by Iran. After his victory in the Gulf War between the United States-led coalition and Iraq in March 1991, President George Bush (1924 –), a Republican, became so popular that his re-election in 1992 seemed assured. This perception discouraged leading Democratic politicians from entering the race for their party's nomination, and inadvertently paved the way for the election as president of a comparatively unknown governor of Arkansas, Bill Clinton (1946–).

The Middle East has been the setting for five major military confrontations since the end of World War II, the latest being the Gulf War. The U.S. dispatched over 550,000 troops to the Persian Gulf—more than it had in Vietnam at the peak of fighting. The armed conflict between Iraq and Iran, lasting from 1980 to 1988, was the longest conventional war in the twentieth century. When the Persian Gulf became a scene of warfare, oil tankers became vulnerable—a third of world petroleum supplies pass through the narrow Straits of Hormuz. This threat to world oil supplies is one of the major reasons why President Clinton established the Fifth Fleet in 1995 for permanent stationing in the Persian Gulf.

ORGANIZATION OF THIS BOOK

The Middle East is divided into two parts. In Part 1, I discuss major regional themes—starting with monotheism. I then assess the strategic importance of the area before turning to its oil riches, and the degree to which the West is dependent on its petroleum. In the remainder of Part 1, I explore the internal dynamics of the region, beginning with the history of the Arab-Jew conflict. I next describe the division within the Arab world, which culminated in the Iraqi invasion of Kuwait in 1990. While progress has been made towards peace between Israel and its Arab neighbors in the 1990s, the decade has also seen the rise of Jewish and Islamic fundamentalism in the area. Therefore, the future for a lasting, comprehensive peace in the region remains uncertain.

In Part 2, I discuss each state or territory separately. In every case, I start with a basic profile of the country, and then give an account of its political and economic history.

Because the histories of most of these countries are interlinked, some overlap in the narrative is inevitable. However, I have avoided, as far as possible, repeating information or insights.

I use the terms "Gulf" and "Persian Gulf," also called "Arabian Gulf," interchangeably. To help the reader place a political leader in time, I state in parentheses—following the first mention of his or her name—the birth and death dates for nonhereditary rulers, and the years of reign for hereditary rulers. I use the suffix A.D. only for the first millennium.

Dilip Hiro

PART 1

The Region

CHAPTER 1

Cradle of Monotheism: Judaism, Christianity, and Islam

Today's major world religions emerged either in India or the Middle East. India offered the world Hinduism and Buddhism, and the Middle East gave birth to Judaism, Christianity, and Islam. Just as Buddhism arose out of Hinduism, so Christianity and Islam arose out of Judaism. Sometimes Judaism, Christianity, and Islam are collectively called Abrahamic faiths, because Abraham was the first prophet to preach monotheism, belief in one God.

JUDAISM

Judaism, the first monotheistic creed, is a compendium of law, tradition, and doctrine that evolved in stages, starting with the prophet Abraham. He was the leader of a nomadic Hebrew tribe that moved west from Mesopotamia, modern Iraq, around 1900 B.C. Son of an idol-maker, Abraham smashed his father's idols and proclaimed faith in the one and only God, whose image was not to be cast.

According to the Book of Genesis of the Old Testament, Abraham had an encounter with the Lord God when he was in the land of Haran, present-day southern Turkey. The Lord God made a covenant with Abraham, and said, "I will make you exceedingly fruitful; and I will make nations of you and kings shall come forth from you. And I will establish my covenant between me and you and your descendants after you throughout their generations for an everlasting covenant, to be God to you and your descendants after you." The first son to be born to Abraham was by Hagar, a maid to the family, and was called Ishmael/Ismail. Later came another son, named Yitzhak/Isaac, by Sarah, his wife.

As Abraham and his entourage passed Shechem, near today's West Bank city of Nablus, God appeared to Abraham, and said: "Unto thy seed I will give this land." Shechem was then part of the land of the Canaanites whose occupation of the region—covering present-day Israel, the West Bank, and southern Lebanon—went back to about 4000 B.C. Abraham finally settled near Hebron where he acquired some land. According to the Book of Genesis, God renewed His original promise to Abraham, the Covenant, with Abraham's son, Isaac, and his grandson, Jacob, who later received the name Israel, which means "prevailing with God." Jacob had 12 sons from whom arose the 12 tribes of Israel. He tried to settle in Shechem, but the local residents objected.

Later, following a widespread famine in the area, Joseph, a favored son of Jacob, led the tribes of Israel into the fertile Nile valley in Egypt. Here the tribes of Israel tended their flocks and prospered until a pharaoh of Egypt enslaved them in about 1700 B.C. Known by now as Beni Israel, that is, "children of Israel" or Israelites, they endured this condition until the mid-thirteenth century B.C. when God called on Moses to lead them out of Egypt. The Israelites then escaped into the Sinai Desert.

During their 40 years of wandering in the Sinai, God gave them the Law through Moses. The Law, with its stress on virtuous action, provided a strong ethical foundation for Israelite beliefs. Moses initiated the Israelites into the worship of the one God, called Jehovah or Yehovah (a derivative of YHVH in Hebrew).

The teachings of Moses were the formal beginning of monotheism. Israelites then began to enter the "promised" land of Canaan from the east, under the leadership of Joshua, the successor to Moses. They settled in the hilly area along the Jordan River, and intermixed with their neighbors, the Maobites. The Israelites were a confederation of tribes led by Judges, such as Gideon and Samson. The Israelites set up altars and sanctuaries in Canaan, with the revered Ark of the Covenant deposited at Shilo. (The Ark was the sacred wooden chest that represented for the Israelites the Covenant and God's presence among them.) As the Israelites spread over Canaan, they came into conflict with the Philistines—who had come originally from Crete and the islands of the Aegan Sea—as the latter began expanding their base from the coastal plain. Supported by the Hebrew tribes who had stayed behind at the time of the great famine several centuries before, the Israelites began confronting the Philistines. In the mid-eleventh century B.C., the Hebrew-Israelites defeated the Philistines.

Around 1030 B.C., they consolidated their gains by founding a state based on the monotheistic religion of Jehovah, with Saul as king. David (ca. 1010–970 B.C), a son of Jesse of Bethlehem, destroyed the last bastion of Philistine power in the region, and established three more Hebrew provinces to the east of the Jordan River. Taken together, King David's domain was known as Eretz Israel ("Land of Israel"). David brought the Ark of the Covenant from Shilo to his capital of Jerusalem, as a shrine for the God of Israel. David's son Solomon (ca. 970–931 B.C.) built the First Temple in Jerusalem.

After Solomon's death, opposition to dynastic rule led to the breakaway of the northern tribes. They called their domain Israel. The southern remnant of Solomon's kingdom, now named Judah, was ruled from Jerusalem by King David's descendants.

During the eighth century B.C., the prophet Amos declared that violations of the moral-ethical code of the Covenant would bring the wrath of God upon the Israelites. In 721 B.C., Israel fell to Assyria, a powerful kingdom to the northeast in Mesopotamia, and many Israelites were expelled from their homeland.

Judah continued to exist; but from 605 B.C., its people, practicing Judaism and called Jews, were exiled by the army of Babylonia, a kingdom in present-day Iraq. Finally, in 586 B.C., the king of Babylonia, Nebuchadnezzar (605–562 B.C.), destroyed Jerusalem and the First Temple, and expelled the Jews, carrying many off to captivity in Babylon. King Cyrus the Elder (550–529 B.C.) of Persia captured Jerusalem in 537 B.C. and allowed the Jews to return. They began constructing the Second Temple and finished it in 515 B.C.

Although the new Covenant of God, promising a kingdom under a descendant of King David, was not fulfilled, King Artaxerxes (464–424 B.C.) of Persia declared the Torah, the first five books of the Old Testament (also known collectively as the Pentateuch), to be the law for Jews. The conquest of the region in 333 B.C. by Alexander the Great (363–323 B.C.), ruler of the Greek kingdom of Macedonia, marked the emergence of Hellenistic Judaism. This was a synthesis of two contrasting cultures: the inclusive, tolerant way of life of Greece, as lived in Athens during the fifth century B.C., and a demanding, exclusivist way of life as prescribed by the Old Testament, the Hebrew Bible.

The banning of Judaism by the Greek ruler, Antiochus IV (175–163 B.C.), in 168 B.C. resulted in the Jewish revolt of 166 B.C. led by Judas Maccabaeus of the Hasmonean family. He succeeded in gaining religious freedom for Jews three years later, but not political freedom. In his attempt to secure the latter, he was killed in 160 B.C. The Jewish commonwealth was revived under Jonathan in 152 B.C. However, with the Torah, written originally in Hebrew, now translated into Greek, Hellenization of Judaism continued.

In 63 B.C., the Roman general Pompey captured the region, named it Judea, and incorporated it into the Roman Empire. Various attempts by Jews to set up an independent Jewish state failed.

Following the death of Jesus (ca. 6 B.C.–28 A.D.), Christianity emerged initially as a sect within Judaism. Restrictive decrees from Rome led to a Jewish revolt in 66–70 A.D., during which the Second Temple was destroyed and the Jews were expelled and scattered across the Roman Empire. Although many Jewish communities existed for centuries in the Middle East, around the Mediterranean, and across Europe, no Jewish state existed until the founding of Israel in the twentieth century except the Khazar (Jewish) kingdom in the Caucasian region between the Caspian and Black Seas from 740 A.D. to 965 A.D.

CHRISTIANITY

Christianity arose out of the birth, crucifixion, and teachings of Jesus, a carpenter from Nazareth, a settlement in the Roman province of Galilee. Born a Jew, Jesus was acclaimed as the Christ—a Greek term meaning "Anointed"—by his principal followers, called the Apostles, who were also Jewish. They regarded Jesus as the Christ who had been sent to earth as part of God's earlier covenants with Abraham, Isaac, and Jacob. Thus, Christianity was considered a Jewish sect.

Following the failed Jewish uprising against Rome in 66–70 A.D., the Jewish element within the Christian community withered. Those believing in the one eternal truth and salvation, as laid down by Christ, followed the rites prescribed by him—especially baptism and the Eucharist. The latter consisted of the consecration and distribution of bread and wine, symbolizing the body and blood of Christ offered in sacrifice.

After the death of Christ, his teachings were assembled and compiled into four books called Gospels, which form the early part of the New Testament in the Christian Bible. While the Apostle Peter exercised religious authority, the Apostle Paul spread Christ's teachings among non-Jews. Christianity evolved as a well-organized religion, and Roman officials felt threatened by it. The pagans hated its monotheistic doctrine and persecuted the early Christians. The situation changed in 313 A.D. when Roman Emperor Constantine I adopted Christianity and made it the state religion.

The breakup of the Roman Empire in 395 A.D. into Western and Eastern sections underminded the unity of the Christian Church. After 325 A.D., various Church councils were held to officially settle controversies. Such a council produced the dogma of the Trinity—the Father (God), the Son (Christ), and the Holy Ghost/Spirit—in the sixth century A.D. Increasingly, the Church was racked by differences on such issues as the number of natures Christ possessed (divine, or divine and human), and the relationship of the Holy Spirit to the Father and the Son. Also, following the barbarian attacks on the Western Roman Empire in the fifth century A.D., the Church, led by the pope in Rome, with Latin as the official language, came to fill the resulting political vacuum. In contrast, in the Eastern Roman Empire, the Byzantine rulers controlled a Church led by the patriarch in Constantinople (now Istanbul), and using Greek as its official language.

Guided by Rome and Constantinople, Christian monks spread the faith among pagans all over Europe. They also made progress in Turkey, North Africa, and the Middle East, but failed to hold on to their gains against the rise of Islam in these regions. After the seventh century A.D., Christians were a minority in the Middle East and North Africa.

ISLAM

The last of the leading monotheistic religions, Islam (Arabic meaning "submission" [to God's will]), draws upon Judaism and Christianity. It was founded by the prophet Muhammad ibn Abdullah (570–632 A.D.), who was born in Mecca, a trading post in western Arabia, into the Hashem clan of the merchant tribe of Quraish, at a time when Judaism and Christianity existed in Arabia and the surrounding lands. Those who follow Islam are called Muslims. They believe that as the last prophet of monotheism, Muhammad synthesized what had been divinely revealed before.

When Muhammad was about 40, his introverted, religious nature drove him to periodic retreats to a cave in the hills near Mecca to engage in solitary contemplation. In the course of these retreats, the first divine revelation "came down" to him on the night of 26–27 Ramadan, the ninth month of the Islamic lunar calendar. In 613 A.D., Muhammad began to preach these revelations to a small group of relatives and friends. His message was to abandon all forms of idolatory and surrender completely to the omniscient, omnipotent, and compassionate God.

Because Muhammad's monotheistic teachings ran counter to the polytheistic idol worship practiced in Mecca and elsewhere in Arabia, his teachings proved unpopular. The growing local hostility made the life of Muhammad and his small band of followers unbearable.

In 622 A.D., they left Mecca for Medina, an oasis town about 300 miles to the northeast. Here the feuding tribes of Aus and Khazraj welcomed Muhammad as an arbiter. Their subsequent acceptance of Islam enabled the tribes of Medina to live in peace as fellow Muslims.

Muhammad became the civil and military governor of Medina, and laid the foundation of the Realm of Islam, based on the Constitution of Medina. Following a series of military victories, Muhammad expanded his domain, and defeated the residents of Mecca in 630 A.D. He entered Mecca at the head of an army of 10,000, and had the town's collection of 360 stone idols overturned from their pedestals. He touched the sacred Black Stone, called the Kaaba, with his stick, and shouted "Allahu Akbar" ("God is Great"), the victorious cry of Islam.

The ranks of Muhammad's followers swelled as the polytheist nomads converted to Islam in droves. Muhammad welcomed them, aware that the fledgling state of Medina needed all the protection it could gather in order to survive his death.

While Muhammad was alive, his divine revelations, delivered in rhythmic prose, were taken down by his followers on palm leaves, camel bones, or patches of leather. After his demise, these were compiled into 114 chapters of varying length to form a book of 6,616 verses, called the Quran/Koran (Arabic for "Recitation" or "Discourse"). Judaism and Christianity appear many times in the divine revelations to Muhammad, and there are numerous references in the Koran to Abraham, Moses, and Jesus. There was also an oral record of what Muhammad had done and said, especially as an administrator, legislator, judge, and military commander. Following his death, elaborate means were used to collect his sayings and doings, which were called the Sunna ("Practice"). Later, 2,700 sayings and doings of Muhammad were codified and published in six canonical collections called the Hadith ("Report"). Together, the Koran and the Hadith form the Sharia ("Way" or "Road"), the Islamic Law.

After Muhammad's death, his duties were assumed by his viceregent, the caliph Abu Bakr, who died in 634 A.D. He was followed by Omar, who ruled for 10 years, and Othman, who was assassinated in 656 A.D. by rebels who accused him of maladministration. During the reign of Omar and Othman, the Islamic state expanded far beyond the Arabian Peninsula, with local governors administering its distant parts, including Syria.

The rule of Caliph Ali, a cousin and son-in-law of Muhammad, was challenged by Muwaiya, the governor of Syria, in 660 A.D. A civil war ensued, dividing Islam into factions. Those who sided with Ali came to be called Shiat Ali, the Followers of Ali. Their opponents, who backed Muwaiya, were later named, rather misleadingly, Sunnis, the followers of *sunna*, social practices inherited from ancestors. Those who took neither side were called Kharajis, meaning Seceders.

Despite these divisions, the spread of Islam was rapid during the two centuries after Muhammad's death, reaching central France in 732 A.D. via North Africa. After defeat by the Franks led by Charles Martel, Muslim Arabs retreated from France, but kept control of North Africa and most of the Iberian Peninsula.

The Islamic empires that emerged in Damascus (Umayyad 661–750), Baghdad (Abbasid 751–1258), Cairo (Mamluke 1250–1517), and Constantinople (Ottoman 1517–1918) followed roughly the model of Muhammad's realm in Medina.

THE MONOTHEISTIC FAITHS

Whereas Islam is related to Judaism and Christianity, it evolved differently from them. Unlike Moses and Jesus, Muhammad founded a state and ruled it, so Islam became interlinked with the state. Its prophet acted as the military commander, made war and peace, collected taxes, laid down the law, and dispensed justice. In contrast, Jesus Christ differentiated between what belonged to God and what belong to Caesar. Since then, Christianity has recognized two separate authorities: Church and State. They exist sometimes in harmony and sometimes in conflict.

With Judaism, the situation is unclear. Rabbinical Judaism arose only after the Jewish state had ceased to exist in 70 A.D. Therefore, Judaism falls between Islam and Christianity when it comes to defining relations between religion and the state.

Islamic scholars argue that the covenant the Lord God made with Abraham applied to all his "nations"—the descendants of Isaac (Israelites and Christians) and those of Ishmael (Arabs). Because Muhammad was descended from Ishmael, they argue that the Muslims are coheirs to the Covenant of Abraham.

All three monotheistic religions regard Jerusalem as holy. For Jews, it is the site of the First and Second Temples, where the Western Wall, a remnant of the Second Temple, still survives. For Christians, it is where the Church of the Holy Sepulcher was built over the supposed burial place of Jesus Christ in 335 A.D. For Muslims, it is the point from where Muhammad undertook his "Night Journey" to heaven. There he encountered the earlier prophets of monotheism, including Adam, Noah, Abraham, Isaac, Jacob, Moses, and Jesus. At the site of the Sacred Rock, where Muhammad was believed to have been carried on a winged animal on the night of his ascent to heaven, a mosque was built by Caliph Abdul Malik ibn Marwan (684–705 A.D.) in 691 A.D., and called the Dome of the Rock. These three holy shrines are contained today in the walled Old City of Jerusalem, which covers only about one-half square mile.

By outlining the historic evolution of the three major monotheistic faiths, this account points up their unity. Yet, in reality, conflict has dogged the chronicles of these religions far more than harmony. This has happened mainly because each of them (especially Christianity and Islam, which were adopted as state religions) became intertwined with the fate of the ruling dynasties in a region that lies at the heart of the Old World.

CHAPTER 2

A Strategic Bridge and Highway

TRADE ROUTES

The strategic importance of the Middle East stems from its position as the meeting point of Africa, Eurasia, and the Mediterranean region. Before the arrival of the railroad in the mid-nineteenth century, animals or watercraft were used to carry people and goods across land or water. Overland transportation by caravans of camels, horses, or mules is slower and dearer than transport or travel by water. In that respect, the Middle East has an advantage over all other regions of the Old World because it is the near-meeting point of the Red Sea, an extension of the Indian Ocean, and the Mediterranean Sea, an extension of the Atlantic Ocean. The two seas are separated only by the narrow isthmus of Suez. The distance between Gaza, the most southeastern point of the Mediterranean Sea, and Aqaba, at the head of the Gulf of Aqaba, a more eastward extension of the Red Sea, is not much longer than the Suez isthmus.

The land between the Mediterranean Sea and the head of the Persian Gulf can also be seen as an isthmus. Although longer than the isthmus of Suez or the Gaza-Aqaba route, the distance was short enough for ancient traders to develop it as a thriving trade route. Alexander the Great, among the early conquerors, realized the potential of the region as a commercial crossroad. His occupation of Palestine in 333 B.C. underlined the economic importance of the area.

Earlier, Egyptian Pharaoh Necho II had connected the head of the Nile Delta with the head of the Gulf of Suez by cutting a canal to create an indirect link between the Mediterranean Sea and the Red Sea. The canal was kept open for most of the next 800 years, until the early fifth century A.D. By then, the Middle East contained the main overland trading routes between Europe and south and east Asia, and had emerged as a zone of commercial importance. Control of these routes became a much-coveted prize for competing empires both inside and outside the region.

In 1497, the Portuguese discovery of a sea route around the Cape of Good Hope, the southernmost tip of Africa, connected Western Europe with India and lands further east and somewhat reduced the significance of the

Middle East. Yet, three centuries later, the French general Napoleon Bonaparte chose to attack Egypt as the first step toward the conquest of British India.

THE TWENTIETH CENTURY

The Middle East maintained its supremacy as the leading commercial crossroad of the Old World in part because of the political unity it enjoyed under the Ottoman Empire (1517-1918). At the turn of the nineteenth century, the land from Turkish Anatolia to Arab Egypt was free of national borders. People and goods moved freely to most destinations in the Empire from Greater/Natural Syria—a region bordered by the Taurus Mountains to the north, the Mediterranean to the west, the Arabian desert to the south, and the Euphrates River to the east. The ports of Tripoli, Beirut, and Alexandria thrived. The Syrian capital, Damascus, handled trade for Transjordan, Palestine, the central Arabian region of Najd, and the western Arabian region of Hijaz. The northern Syrian port of Aleppo served a vast hinterland, covering Anatolia, the Mosul area in northern Iraq, Mesopotomia, and Persia.

There are several reasons why the Middle East is still of great strategic and economic importance in the late twentieth century. Once the Mediterranean Sea and the Red Sea were connected directly by the Suez Canal in 1869, the Middle East regained its position as the foremost intercontinental highway. The Suez Canal, as an international waterway open to all countries, continues to hold that position today. Due to the discovery of vast reserves of petroleum in the countries surrounding the Persian Gulf in the first half of the twentieth century, and the accelerated extraction of these reserves in the second half of the century, the economic clout of the area has risen sharply. Finally, the advent of air travel has not diminished the strategic importance of the Middle East. The routes connecting North America and Europe with southern and southeastern Asia and Australia pass through the region. The Middle East is thus a link between the earth's most populous areas: the North Atlantic basin and southern and southeastern Asia.

Among the countries covered by this book, Turkey well illustrates the region's strategic significance. Turkey's hinterland of Anatolia is in Asia, but its commercial heart is in Istanbul, a city that spans Europe and Asia. Until the collapse of the Soviet Union in 1991, Turkey shared borders with it. For these geopolitical reasons, the Western powers accepted Turkey as a member of the North Atlantic Treaty Organization (NATO) in 1952, admitted it to the Council of Europe, and granted it associate membership in the European Economic Community (now the European Union). When, in the 1970s and 1980s, the civil conflict in Lebanon and the war between Iran and Iraq deprived Baghdad of its outlets for oil in the Mediterranean Sea and the Persian Gulf, the Turkish port of Dortyol on the Mediterranean emerged as the most suitable terminal for Iraqi oil. This development only further underlined the current strategic significance of both Turkey and Middle Eastern oil.

CHAPTER 3

The Oil Jugular of the Western World

The advent of the gasoline-powered automobile in the late nineteenth century ushered in a new era in human civilization. Since petroleum is the source of gasoline, modern life became increasingly dependent on it. However, humans have known about petroleum since antiquity. Archaeological excavations in Iraq and Iran show that oil in the form of bitumen was used in ancient times for building roads and for coating walls and the hulls of ships.

Petroleum, or crude oil, is a mixture of hydrocarbons found underground in a gaseous or liquid state. In its liquid form, it is often greenish or dark brown, and sometimes black. Mining oil involves prospecting, drilling, and extraction. (The first modern petroleum well was drilled in 1859 in Titusville, Pennsylvania.) After its extraction or recovery, oil is refined by distillation, a process which separates it into fractions of varying volatility. These are put through chemical conversion processes, known as cracking and re-forming, to produce a variety of end-products: asphalt, cleaning agents, explosives, fertilizers, fibers, gasoline, jellies, jet fuel, kerosene, medicines, naptha, paints, plastics, and synthetic rubber and waxes.

THE DISCOVERY OF OIL

In the Middle East, the first commercial oil drilling occurred in 1908 at Masjid-e Suleiman in southwest Iran (then called Persia). Five years later, when the powerful British navy decided to switch from coal to oil, the importance of petroleum rose. To ensure supplies, Great Britain acquired a controlling share in the Anglo-Persian Oil Company (APOC), then engaged in petroleum mining in Persia. As the leading imperial power in the Persian Gulf region, Great Britain imposed a series of agreements on the rulers of Kuwait (1913), Bahrain (1914), Qatar (1916), and the Lower Gulf emirates and Oman (mid-1920s), whereby they were barred from giving oil concessions to non-British companies without London's prior permission.

The terms of oil concessions to British interests included long duration (60 to 95 years), vast areas, exemption from local taxes, and paltry royalties to the host country. The royalty was treated as a rental related to the size of yield from the last, irrespective of the price of the mined commodity. It varied between 3 to 8 British pence (8-20 American cents) per barrel of oil (42 U.S. gallons).

After World War I, APOC acquired three-quarters of the shares of the Turkish Petroleum Company (TPC), which consisted originally of British, French, and German interests. TPC had begun operating in Iraq in 1912 after winning an oil concession from the Ottoman sultan. Great Britain and France tried to keep American companies out of the region, arguing that they had ample opportunities to exploit vast reserves at home. But, pressured by Washington, they accepted two American corporations as partners in their operations in Iraq, which proved commercially successful in 1927.

Petroleum on a commercial scale was next discovered in Bahrain in 1932, and in Kuwait and Saudi Arabia in 1938. By then, the Anglo-Persian Oil Company had become the Anglo-Iranian Oil Company (now British Petroleum), following the renaming of Persia as Iran in 1933. The Turkish Petroleum Company had been transformed into the Iraq Petroleum Company (IPC) in 1931. It was owned equally by British, Dutch, French, and American corporations, with the European interests represented by government-owned companies, and the American by two private corporations. After a halt in production during World War II, petroleum output rose sharply as more oilfields were discovered and tapped. By the late 1960s, Persian Gulf oil production amounted to about one-third of the global total.

OIL PRODUCTION SINCE WORLD WAR II

Between 1945 and 1967, consumption of oil and oil products increased tenfold in Western Europe, providing about half of its total energy needs. The switch from coal to oil was motivated as much by environmental considerations as by economics. A heat unit obtained from oil cost only 30 to 40 percent as much as one obtained from locally mined coal.

The United States also registered a dramatic increase in the use of petroleum and petroleum products. Unlike Western Europe, however, the U.S. had substantial oil reserves. Because the cost of oil production in the U.S. was many times the cost in the Persian Gulf, President Dwight Eisenhower (1890-1969) tried to safeguard the local oil industry by imposing an import quota on petroleum in 1959. He fixed the quota at 12.3 percent of the domestic output, or 11.3 percent of the total consumption. But as consumption rose sharply, and as oil drillers in the U.S. encountered more dry holes, pressure built to relax the quota. President Richard Nixon (1913-1994) did so in 1970.

By then, the Organization of Petroleum Exporting Countries (OPEC), which was formed in 1960, had emerged as an important player in the world oil market. Most of its 13 members were from the Middle East and North Africa.

The Middle East, and particularly the Persian Gulf, remains the world's most dominant oil region. In 1993, of the world's proven oil reserves of 1009 billion barrels, the Middle East had 669.2 billion barrels, or 66.3 percent of the aggregate. Of this, 65.2 percent was in the six Gulf states of the Arabian Peninsula, Iran, and Iraq, with the rest in Egypt, Syria, and Yemen. (U.S. and Canadian deposits, at 31.2 and 7.4 billion barrels, respectively, together amounted to 3.8 percent of the global total.)

In 1993, the oil output from the Gulf region was 35 percent of the world aggregate, and 85 percent of the OPEC total. Most of the Gulf oil was exported. The cumulative deposits of the Middle East were expected to last almost 100 more years. In contrast, the petroleum reserves of the U.S. and Canada were expected to be exhausted in less than 10 years.

OIL AND WORLD POLITICS

The Arab oil embargo against the countries that supported Israel in the October 1973 Arab-Israeli War dramatized the dependence of the U.S. on Middle Eastern oil. The boycott, which lasted from October 1973 to March 1974, applied to the U.S. and a few other Western countries, including Holland. It reduced the annual U.S. Gross Domestic Product by an estimated $10-20 billion. Despite periodic attempts to curtail petroleum consumption in the United States, American dependence on oil imports has risen dramatically. In 1958, the U.S. produced more than nine-tenths of its petroleum needs. By 1983, the proportion was down to roughly seven-tenths, and by 1993 it fell to about half.

Except during 1973-74, the U.S. and Saudi Arabia, the world's largest oil producer, have had close relations since the 1930s. This relationship has allowed the U.S. and other industrialized nations to receive adequate oil supplies at cheap prices. In terms of the 1993 U.S. dollar, a barrel of oil cost between $9 and $75 during the period between 1861 and 1880. A century later, in 1960, the price was $9 a barrel. The 1973 Arab-Israeli War and the 1979 Islamic revolution in Iran pushed it to a peak of $51 a barrel in 1981. It then declined to $17 in 1993 and 1994, a doubling of the price since 1960. Taking into account an average annual inflation rate during the period of 6 percent for the industrialized world—as represented by the 25-member Organization of Economic Cooperation and Development (OECD)—oil was one-third cheaper in the mid-1990s than it was in the late 1950s.

The reliability of oil supplies is as important as price to the Western and Japanese economies. A substantial proportion of Persian Gulf Oil passes through the Straits of Hormuz, which connect the Persian Gulf with the Arabian Sea, on its way to buyers in the West and Japan. During the 1980-88 Iran-Iraq War, Tehran periodically threatened to block the Straits of Hormuz. Washington publicly declared the Straits an international waterway, and refused to allow a continued blockade of those waters. Contravening its public policy of neutrality, the U.S. then began to favor Iraq.

In 1990, after the Iraqi invasion of Kuwait, U.S. President George Bush reckoned that Iraqi President Saddam Hussein (1937–), by annexing Kuwait, would double the oil reserves under his control to about 20 percent of the world total. This would enable him to challenge the role of pro-American Saudi Arabia, with 25 percent of the world's reserves, as the pacesetter in oil pricing. The U.S. economy would thus become a hostage to the whims of Saddam Hussein. As U.S. president, Bush could not let that happen. He therefore created a 29-nation anti-Iraq Coalition under American leadership and expelled Iraq from Kuwait in the 1991 Gulf War. For this reason, many commentators and historians have described the Gulf conflict as an oil war.

Given the high concentration of petroleum reserves in the Persian Gulf area, the vulnerability of the oil shipping lanes, and the extreme sensitivity of price to demand and supply, political stability in the Middle East is crucial for the economic health of the West and Japan. The most serious threats to regional stability—the Arab-Jew conflict and Islamic militancy—are discussed in the next chapter.

CHAPTER 4

The Conflict Between Arabs and Jews

Today's Arabs are overwhelmingly Muslim. They claim descent from Ishmael, Abraham's son by Hagar, and often appear in the Bible as Ishmaelites. In the Old Testament, the Second Book of Chronicles (17:11) alludes to "some Arabs" bringing 7,700 sheep and 7,700 goats as presents to King Jehosophat of Judah (*ca.* 870–851 B.C.), the term describing nomadic people from the eastern bank of the Jordan River. An inscription of King Shalmaneser III of Assyria in the eight century B.C. refers to "Gindibu the Aribi" as a member of the group of rebelling notables whom he had defeated. Later inscriptions in Assyria and Babylon are full of references to Aribi or Arab, a term used for nomads inhabiting the northern and central Arabian Peninsula. During the Greek and Roman periods, Arab meant somebody living in the Arabian Peninsula.

The word "Arab" is a derivative either of a Semitic root linked to nomadism, or of "abhar," meaning "to pass or move." Nomadic Arabs worshipped nature—rocks, water springs, trees–or idols until the arrival of Islam in the mid-seventh century. The Arabs who had settled in the oases came under the influence of such pre-Islamic religions as Judaism.

In 622 A.D., Prophet Muhammad migrated from Mecca, his birthplace, to Medina, the abode of the pagan Aus and Khazraj tribes, as well as of Jewish tribes. When Muhammad promulgated the Constitution of Medina, it was signed by the Jewish leaders. The Jews thus became an integral part of the Medinese polity, and the newly converted Muslims regarded them as allies. Unlike Muslims, Jews were not required to bear arms, an activity then undertaken primarily to spread Islam, although they were required to pay extra taxes.

In the deadly rivalry that arose between Mecca and Medina, some Jewish leaders sided, both overtly and covertly, with the Meccans. As a result, relations between the Medinese Muslims and Jews soured. When Muhammad warned the Jews that if they expected to be protected by his forces they would have to renew their pledge to the Constitution of Medina, they did. But as hostility between Mecca and Medina escalated into a bloody battle in 630 A.D., ending in the defeat of the Meccans, the relationship between Muhammad and the pro-Meccan Jewish tribes became strained. In the battle between the two sides that followed later that year at Khaibar, Muhammad won. Although the Jewish tribes that stayed out of the fray were allowed to continue their existence as before, the overall presence of the Jews in the region fell rapidly. Since then, relations between Jews and Arab Muslims have fluctuated between extremes of total harmony and bloody warfare.

Certain common features of Jews and Arab Muslims are worth noting. They share religious injunctions to circumcise male children and abstain from pork. Their languages, Arabic and Hebrew, belong to the same Semitic family. Today, Israeli Jews from Arab countries speak Hebrew more correctly than those from Europe or the U.S.

After Jews were expelled from Catholic Spain in 1492, they took refuge in the Muslim countries around the Mediterranean, where they lived in peace. Along with Christians, they were recognized as the "People of the Book" by the Ottoman sultan, whose empire included Palestine from 1517 onwards. In the Ottomon lands, Jews lived in harmony with Muslims and Christians.

THE ISSUE OF PALESTINE, THE HOLY LAND

The current Arab-Jew conflict centers around Palestine, also known as the Holy Land because it is sacred to Jews, Christians, and Muslims. As a territory ruled in the pre-Islamic era by Egyptians, Assyrians, Israelites, Babylonians, Persians, Greeks (under Alexander the Great and his successors), Maccebeans (Jews), and Romans, both its name and borders have varied enormously. In Old Testament times, Palestine was wherever the 12 Israelite tribes lived. Depending on the particular Bible quote, Palestine's frontiers could be stretched from the Nile in Egypt to the Euphrates in Iraq, or confined to the land between the Mediterranean Sea and the Jordanian desert.

In the second century A.D., the Roman emperors called the southern third of their province of Syria, including former Judea, Syria Palestine. Starting in 637 A.D., Palestine came under Muslim rule. Except for the brief Crusader reign from 1099 to 1187, Muslim rule continued until 1917 under the Arab or Turkish dynasties of the Umayyads, Abbasids, Fatimids, Ayubids, Mamlukes, and Ottomans.

During the last century of Ottoman Turkish rule in Palestine, the major European powers gradually weakened Ottoman authority. In 1831, the Egyptian general Muhammad Ali revolted against the Ottomans with British support. He lasted until 1839, when the European powers imposed the Capitulations on the Ottoman sultan. Providing unilateral commercial, religious, and diplomatic privileges to the Europeans, the Capitulations were modeled on the unilateral charters granted by the Byzantine rulers, Crusaders, and Mamlukes to the Italian city-states.

France acquired the right to act as the guardian of Catholics in the Ottoman Empire. Russia became the protector of the Orthodox Christians. As Christian nations, France, Russia, and Great Britain set up missions in the walled Old City of Jerusalem. Of the Old City's estimated 10,000 residents, almost 3,000 were Jews. In 1860, Sir Moses Montifeori of the London Mission for the Jews built a windmill and houses for Jews outside the Old City. By then, the term Palestine, which had disappeared for many centuries, reappeared, and Western travelers used the terms Palestine and Holy Land interchangeably.

Zionism

In 1862, Moses Hess, a German Jew, advocated the return of Jews to Palestine to create a spiritual center there for the Jewish Diaspora, the Jewish community living outside Palestine. Ever since the expulsion of the Jews from Jerusalem in 586 B.C., the return to

Zion (the hill in ancient Jerusalem on which King David's palace was built) had been an idea expressed in the Jewish liturgy. Hess's idea was adopted by the Hovevei Zion (Lovers of Zion) societies that sprang up in Russia soon after the pogroms of 1881-82 that followed the assassination of Tsar Alexander II. They believed in religious Zionism, which called on Jews to return to Zion for religious reasons. They organized the first immigration wave (aliya) into Palestine. It was a failure. Most of the Jews who immigrated found life in Palestine unbearable and departed.

Theodor Herzl (1860–1904), an Austro-Hungarian Jewish journalist, gave a political dimension to the concept of Zionism. In his 1896 pamphlet, *Der Judenstaat* (*The Jewish State*), he argued for a Jewish homeland to be set up preferably, but not necessarily, in Ottoman Palestine, through an international agreement. The next year he convened the first Zionist Congress in Basle, Switzerland. It established the Zionist Organization—renamed the World Zionist Organization (WZO) in 1960—which stated that "Zionism strives to create for the Jewish people a home in Palestine secured by public law."

Most of the Hovevei Zion societies affiliated themselves with the WZO, which was based in Vienna, Austria. The Ottoman sultan turned down Herzl's proposal for autonomy for Palestine, which was not a single administrative unit in the empire. Its southern zone was called the *sanjak* (district) of Jerusalem; its northern area was part of the *wilayat* (province) of Beirut; Jerusalem and its suburbs were administered directly by Constantinople. Great Britain offered the WZO 6,000 square miles of virgin land in Uganda, East Africa, in 1903, but the Organization's 7th Congress in 1905 rejected the overture.

With the failure of the Russian revolution of 1905, and the subsequent repression and programs, the migration of Russian Jewish youths to Palestine increased, and so did support for the Zionist movement among European Jews. Since many of the Russian settlers were socialists, either Marxist or non-Marxist, a socialist Zionism arose in Palestine, which by 1914 had some 90,000 Jews. However, when the Ottomans joined the Germans in World War I, many Jews left Palestine, so that at the end of the conflict there were 60,000 Jews in a total population of 650,000.

Following the outbreak of World War I, political Zionism became dominant, and its leadership passed to the Russian Jews settled in Great Britain. Two such figures, Chaim Weizmann and Nahum Sokolow, played crucial roles in securing a declaration by Lord Balfour, British foreign secretary, in November 1917, concerning Palestine's future as a "national home" for Jews. Even though there was then no political-administrative entity called Palestine, the Balfour Declaration referred to the "establishment in Palestine of a National Home for the Jewish people." In 1922, the Declaration was incorporated into Great Britain's League of Nations mandate over Palestine. The mandate was a new concept of trusteeship devised by the League's Supreme Council to be applied to the Arab sector of the defeated Ottoman Empire. The mandate provided for the recognition of "an appropriate Jewish agency" for "advising and cooperating with the administration of Palestine in such economic, social, and other matters that may affect the establishment of the Jewish national home and the interests of the Jewish population in Palestine." The WZO performed this role until 1929, when it ceded its position to the newly formed Jewish Agency for Palestine.

Instead of preparing Palestine for independence—something required of London by the League of Nations mandate—Great Britain contrived to hold on to it, and, in line with the Balfour Declaration, encouraged Jewish immigration. Between 1918 and 1931, the percentage of Jews in the Palestinian population doubled from 9 to 18 percent. Arabs protested, but the situation did not change, and they rioted in 1926 and 1929. The next wave of Jewish immigration, from 1932 to May 1939 (when a British policy paper restricted Jewish intake), brought a further 225,000 Jewish immigrants into the country, mainly from

Germany where the rise of Adolf Hitler to power in 1933 made life for Jews increasingly intolerable. The Jewish population in Palestine reached 446,000 in 1939.

The 1920s and 1930s witnessed the development and consolidation of Jewish life in Palestine, funded by the WZO, which was in turn financed mainly by American Jews. The Jewish community in Palestine was represented by an elected national council, the Vaad Leumi; a trade union federation, the Histadrut; and a militia, the Haganah.

In 1937, the Arabs rejected the recommendation by a British commission, headed by Lord Peel, to create a Jewish state on the coastal plain and Galilee, and an Arab state to be attached to the neighboring Transjordan. Having failed either to slow Jewish immigration or convince the British to grant Palestine independence, the Palestinian Arabs mounted a revolt in 1936, which ended after three years and the deaths of 3,232 Arabs, 329 Jews, and 135 Britons.

Responding to this, and anxious to retain Arab goodwill and access to the crucial Iraqi oilfields, Great Britain issued a White [policy] Paper in May 1939. This document limited Jewish immigration to 75,000 over the next five years, and offered an outline of an independent, binational state to be set up in Palestine by 1949. However, illegal immigration grew.

Tensions were eased by World War II, in which both Arabs and Jews cooperated with Great Britain. 43,000 Jews joined the Allied military, 10,000 of them becoming part of the British Nile Army. In Europe, the Nazi Holocaust made many Jews more determined than ever to create an independent Jewish state. After the war, in April 1946, an Anglo-American commission on Palestine recommended that Great Britain continue the mandate.

The Founding of Israel

The decision of the WZO—then known as the Zionist Organization—in December 1946 to demand an independent Jewish state in Palestine ended whatever hopes London had of solving the problem on its own. It therefore placed the issue before the General Assembly of the United Nations (UN), the successor to the League of Nations. The UN Special Committee on Palestine recommended in August 1947 that Palestine be partitioned—with 42.5 percent of the land going to the Arabs, who formed 70 percent of the population; and 56.5 percent to the Jews, who were 30 percent of the population and owned 6 percent of the land. The remaining 1 percent of the area, covering Jerusalem and its suburbs, was to be placed under international control.

On 29 November 1947, the UN General Assembly adopted Resolution 181, specifying partition. The 33 votes in favor included the Soviet Union and other members of the Communist bloc, while the 13 votes against and 10 abstentions included Great Britain. The Arab states challenged the right of the UN General Assembly to partition a country against the wishes of the majority of its inhabitants, proposing that the International Court of Justice rule on the matter. Their proposal was defeated by a vote of 21 to 20 in the General Assembly.

The WZO accepted the UN plan, but the Arabs rejected it. The inter-ethnic violence, which erupted immediately, intensified, as Great Britain's withdrawal date—May 15, 1948—approached. By that date, some 300,000 Arabs had fled from the areas allocated to the Jews by the UN partition plan. Once the State of Israel was proclaimed on May 14, 1948, fighting broke out between the Zionist forces and the armies of the five members of the Arab League, which had declared war against Israel. The Arab League countries were Egypt, Jordan, Iraq, Syria, and Lebanon.

During this war, which ended in January 1949, Israel occupied the Jewish sector allocated to it by the United Nations and annexed half the area allotted to the Arabs by the UN, thereby curtailing their share to 23 percent of Palestine. The number of Palestinian Arabs remaining in this territory was reduced from 920,000 to 160,000 by their flight into the adjoining Palestinian Arab territories (later to be called the West Bank and the Gaza Strip), Jordan, Syria, and Lebanon. They became refugees there. Of the two remaining Palestinian areas, the larger, the West Bank of the Jordan River, was later annexed by Jordan (a move not recognized by any other Arab state), and the smaller, the Gaza Strip, was administered by Egypt.

Following talks between the warring parties on the Greek island of Rhodes, Israel signed armistice agreements with Egypt, Lebanon, Jordan, and Syria during 1949. Iraq, which claimed common borders with Israel, did not conclude any such agreement with Israel. These arrangements did not lead to peace treaties between the belligerents. The Arab states refused to recognize Israel, which they saw as an entity created by the West and imposed on the oil-rich Arab world to divide and dominate it. The rise of Arab nationalism, which opposed Western imperialism as well as Zionism, especially in Egypt and Syria, strengthened this viewpoint.

Arab-Jewish Relations Since 1956

The conquest in 1956 of Egypt's Sinai Peninsula by Israel—in collusion with Great Britain and France—proved to Arab nationalists the links between Zionism and European imperialism. During this conflict, known as the Suez War, Israel occupied the Gaza Strip before capturing the Sinai Peninsula. Due to United Nations intervention, backed strongly by the U.S. and the Soviet Union, the invaders failed to make further gains. Later, under pressure from the UN, the Soviet Union, and the U.S., Israel vacated both Sinai and the Gaza Strip.

The uneasy peace between Israel and its Arab neighbors broke down in June 1967, when Israel won a war that lasted barely six days. It occupied not only the West Bank and Gaza Strip, but also the Sinai Peninsula of Egypt and the Golan Heights of Syria. Israel declared that it was prepared to give up the occupied Arab lands in return for peace treaties with its Arab neighbors. The Arab response was simple and unanimous: No talks, no treaty, no recognition. They reaffirmed the right of Palestinians, represented by the Palestine Liberation Organization (PLO), to form their own independent state. As Israel began establishing Jewish colonies on the occupied Arab territories, the PLO intensified its guerrilla operations against Israeli targets inside and outside Israel and the changes of a peaceful end to the Arab-Jew conflict dwindled.

In October 1973, Egypt and Syria attacked the Israeli forces in the occupied Sinai Peninsula and Golan Heights. Before this war ended three weeks later, Egypt regained part of the Sinai. The armed conflict revived the peacemaking efforts of the United Nations, but the initiative soon passed to the U.S. The mediation efforts of President Jimmy Carter led to a peace treaty between Israel and Egypt in March 1979.

But the core of the Arab-Jew conflict, the Palestinian problem, remained unresolved, and a comprehensive peace in the region remained elusive. The PLO, based in the Lebanese capital of Beirut since 1972, reasserted its right to establish the State of Palestine. In contrast, Israel was prepared to consider nothing more than giving the Palestinians in the West Bank and Gaza Strip limited autonomy to run their municipal affairs.

In 1982, Israel invaded Lebanon and encircled Beirut, forcing the expulsion of the PLO from the city. The PLO moved to the distant Tunisian capital of Tunis in North Africa. Israel accelerated its colonization of the West Bank and Gaza Strip.

The removal of the PLO from the region, and the relentless encroachment on Palestinian land by Jewish settlers, pushed the Palestinians to act on their own. In late 1987, they launched the *intifada,* a grass roots resistance movement. Repressive action by the Israeli security forces, involving firings, curfews, harassment, arrests, and house searches and demolitions, severely disrupted Palestinian life, but failed to end the *intifada*.

Externally, Israel noted with unease the rising power of Iraq, which had emerged from an eight-year war with Iran in 1988 with its military strength enhanced. Iraq began to inspire the PLO and even moderate Jordan. On the other hand, the accelerating disintegration of the pro-Arab Soviet bloc, which began in late 1989 and sharply increased the inflow of Soviet Jews into Israel, heartened the Jewish state. In August 1990, Iraq's aggression against Kuwait created an open breach in Arab ranks and unwittingly strengthened Israel's hand.

CHAPTER 5

The Arab Split: Iraq's Invasion of Kuwait

The Iraqi invasion and occupation of Kuwait in 1990 was the worst blow to pan-Arabism since the founding of the Arab League, a collective of Arab states, in 1945. Ironically, the culprit in 1990 was Iraqi President Saddam Hussein, who had portrayed his war with Iran in the 1980s as a struggle for "all of the Arab homeland" against Persian expansionism "masquerading as pan-Islamism."

Pan-Arabism maintains that no matter where Arabs (meaning those who speak Arabic) live, they are part of a single nation. It first manifested itself among the inhabitants of the Arab territory of the Ottoman Empire during the last quarter of the nineteenth century. World War I provided Arabs with an option to further their nationalist cause by siding with the anti-Ottoman forces. By declaring an Arab revolt in 1916, Hussein ibn Ali al Hashem, the governor of Hijaz in western Arabia, emerged as the leader of pan-Arabism. He wanted to see the Arab territories unified as a single, independent Arab state after the Ottoman defeat. But Hussein's plans came to nothing because it clashed with the clandestine pact between Great Britain and France, signed by British representative Mark Sykes and French representative Georges Picot in May 1916.

In the inter-war period, the al Hashems, ruling Iraq and Transjordan, remained the repositories of pan-Arabism. This changed in 1948 when King Abdullah ibn Hussein al Hashem of Jordan (1922–1951) tried to annex parts of Palestine by making a secret deal with the Zionists. Pan-Arab nationalists now viewed him as a traitor to their cause.

After the Arab-Israeli War of 1948–1949, and the establishment of Israel, pan-Arabism centered around the Arab struggle for the retrieval of Palestine from the Zionists. Following the successful coup in 1952 by the republican Free Officers Group against corrupt King Farouq (1936–1952) of Egypt, the most populous and strategic Arab country, the mantle of pan-Arab leadership fell on Egyptian President Gamal Abdul Nasser (1918–1970). Before Nasser, Egypt had contributed little to pan-Arabism, except to provide headquarters for the Arab League.

The first move to further pan-Arabism came in early 1958 when Egypt and Syria combined to form the United Arab Republic (UAR). When pro-Western King Faisal II al

Hashem (1939–1958) was overthrown by the Free Officers in Iraq in mid-1958, nationalist, republican Iraq was widely expected to join the United Arab Republic. But Iraq did not join, and in September 1961, Syria broke away from the UAR, badly damaging the prospect of a unified Arab state or federation.

Yet the idea of two or more Arab countries forming an alliance for a specific purpose persisted. On the eve of the June 1967 Arab-Israeli War, President Nasser led a joint military command of Egypt, Syria, and Jordan. The 1967 conflict ended in Arab defeat, with Israel occupying the West Bank and Gaza Strip, as well as the Sinai Peninsula of Egypt and the Golan Heights of Syria. The outcome of the war focused pan-Arabism on the recovery of all Arab territories lost to Israel by Egypt, Syria, and Jordan.

The objective of the October 1973 Arab-Israeli War, started by Egypt and Syria, was to recover these Israeli-occupied territories. The Egyptian-Syrian alliance, backed by the military and oil muscle of the rest of the Arab world, thus became the latest example of pan-Arabism. Although only Egypt made limited military gains, the 1973 war was the first time since the founding of the Arab League that the Arab world had acted in such unison. The war subsequently proved to be the pinnacle of pan-Arabism.

Egyptian President Anwar Sadat (1918–1981) severely damaged Arab unity by signing a peace treaty with Israel in 1979. His actions destroyed the Arab consensus against unilateral peace treaties with Israel. Egypt regained the Sinai Peninsula but lost its leadership of pan-Arabism, which passed to Syrian President Hafiz Assad (1930–). He committed himself to securing the retrieval from Israel of the Golan Heights, the West Bank and Gaza Strip, and the border strip of Lebanon occupied by Israel in 1978.

After invading Iran in September 1980, Iraqi President Saddam Hussein tried to portray the war as a common Arab struggle against Persian expansionism. He was only partially successful. He received massive grants and loans to carry on the war from the rulers of Saudi Arabia and Kuwait, and lesser amounts from the rulers of other oil-rich Gulf states. They gave out of self-interest, reckoning that if the Islamic Republic of Iran won it would export revolution to their countries

After the war ended in August 1988, the ruler of Kuwait, Shaikh Jabar III al Sabah (1977–) pressed Saddam Hussein to repay Kuwaiti loans of about $12 billion. He refused, arguing that the conflict with Iran had as much to do with the future of Kuwait as with that of Iraq. To pressure Iraq economically, Kuwait and the United Arab Emirates flooded the oil market with their exports, and depressed the price of oil by about one-third, to between $11 and $13 a barrel in the spring of 1990. This economic pressure hurt Iraq, a major exporter of oil. Saddam Hussein warned Shaikh Jabar III, and then dispatched troops to the Iraqi-Kuwaiti border when Jaber ignored the warning.

THE KUWAIT CRISIS AND THE GULF WAR

Relations between Iraq and Kuwait had soured before. Something like this had happened twice since Kuwait's independence in 1961. Each time the Kuwaiti ruler had fended off the threat by offering funds to Iraq. Saddam Hussein expected the past pattern to repeat itself, with Kuwait foregoing its previous loans and even offering fresh economic aid.

But this time, advised by Egypt and the U.S., Kuwait stood firm. It also used the crisis to pressure Iraq to finalize the demarcation of the Iraqi-Kuwaiti frontier. Last-minute talks between the two sides in the Saudi city of Jiddah on 31 July 1990 failed. Stung by Kuwait's unexpected obduracy, Saddam Hussein ordered an invasion of his tiny neighbor.

At 2 a.m. local time on 2 August 1990, Iraqi forces invaded and occupied Kuwait. Shaikh Jabar III and other members of the royal family fled to Saudi Arabia. The 15-member United Nations Security Council passed a resolution, by 14 votes to 0, condemning Iraqi aggression against Kuwait and demanding an immediate withdrawal. The next day the Arab

League condemned the Iraqi action by 14 votes to 1, with 5 abstentions and one walkout. The UN Security Council passed Resolution 660 on 12 August by 13 votes to none. The resolution imposed mandatory sanctions and an embargo on Iraq and occupied Kuwait. Invited by Saudi King Fahd ibn Abdul Aziz (1982–) to bolster his country's defenses, United States President George Bush ordered American fighter aircraft and troops to leave immediately for Saudi Arabia.

On 12 August, Saddam Hussein offered a peace initiative, including "preparation" of withdrawal by Israel from the occupied Arab territories in "Palestine, Syria and Lebanon," and the formulation of arrangements for the "situation in Kuwait" in line with the UN resolutions. Washington did not respond.

In early October, Amnesty International, a London-based human rights organization, published a report portraying widespread arrests, torture, and summary executions in Kuwait by the occupying Iraqi forces. On 8 November, President Bush doubled the U.S. troops in the gulf to 400,000. A week later, Saddam Hussein proposed talks between Iraq and Saudi Arabia on regional problems, and between Iraq and the U.S. on wider issues. Neither Saudi Arabia nor the U.S. responded to this offer.

In Washington, expert testimony before the U.S. Senate Armed Services Committee in late November showed a large majority favoring the economic option over the military in forcing Iraq out of Kuwait. On 29 November, the UN Security Council adopted Resolution 678 by a vote of 12 to 2, with Cuba and Yemen voting against and China abstaining. The resolution authorized the states supporting Kuwait to use "all necessary means" to implement the earlier resolutions and "to restore international peace and security in the area," unless Iraq fully implemented the resolutions before 15 January 1991.

On 12 January 1991, the U.S. Senate authorized President Bush, by a vote of 53 to 47, to use the American military pursuant to UN Security Council Resolution 678; the House of Representatives concurred by a vote of 250 to 183. Two days later, Iraq's parliament unanimously decided to go to war rather than withdraw from Kuwait, and empowered President Saddam Hussein to conduct it.

Iraq faced a 29-nation coalition led by the U.S. Baghdad had 545,000 troops in Kuwait and southern Iraq, equipped with 4,200 tanks, 150 combat helicopters, and 550 combat-ready warplanes. The 425,000 U.S. troops, included 250,000 soldiers, 75,000 marines, 60,000 naval personnel, and 45,000 air force personnel. They were equipped with 2,200 tanks, 500 combat helicopters, and 1,500 warplanes. By the end of the war, U.S. troops in the region exceeded 550,000. The British and French forces together amounted to 45,000. The 12 NATO members involved deployed 107 warships in the Gulf, the northern Arabian Sea, the Gulf of Oman, the Red Sea, and the eastern Mediterranean, with most of them enforcing the UN embargo. U.S. naval personnel were armed with 700-plus nuclear weapons on warships and submarines. The Arab and Muslim troops totaled 220,000. The non-U.S. component of the coalition was equipped with 1,200 tanks, 150 combat helicopters, and 350 warplanes. The overall commander of the coalition was General Norman Schwarzkopf of the U.S. army. Based in the Saudi Arabian capital of Riyadh, he worked in close cooperation with Saudi General Prince Khalid ibn Sultan, the commander of the Arab-Islamic forces.

On the night of 16 January, the coalition mounted an air campaign code-named Operation Desert Storm, with aerial bombing and firing of cruise missiles from American warships. On 18 January, Iraq fired 12 Scud ground-to-ground missiles at Tel Aviv and Haifa in Israel, and four days later three more Iraqi Scuds landed in Tel Aviv. It also fired Scuds at Riyadh. Coalition air sorties in the first week totaled 12,000 (with half being combat sorties), and cruise missile firings numbered 216. During the second week, the total of daily air sorties rose to 3,000, with the U.S. share at 87 percent. In the fourth week in February, the coalition concentrated on destroying Iraq's transport infrastructure of bridges and roads. By the fifth week, the total of coalition air sorties reached 86,000. By the end of the war, the total of coalition air sorties reached 106,000.

On 21 February, Iraq welcomed the Soviet Union's eight-point peace plan, which included a ceasefire, Iraq's evacuation of Kuwait, the end of UN sanctions once two-thirds of the Iraqi force had left, and the abrogation of the remaining UN resolutions once all Iraqi troops had departed. Bush rejected the package, and announced a list of 12 conditions, including total Iraqi withdrawal within a week, by 17.30 GMT (Greenwich Mean Time) on 23 February.

At 12:00 GMT on 23 February, Iraq said that, in accord with its acceptance of the Soviet peace plan, it would withdraw from Kuwait immediately and unconditionally. At 16:30 GMT, the UN Security Council began a closed door session; the Western powers stated that they were not interested in bridging the gap between the Soviet plan and the U.S. terms. At 18.00 GMT, Bush ordered General Schwarzkopf to expel the Iraqis from Kuwait. By then, retreating Iraqis had begun setting Kuwaiti oil wells ablaze.

On 24 February, the U.S.-led coalition launched its ground campaign, Operation Desert Saber, with ground troops advancing on two axes. The next day, at 21:30 GMT, the Soviet Union presented a new peace plan, which Iraq accepted an hour later. Baghdad ordered a withdrawal from Kuwait as part of its compliance with Security Council Resolution 660. On 26 February, at 11:50 GMT, Iraqi forces left Kuwait City.

American troops blocked all exits for the Iraqi forces in the Kuwaiti theater of war. Killing of the retreating Iraqi soldiers continued until a ceasefire 40 hours later. On 27 February, at 5:30 GMT, Iraq said that it had completed its evacuation of Kuwait. By then, some 640 Kuwaiti oil wells were ablaze. The next day at 2:00 GMT, Bush ordered a truce if Iraqi troops put down their arms. At 4:40 GMT, Iraq did so, and a temporary ceasefire went into effect at 5:00 GMT, thus ending 42 days of warfare.

Consequences of the Gulf War

Iraq did not officially announce its human losses. The U.S. Defense Intelligence Agency issued an estimate of 100,000 with an error factor of 50 percent. Earlier, Iraq's deputy premier, Sadoun Hamadi, had estimated that in the first 26 days of the war coalition bombing had killed 20,000 Iraqis. At this rate, a further 12,600 deaths can be estimated for the 41,000 sorties flown after Hamadi's statement was made. Iraqi fatalities for the ground campaign were estimated at 25,000 to 30,000. This gave a grand total of 57,600 to 62,600 Iraqi deaths. The American death toll (in combat and accidents during seven months) was 376. Iraq lost 30 warplanes, and the coalition 21.

As for the cost of the war, Iraq did not release any official figures. The coalition total of $82 billion broke down as follows: Japan $13 billion, Kuwait $22 billion, Saudi Arabia $29 billion, and the United States $18 billion. Saudi Arabia put its indirect costs at $22 billion.

In April 1991, UN Security Council Resolution 687 required Iraq to implement a UN-monitored program of disarming itself of weapons of mass destruction and of intermediate and long-range ground-to-ground missiles before UN sanctions against it could be lifted.

Whether by chance or design, Saddam Hussein had struck a body blow to pan-Arabism. Before his aggression against Kuwait in 1990, the Arab League held a summit every year. After it, no summit conference has been held, and none is planned. The loathing for Saddam Hussein, especially by King Fahd of Saudi Arabia and Shaikh Jabar III of Kuwait, was so strong that they could not bring themselves to attend any meeting where he was present. This development became all the more ironic in 1993 when life-long enemies Yasser Arrafat (1929–), the Palestinian leader, and Yitzhak Rabin (1922–1995), Israeli prime minister, made peace and shook hands in public.

CHAPTER 6

The Emerging Peace: An Israeli-Palestinian Accord

The 13th of September 1993 will long be remembered as an important and stunning day in Middle Eastern history. On that Monday, Palestinians and Jews made peace after a century of bitter conflict with an accord that granted self-rule to the Palestinians in the Gaza Strip and the West Bank town of Jericho. The accord was signed in a solemn ceremony on the sunlit lawn of the White House in Washington D.C. before an audience of 3,000 American and foreign dignitaries. Seconds after the signing by Israeli foreign minister, Shimon Peres, and his PLO counterpart, Mahmoud Abbas, came the surprise. With hundreds of millions of people watching the ceremony on television worldwide, Yasser Arafat (1929–), the 64-year-old PLO chairman, stretched out his hand to Yitzhak Rabin (1922–1995), the 71-year-old Israeli prime minister. Rabin hesitated. President Clinton nudged him gently. Slowly Rabin lifted his hand and acquiesced in the most publicized handshake in history—the symbolic reconciliation of two men who had been mortal foes for 25 years. The distinguished audience rose to its feet with a collective gasp, and clapped rapturously as Arafat, in his military uniform and *keffiyeh* head dress, shook hands with Rabin, in his business suit. This was the climax of talks which had been in strictest secrecy for nine months. But those negotiations were rooted in a wider process that can be traced back to the defeat of Iraq in the Gulf War in early 1991.

THE 1993 ACCORD

Saddam Hussein's invasion and annexation of Kuwait severely split the Arab League, and mortally weakened pan-Arabism. The decimation of powerful Iraq changed the situation regionally and in the Arab world. Robbed of any radical option by the outcome of the war, the PLO turned to such moderate, pro-American Arab states as Egypt. The PLO made itself amenable to compromise, basically on Israel's terms. This development became clear a year later when the Arab neighbors of Israel and the Palestinians agreed to negotiate with the Jewish state not collectively un-

Israeli Prime Minister Yitzhak Rabin, U.S. President Bill Clinton, and PLO Chairman Yasser Arafat on the White House lawn, 13 September 1993. Photo: Courtesy of Government Press Office, Jerusalem.

der United Nations auspices, as they had hitherto unanimously insisted, but bilaterally, as Israel had proposed.

The Gulf War also made Israel more amenable to seeking peace seriously. The long-range Scud surface-to-surface missile attacks on Tel Aviv and Haifa by Iraq made Israel realize that its major cities were no longer immune to direct hits by the enemy. Israelis also realized that having or not having the West Bank as a buffer made little difference to the country's overall security.

These factors encouraged U.S. Secretary of State James Baker to press Israel and its Arab neighbors to attend a peace conference. Israel, then ruled by a right-wing coalition led by Yitzhak Shamir (1915–), was agreeable only if its preconditions were met. The conference was to be cochaired by the United States and the Soviet Union (later Russia), and not by the United Nations. And after the preliminary session, Israel would conduct bilateral talks with each of the Arab parties. While there would be Palestinians in a joint Jordanian-Palestinian delegation, they would not be members of the PLO. On 18 July 1991, following Syrian President Hafiz Assad's dramatic concessions on his terms for attending a peace conference, Baker met him in Damascus. On 30 September, the Palestine National Council, the parliament-in-exile of Palestinians, agreed to attend such a gathering.

The conference opened in Madrid, Spain, on 31 October 1991 under the co-chairship of the U.S. and Russia; it was attended by Israel, Syria, Lebanon, and Jordan, whose delegation included Palestinians from the occupied territories of the West Bank and Gaza Strip. All parties agreed to honor United Nations Security Council Resolution 242 (November 1967), which called for the withdrawal of Israel from the occupied Arab territories in exchange for the peaceful existence of all the states in the region.

The Madrid conference was followed by bilateral talks between Israel and the three Arab parties, held outside the Middle East. The bilateral negotiations between Israel and Jordan evolved into separate talks between the Israeli delegates and the Jordanians, and the Israeli delegates and the Palestinians, with the latter taking their orders from the PLO. These negotiations went on against the background of the Palestinian *intifada*, in the West Bank and Gaza Strip. In the early 1990s, the campaign against Palestinians working as Israeli agents intensified, and destroyed the Israeli secret police's 20,000-strong intelligence network. This development prevented the occupying Israeli authorities from re-imposing full control and restoring law and order. The continuing disorder and the refusal of the Palestinians to call off the *intifada* convinced the Israeli government of the futility of continued suppression and denial of the Palestinian right to self-rule, and paved the way for the recognition of the PLO under certain conditions. But such recognition had to wait for the defeat of the right-wing government of Yitzhak Shamir in a general election in June 1992.

Palestinian negotiators soon ended the charade of their disassociation from the PLO by holding public meetings with PLO chairman Arafat. They thus undermined Israeli claims that Israel was not negotiating with the PLO. The newly elected government of Yitzhak Rabin, a Labour leader, lifted the official ban on contacts with the PLO in January 1993. That month, at the behest of Mona Juul and Terje Rod Larsen, two Norwegian mediators familiar with the situation in Israel and the occupied territories, the Israelis entered into secret talks with PLO officials in Norway. Eight months of negotiations led to an accord initialed in the Norwegian capital of Oslo in late August 1993.

In early September, Prime Minister Rabin recognized the PLO after Arafat had accepted the existence of Israel within secure borders and foresworn violence against Israel. They did so by exchanging letters. The stage was thus set for Israel and the PLO to sign the agreement initialed in Oslo.

The accord, described as a Declaration of Principles (DOP), specified a gradual approach to meeting the Palestinian demands. In the first stage, Palestinians were to exercise autonomy in the Gaza Strip and the West Bank town of Jericho. In the second stage, autonomy was to be extended to the rest of the West Bank, and elections were to be held in the West Bank and Gaza Strip for a Palestinian Council charged with administrative and legislative powers. In the final stage, talks were to begin by May 1996 to settle the status of Jerusalem and agree on the terms of the final settlement between Israel and the Palestinians. During the interim phase, external security of the West Bank and the Gaza Strip was to rest with Israel.

The famous handshake between Arafat and Rabin on the White House lawn in 1993 marked the end of an era of hostility between Arabs and Jews that dated back to the World Zionist Congress resolution of 1897 calling for creation of a "home" for the Jewish people in Palestine. Among other things, what drove Rabin to sign an accord with the PLO was his realization that the influence of political Islam among Palestinians was growing fast. The PLO, as a secular, nationalist organization was preferable to Hamas (meaning Zeal), the Islamic Resistance Movement, or the smaller Islamic Jihad. Were he to persist in his nonrecognition of the PLO, he or his successor would be forced to make a deal at some point with Hamas and the Islamic Jihad, who were gaining ground at the expense of the PLO. The assassination of Rabin in November 1995 by a fanatic Jewish Israeli made no difference to this assessment, which was shared by his successor, Shimon Peres. As Israel's foreign minister since June 1992, Peres had been actively involved in secret talks with the PLO. However, the rise of militant Islam was not limited to Palestinians. It was a much wider phenomenon with a long history.

CHAPTER 7

Islamic Fundamentalism in the Region: A Rising Tide?

Popular belief in the United States associates Islamic fundamentalism with the Iranian revolution of 1979 and sees the movement as one of fanatics bent on harming Western interests. The bombing by Muslim fundamentalists of the World Trade Center in New York on 26 February 1993, which killed six people and injured more than a 1,000, confirmed this prevalent view. The speed with which the American people and media wrongly attributed the bombing in Oklahoma City on 19 April 1995, which resulted in 168 deaths, to Islamic fundamentalists showed how widespread this perception had become.

On the other hand, few in the United States and elsewhere in the Western world realize that the oldest Islamic fundamentalist state of modern times, Saudi Arabia, is firmly allied with the West. Its oil pricing policy, and its stance before and during the 1991 Gulf War, are evidence of its strong Western links. But whatever the popular perceptions, Islamic fundamentalism has in recent times clearly had a strong impact on the Western mind. This is partly because most of the countries experiencing Islamic fundamentalism are situated in the strategically important Middle East and North Africa, and partly because several of these are rich in oil, a commodity on which Western economies are heavily dependent.

The term *fundamentalist* is open to different interpretations. Muslim Arabs argue that there is no such word as *fundamentalism* in Arabic. Western specialists know that the "fundamentalist" has a particular connotation in the American psyche due to the history of Christian fundamentalism in the U.S.

Christian fundamentalism rests primarily on the belief that both the Old and New Testaments are literal expressions of divine truth, particularly in their moral-ethical commandments and socio-political injunctions. The Bible is seen as absolutely infallible. *Fundamentalism* came into vogue in the U.S. in the 1920s following the publication of the 12-volume *Fundamentals: The Testimony to Truth*. Fundamentalism was presented as a doctrine opposed to modernism and liberalism, which were popularly associated with most mainline denominations within American Protestantism, an idea that still persists.

To get around the charged definition of fundamentalism, some specialists prefer the terms "revivalism" or "resurgence." The history of Islam, as well as of Christianity and Judaism, shows many examples of revivalist movements. The nature of every religion is to revitalize itself periodically. However, within the monotheistic family of religions Islam is special. Because Muhammad founded a domain and ruled it, Islam became intertwined with the state. Islam thus evolved as a complete social system that governs both the private and public lives of the believers. Being human, they fail to live up to these strict, all-pervasive standards. Every so often an extraordinarily pious leader rises and calls for an end to back-sliding. Islamic history is full of *mujtahids* or *mahdis*, reformers who strove to return the faithful to the fundamentals of Islam and to purify doctrine. Nowadays such personalities are invariably called "fundamentalist" in the Western media.

In medieval times, the drive for purification meant ridding Islam of superstition or scholastic legalism. Today, the response is both internal and external: to release Islam from its scholastic cobwebs as well as to rid it of ideas imbibed from the West.

In a Muslim-majority country, the single criterion for determining whether or not a law is fundamentalist is to ask if it derives *solely* from the Sharia, the Islamic Law. If yes, then it is fundamentalist. By this definition, Saudi Arabia is the oldest Islamic fundamentalist state in the world today. It has known nothing but the Sharia since its inception in 1932.

Prior to its demise in 1918, the Ottoman Empire was run according to the Sharia. In the eighteenth century, the Ottoman sultan came also to be called the caliph or vice-regent of Islam. In their dealings with the West, the Ottomans argued that the sultan's spiritual status was similar to that of the Roman Catholic pope or Orthodox patriarch, and that he enjoyed the spiritual allegiance of Muslims outside his empire.

After World War I, the nucleus of the Ottoman Empire became the Republic of Turkey under the secular rule of Mustafa Kemal Ataturk (1881-1938). He abolished the caliphate in 1924, thus ending an institution dating back to 632 A.D. and creating a religious vacuum in the Muslim world. This void was soon filled by a grass-roots movement in Egypt, a country that had come to occupy a prominent position in Islam.

EGYPT

In 1928, Hassan al Banna, a teacher, set up the Muslim Brotherhood. Starting out as a youth club, it turned political in the mid-1930s. Among other things, it supported the 1936–1939 Palestinian Arab uprising against the British mandate and Zionist colonization. It declared that Islam, based on the Koran and the Hadith, is a comprehensive, self-evolving system, applicable to all times and places. The Brotherhood believed in pan-Islamism, maintaining that all Muslime belonged to a universal Islamic *umma* or community.

During World War II, the Brotherhood's ranks swelled with students, civil servants, artisans, petty traders, and middle-income peasants. After the war, it participated in the escalating anti-British struggle. It claimed 500,000 members with as many sympathizers, organized in 5,000 branches. Its volunteers fought in the 1948 Arab-Israeli War.

Blaming Egypt's political establishment for the debacle in that conflict, the Brotherhood resorted to terroristic and subversive activities. The government declared martial law and banned the party in December 1948. Three weeks later, Premier Mahmoud Fahmi Nokrashi Pasha was assassinated by a Brotherhood member. In February 1949, Hassan al Banna was assassinated by secret service agents in Cairo.

The Egyptian Brotherhood set up sister organizations in Syria, Transjordan (now Jordan), and Palestine. In Egypt, the Brotherhood reached a climax in 1949. Although officially banned, it was still an important political force at the time of the Free Officers' coup in 1952. But in the course of popularizing pan-Arabism and then Arab socialism, Egyptian President Abdul Gamal Nasser suppressed the Muslim Brotherhood. The mantle of pan-Islamism then passed to Saudi King Faisal ibn Abdul Aziz (1964–1975), who unsuccessfully promoted it in the mid-1960s as a competing ideology to Nasser's Arab socialism.

In 1969, an abortive attempt by Michael Rohan, an Australian Christian fundamentalist, to set fire to Islam's third holiest shrine, the al Aqsa Mosque in Jerusalem, created a wave of outrage in the Muslim world. This enabled King Faisal to sponsor the Islamic Conference Organization (ICO), composed of Muslim states throughout the world. The ICO set up its headquarters in the Saudi city of Jiddah. As a multinational body representing governments, the ICO paralleled the Arab League.

When Anwar Sadat succeeded Nasser in 1970, he reversed Nasser's policy and promised that the Sharia would be the chief source of legislation. He released all Brotherhood prisoners. He ordered General Abdul Munim Amin, a Muslin Brotherhood sympathizer, to establish, train, and arm 1,000 Islamic associations—which later collectively became known by their Arabic title, al Gamaat al Islamiya (The Islamic Groups)—in universities and factories to fight "atheist Marxism." The program was so successful that the al Gamaat acquired an independent existence. Its members called on Sadat to intensify the struggle against Israel.

The October 1973 Arab-Israeli War, described as victory by the Egyptian authorities, produced a lull in al Gamaat circles. But the economic crisis that followed the war, and Egypt's step-by-step rapprochement with Israel, created a favorable climate for the rise of Islamic fundamentalism. Fearful of the popular appeal of the Brotherhood, Sadat denied it a license to contest the 1976 general election as a distinct group. The Brethren then ran either as independents or as members of the ruling Arab Socialist Party (ASP). Nine got elected as independents, and another six as ASP members.

Sadat's economic policies increased the disparity between the poor and the rich. In 1979, he made peace with Israel without successfully addressing the crucial Palestinian problem. For these reasons, the Brotherhood leaders turned against him. Al Gamaat students, defying heavy penalties for public protest, demonstrated, shouting such slogans as "No peace with Israel," "No privilege for the rich," and "No separation between Islam and the state."

Another fundamentalist group, al Jihad al Islami, often called al Jihad, emerged in the late 1970s. One of its leaders was Shaikh Omar Abdul Rahman, a blind cleric. Its ideologue, Muhammad Abdul Salam Faraj, argued that a true Muslim must struggle for the revival of the Islamic *umma* and that those Muslim groups or leaders who had turned away from the Sharia were apostates. One such leader was Anwar Sadat.

On 6 October 1981, Lieutenant Khalid Ahmad Islambouli and three soldiers under him, armed with automatic weapons and hand grenades, attached the review stand at a military parade in a Cairo suburb, killing Sadat and seven others. All the attackers were members of al Jihad.

President Hosni Mubarak (1928–), who succeeded Sadat, suppressed fundamentalists. At the same time, he engaged clerics to reeducate the imprisoned Muslim Brethren and other fundamentalists, two-fifths of whom were college or university students.

Since Egypt's 1983 election law, like its predecessor, banned parties based on religion or atheism, the Brotherhood was barred from contesting the 1984 parliamentary poll. Outside parliament, the Brotherhood, working together with its secular sympathizers, succeeded in capturing, electorally, the syndicates of journalists, lawyers, doctors, and engineers. Meanwhile, al Gamaat activists continued their social welfare work in religious education and health clinics through local mosques.

In the 1987 elections, the Brotherhood allied with a sympathetic secular party. The alliance won 17 percent of the vote, and 60 seats in a chamber of 448. The Brotherhood deputies demanded the enforcement of the Sharia, the ending of Egypt's military and economic ties with the U.S., and the abrogation of the peace treaty with Israel. As for extra-parliamentary fundamentalists, the government arrested hundreds of al Jihad members following clashes between Muslims and Christians in the spring of 1987. The departure in 1989 of Shaikh Omar Abdul Rahman first to Sudan, and then to the U.S., further weakened al Jihad.

Like other opposition parties, the Brotherhood boycotted the 1990 election when the government rejected their joint call to lift the state of emergency (in force since 1970) and conduct the poll under the supervision of a nongovernmental body instead of under the interior ministry.

During the Gulf War crisis, the Brotherhood, a traditional ally of Saudi Arabia, supported Iraqi President Saddam Hussein. The Brotherhood fueled pan-Islamic feelings at the expense of the West. Its absence from parliament meant the Brotherhood could no longer act as an intermediary between the government and such militant Islamic groups as al Jihad and al Gamaat, which intensified their anti-regime campaign.

In the spring of 1992, many Egyptian fundamentalists returned home from Afghanistan, where they had participated in the successful *jihad* or holy war against Soviet troops and the leftist Afghan regime. In Afghanistan, they had been trained by Pakistani intelligence and the American Central Intelligence Agency in subversive and terrorist actions. Now they decided to use these skills against the Egyptian regime, which they considered unrepresentative, unIslamic, and a handmaiden of Washington.

To hurt the Egyptian economy, al Gamaat activists began in October 1992 to attack foreign tourists. The government responded with an iron hand, and fundamentalists were killed in frequent encounters with security forces. Those arrested were tried by military courts, which handed out capital punishment in many cases. By early 1995, the total number of people killed in political violence over the past three years exceeded 700. Of 10,000 imprisoned fundamentalists (an official figure, believed to be about half of the total), two-thirds belonged to al Gamaat. In June 1995, al Gamaat claimed to have made an unsuccessful attempt to assassinate President Mubarak while he was on his way to attend an Organization of African Unity summit in the Ethiopian capital of Addis Ababa. Mubarak intensified his campaign against the fundamentalists.

Many in Egypt and abroad approve of Mubarak's strategy. They want him to maintain his hard-line policy, and ostracize both moderate (the Muslim Brotherhood) and militant (al Gamaat and al Jihad) fundamentalists. Others say he should co-opt the Brotherhood into the political system, and thus divide and weaken the fundamentalist camp. The U.S. prefers the latter policy; its embassy in Egypt maintains contacts with the Muslim Brotherhood. Mubarak is adamant about treating all fundamentalists, moderate or radical, as pariahs and using state power to crush them with force.

JORDAN

In Jordan, the Muslin Brotherhood, long recognized as a religious body, participated in the November 1989 parliamentary election through its political wing, the Islamic Action Front (IAF). The IAF emerged as the single largest group with 23 deputies in a house of 80. Another nine deputies, describing themselves as independent Islamists, worked closely with the IAF.

The Brotherhood in Jordan goes back to 1943–1945, when Hassan al Banna visited the country to set up Muslim Brotherhood branches in many Jordanian towns. When the Brotherhood was first banned in Egypt in 1948, hundreds of its activists went into exile in other Arab states, including Jordan. More activists came to Jordan in 1954 when the Brotherhood in Egypt was dissolved by President Nasser. Because Nasser tried to overthrow King Hussein of Jordan (1952–), the Jordanian Brotherhood turned increasingly pro-Hussein. When his throne was threatened by opposition demonstrations in 1956, it actively sided with him. In return, the king's 1957 ban on political parties exempted the Brotherhood because it was registered as a religious charity. In the decade following the 1967 Arab-Israeli War, King Hussein drew closer to Saudi Arabia for financial and ideological reasons. He also began co-opting Brotherhood leaders into his regime.

During the Gulf War, the Brotherhood supported Iraqi President Saddam Hussein mainly because he took a strong pro-Palestinian line. Partly in deference to the views of IAF deputies and their allies, King Hussein refused to join the coalition against Iraq.

After the Gulf War, Hussein quickly repaired his relations with the West, particularly the U.S. He prevented the IAF and the Brotherhood from becoming an overwhelming political force by modifying the electoral law by decree. The November 1993 general election was the first to be conducted officially on a multi-party basis. IAF leaders decided *not* to aim at winning a majority in parliament, and thus force the monarch's hands. They contested only 36 of the 80 seats, winning 16 seats and emerging again as the largest group in parliament. Most of the remaining places went to independents, with other political parties getting a single seat each.

Although the IAF opposed the Israeli-Jordanian Peace Treaty signed in October 1994, mustering a third of the parliament against it, the party did not carry its opposition to the streets. Thus fundamentalists remain an important part of the Jordanian political landscape.

PALESTINIANS

Just as the IAF rejected the 1994 Israeli-Jordanian Peace Treaty, Hamas and Islamic Jihad, two radical Muslim organizations in the West Bank and the Gaza Strip, rejected the 1993 Israeli-PLO Accord signed in Washington. Both these groups grew out of the Muslim Brotherhood branches that Hassan al Banna set up in many Palestinian towns between 1942 and 1945. During the 1948–1949 Arab-Israeli War, many Brotherhood activists volunteered to fight alongside Arab armies. The subsequent loss of more than three-quarters of Palestine to Israel embittered these activists. Following the war, the Gaza Strip came under Egyptian authority, and the West Bank under Jordanian. The fate of the Brotherhood in the Gaza Strip became intertwined with its Egyptian counterpart, and that of the Brotherhood in the West Bank with its Jordanian counterpart.

During the 1967 war, Israel occupied the West Bank and Gaza Strip. To weaken the nationalist, secular PLO in the occupied territories, Israel issued a license in 1973 to Shaikh Ahmad Yasin, the Brotherhood leader in the Gaza Strip, to set up the Islamic Centre as a charity to run social, religious, and welfare institutions. Israel helped the Islamic Centre/Muslim Brotherhood, which was funded largely by private and official benefactors in the oil-rich Gulf states, to grow as a counterpoint to the PLO.

President Sadat's assassination in 1981 by fundamentalists caused the Israeli government to have second thoughts. The Israelis arrested Yasin in 1983 for illegal possession of arms, and sentenced him to a long jail sentence. He was released two years later as part of a prisoner exchange deal between Israel and the Popular Front for the Liberation of Palestine—General Command. Yasin built on the popularity he had gained as a political convict of Israel, and rapidly increased the membership of the Islamic Centre/Muslim Brotherhood. However, his policies were not considered radical enough by some members, who broke away and secretly formed the Islamic Jihad in 1985–1986.

With the outbreak of the Palestinian *intifada* in late 1987, Yasin and other leaders of the Brotherhood decided to join the resistance movement against the Israeli occupiers. The result was the founding of an activist organ for the Brotherhood called Hamas, which is an acronym for *Harakat al Muqawama al Islami*, meaning Movement of Islamic Resistance. Hamas in turn set up an armed wing named after Izz al Din Qassam, a Palestinian leader killed in an armed confrontation with the British in 1935. The arrest of Yasin in 1989, in the midst of the *intifada*, did not much affect Hamas.

Israel's deportation of 413 leaders of Hamas and Islamic Jihad to south Lebanon in December 1992 proved counterproductive. The fate of these deportees—many of them doctors, lawyers, teachers, and other professionals—attracted much world media attention.

Both Hamas and the Islamic Jihad opposed the 1993 Israeli-PLO Accord. After the PLO set up the Palestinian Authority in the Gaza Strip in May 1994, with nearly two-fifths of the Strip still under Israeli control, these groups reiterated their earlier position: Jewish settlers and Israeli troops in the Palestinian territories were occupiers to be resisted by all means. Both groups carried out suicide bombing attacks on Israeli soldiers in Israel.

Opinion polls put support for Hamas in the Gaza Strip, which contains half of the 2 million Palestinians living outside the pre-1967 Israel (but inside the British mandate Palestine) at 35 percent. In contrast, support for the smaller, more radical Islamic Jihad was minimal. Both groups boycotted the elections to the Palestinian Council held in January 1996. While Hamas depended on contributions from sources at home and in the Arab world, the Islamic Jihad was known to be dependent on funds from Iran.

IRAN

After the collapse of the Ottoman Empire in 1918, the first country to strictly apply the Sharia was the Kingdom of Saudi Arabia in 1932. Iran did not follow suit until nearly half a century later. But the Islamic revolution in Iran in early 1979 transformed a secular, pro-Western state into an Islamic entity and thus left a deep mark on the region, the Muslim world, and the West. The Iranian monarch, Muhammad Reza Shah Pahlavi (1941–1979), was a close friend of the West, particularly the U.S. His overthrow by a popular revolutionary movement led by a cleric, Ayatollah Ruhollah Khomeini (1903–1989), stunned and puzzled the United States.

Relations between the U.S. and Islamic Iran deteriorated rapidly. After the taking of 67 American diplomats as hostage in Tehran in November 1979, the U.S. broke diplomatic ties with Tehran and imposed economic sanctions against Iran. (The hostage crisis and allied matters are discussed fully in Chapter 10.)

The West's initial fears that Islamic revolution would spread immediately to the other countries of the oil-rich Persian Gulf did not materialize, but the prospect still loomed. Therefore, Western leaders looked the other way when Iraqi President Saddam Hussein invaded Iran in September 1980. They did not use the United Nations Security Council to condemn Iraq for its aggression. Indeed, they were quietly pleased that a powerful neighbor had attacked Iran. They hoped that the chaotic state of Iran's military, which was equipped with American weapons for which it could get no spare parts, would defeat and destroy the Islamic regime. This was not to be.

Against all expectations, the conflict dragged on for eight long years. During the latter phase of the war, France overtly and the U.S. covertly helped Iraq. Thus, Iraqi President Saddam Hussein, aided by the Gulf states and the West, succeeded in containing whatever threat, ideological or otherwise, Iran posed to Iraq and other Arab states in the Persian Gulf region.

Iran failed because it did not have the resources to match those employed by an enemy assisted by the Arab states in the Gulf and by the West, especially France. What's more, the large majority of Muslims in Iran are Shia, whereas Sunnis are the dominant group in the Arabian section of the Gulf. By playing on this fact, the Arab rulers in the region were successful in eroding whatever popular goodwill Iran had enjoyed during the early period of its Islamic revolution. Ironically, the first Muslim fundamentalist movement arose in Egypt, a Sunni country. Iran's failure to defeat Iraq had little impact on the situation outside the Gulf region, except on the Shia minority in Lebanon. The emergence of fundamentalists as the most popular force in Algeria in late 1991 had nothing to do with Iran. The resurgence of militant Islamic groups in Egypt in 1992 had to do with events in Afghanistan, where the U.S., Pakistan, and Saudi Arabia funded, armed, and trained fundamentalists from all over the Muslim world to fight the Soviets and local leftists.

Iran's success in helping to form the Hizbollah ("Party of God") among the Shias of Lebanon came in the wake of Israel's invasion of Lebanon in 1982. Since then, Hizbollah, like the Palestinian groups in the occupied territories, has committed itself to ending the Israeli occupation of south Lebanon by "all means." The Hizbollah is more than a resistance movement, it is a political party, with eight deputies in the Lebanese parliament, and a social welfare organization.

CONCLUSION

The absence of legal, electoral avenues to change increasingly corrupt, repressive regimes in such pro-Western countries as Egypt has led many citizens to support Islamic fundamentalists. With the collapse of the Soviet Union, and the worldwide decline of Marxism, the only viable alternative many see to a badly functioning capitalist system is militant Islam. However, Muslim fundamentalism has evolved differently in different countries. Egyptian fundamentalism is distinct from Jordanian or Iranian fundamentalism. Of the five Arab political entities bordering Israel—Egypt, Jordan, Syria, the Palestinian Authority, and Lebanon—all except Syria have an ongoing fundamentalist movement. That fact casts a long shadow over the prospect of a lasting peace in the Middle East. No matter how well or badly the peace process between Israel and the Arab world proceeds in the coming years, the overall future of the region remains uncertain.

CHAPTER 8

Peaceful Future Uncertain

The Middle East peace process is based on United Nations Security Council Resolution 242, which was passed five months after the June 1967 Arab-Israeli War. It emphasizes "the inadmissibility of the acquisition of territory by war" and the need for "a just and lasting peace in which every State in the area can live in security."

A substantial minority of Palestinians believe that the 1993 Israeli-PLO Accord is not just; they want Israel to vacate the West Bank, Gaza, and East Jerusalem, and allow Palestinians to establish an independent, sovereign state. Many of the Palestinians who support the Accord see it as a means, albeit implicit, to ultimate independence. But most Israelis at present seem unprepared to accept an independent Palestine next door.

The key element in the Accord is the 88-member Palestinian Council, which was elected on the basis of universal suffrage in January 1996. Although its legislative powers are limited to socio-economic affairs, it is widely expected to have an impact on the Israeli-Palestinian negotiations on the final agreement, scheduled to begin in May 1996. Given the political freedom that exists in Israel, with which Palestinians are now intimately involved, it will be hard for Yasser Arafat—elected directly as president of the Palestinian Council—to control it tightly and create an authoritarian entity in the areas he administers. Having struggled long and hard against Israeli occupation, the Palestinians are unlikely to accept any muzzling of their freedom of speech and association by Arafat or any other leader.

To ensure the future security of Israel, its leaders want the country to establish strong economic links with Arab states. To them, economic cooperation is vitally important. It will help create wealth and prosperity, and give Arabs and Jews alike a stake in a thriving economic system. Hence, Israel has been as keen to move forward on the multilateral track of the peace process as on the bilateral track. It wants very much to penetrate the lucrative markets in the oil-rich Gulf states.

But nothing substantial will happen in the economic field until and unless there is peace between Israel and Syria, which in turn will open the way to a similar accord between Israel and Lebanon. President Assad's demand of total Israeli withdrawal for total peace has almost unanimous support in his country and elsewhere in the Arab world. But he has little to show so far for four years of hard bargaining. If he were to die without resolving this problem, his successor, lacking his stature, will have a difficult time tackling the issue.

Nor will serious negotiations between Israel and Lebanaon—if and when they commerce—prove smooth. Lebanon now has a Muslim majority, with Shias the single largest sect. Many of them look to Iran, the world's largest Shia state, for spiritual and political guidance. Iran considers the emergence of Israel as illegitimate. But Iran's extraordinary geostrategic importance, vast oil and gas reserves, and large population make it unlikely that the U.S. policy of ostracizing Tehran will be adopted by American allies in Europe and Japan, or by such major non-Western powers as Russia, China, and India. In any event, Iran has little ability to export Islamic revolution. Persistently low oil prices have weakened Iran financially, and Iranian leaders are having to focus on tackling the economic crisis and containing rising unrest at home.

The future of Islamic fundamentalism in the Muslim world will be settled more by what happens in Algiers than by what happens in Tehran. Algeria is an Arab country and a Sunni country; the Sunni sect commands the loyalty of 85 percent of the world Muslim community. Were the Algerian fundamentalists to negotiate a return to parliamentary politics, and gain power through the ballot, as they were poised to do in early 1992, it would have a ripple effect on Algeria's immediate neighbors and on Egypt, and would destabilize the regimes in these countries.

In Iraq, the political situation remains unresolved. Five years of UN economic sanctions have impoverished most Iraqis. They are so busy surviving that there seems little prospect of popular insurrection. Northern Iraq remains outside the control of Baghdad. Opposition forces, encouraged by the defection in August 1995 of two senior officials who are married to the daughters of Saddam Hussein, continue to forecast the downfall of the Iraqi president. If this happens, it is unlikely to be a surgical operation that leads to a smooth transition to a pro-Washington coalition of Iraqi forces. On the contrary, the country will most likely slide into a bloody civil war into which Saudi Arabia, Jordan, Syria, Turkey, Iran, and even the U.S. will be drawn. Since the conflict will be in an oil region, bristling with weapons, the price of petroleum will rise and damage the economies of the West and Japan. It is chastening to remember that the civil war in Lebanon lasted 15½ years.

In the Persian Gulf proper, the royal autocracies in the oil-rich states show little sign of sharing power with their subjects. Prominent among them is Saudi Arabia, which is so closely bound with the United States that any dramatic change there can only result in these ties being loosened. Such a change would impact immediately on the price of oil, a vital commodity for the industrialized nations of the globe. Given all these variables and points of potential conflict in this unpredictable region, the future remains uncertain.

PART 2

The Countries

Middle East 1996

CHAPTER

Turkey

The Republic of Turkey, the second most populous state of the region after Iran, is the successor to the Ottoman Empire, the heart of the Islamic world for four centuries, from 1517 to 1918. The Ottoman Empire included the Arab countries of the modern Middle East, as well as Palestine. Present-day Turkey, populated by Osmanli (or Ottoman) Turks, is a bridge between Asia and Europe. Indeed, the bridge over the Bosporus Straits in Istanbul connects the small European segment of the country with its vast Anatolian mainland in Asia.

PROFILE

Area & Population: Turkey is roughly rectangular in shape, extending some 1,000 miles from east to west and 300 miles from north to south, with an area of 300,948 square miles. Its European part, called Thrace, occupies 9,000 square miles. Its estimated population in 1993 was 60,641,000.

Cities: The capital, Ankara, is the second largest metropolis, with 2,559,500 residents. The largest city, Istanbul, has a population of 6,620,200. Next in size are Izmir (1,757,400), Adana (916,150), Bursa (834,600), Gaziantep (603,400), and Konya (513,300).

Constitution: In 1982, a draft document amending the 1961 constitution, which was based on the 1923 original, was approved by a national referendum. It reaffirms that Turkey is a secular, parliamentary democracy based on the principles started by the republic's founder, Mustafa Kemal Ataturk. It specifies a single-chamber Grand National Assembly with a minimum 400 members for a five-year term, and a president elected by the Assembly for a seven-year term. It authorizes the president to veto legislation, and appoint judges to the Constitutional Court, which, among other things, is empowered to pass judgments on the issues concerning civil and human rights specified in the constitution.

Economy: At the national Gross Domestic Product (1993) of $173.7 billion, the per capita GDP was $2,950.

Education: Free education is provided at all levels by the ministry of national education, youth, and sports. Literacy among the population aged 15 and over (1990) was 80.7 percent (female 71.1 percent, male 89.7 percent).

Ethnic Composition: Turks 79.3 percent, Kurds 16.6 percent, Arabs 1.9 percent, and others 2.2 percent.

Geography: Anatolia comprises 97 percent of Turkey. Although bordered by the Mediterranean Sea to the south, the Aegean Sea to the west, and the Black Sea to the north, Turkey has 1,630 miles of land border with Greece, Bulgaria, Georgia, Armenia, Azerbaijan, Iran, Iraq, and Syria. Most of Turkey's coast is lined with mountains that fall away inland to a series of plateaus. Deprived of sea winds by the surrounding mountains, the central plateau is arid. In contrast, the Aegean seaboard, with a Mediterranean climate, receives rain during winter. The rainfall in the northern seaboard along the Black Sea is high and more frequent. The Taurus Mountain range, bounding the plateaus to the south, turns inland to merge with the eastern massif. Mount Ararat, Turkey's highest peak at 16,955 feet, is near the Armenian border. Both the 1,680 mile-long Euphrates River and the 1,180 mile-long Tigris River rise in eastern Turkey.

Governmental System: Turkey is a republic, with a president elected by parliament.

Military: Turkey's total armed forces number 503,800 actives and 952,300 reserves. Military expenditure as percent of GDP in 1992 was 3.9 percent.

Mineral Resources: Turkey's mineral resources include antimony, bauxite, borax, chromite, coal, copper, iron ore, lead, manganese, mercury, rock salt, and zinc. Its annual output of iron ore is about 5.5 million tons, and of coal nearly 5 million tons. At 613,000 tons a year, its chromite production is one of the largest in the world. Its oil deposits amount to 10 billion barrels, or 0.1 percent of the global total; its output is 50,000 barrels/day.

Religious Composition: Muslim 99.6 percent, of which Sunnis are 90 percent and Alavis/Alawis (a sub-sect among Shias) 9.6 percent; Christian 0.4 percent.

HISTORY BEFORE 1918

Turks are divided broadly into three groups: Eastern/Central Asian Turks, Tatars/Turko-Tatars, and Western Turks. Consisting of Ottomans and Seljuks (also called Oghuzs), Western Turks are dominant in western Asia and eastern Europe. The original Turks were hunting people in the Altai Mountains of western Mongolia at a time when the steppes were occupied by Scythians, Huns, and other pastoral nomadic peoples, and the plains of Mongolia by the Kyrgyz/Kazakh people. As the Turks moved westwards, they adapted a pastoral nomadic life and occupied the steppes, reaching the shores of the Caspian Sea in the middle of the first millennium A.D. They were followed form the ninth to the eleventh centuries by the Seljuks, who played an important role in the ethnogeny of Turkmens (a Persian word meaning Turk-like), the term used for a group that speaks the Turkmen language, a member of the south Turkic group. In the tenth century, Mongols conquered Mongolia displacing the Kyrgyz/Kazakh people, and causing a migration of Turks and Turko-Mongols over the next several centuries. The Kyrgyzs/Kazakhs moved south to the present-day central Asian regions of Kyrgyzstan and East Kazakhstan, which until 1991 were part of the Soviet Union. Other Turks made forays into the adjoining Syr Daria region of the contemporary central Asian Republic of Uzbekistan.

Of the various Turkish realms that sprang up in the region, the Ottoman principality emerged as the most powerful under Osman I (1259–1326), a leader of Osmanali Turks who had embraced Islam. Its capital was Bursa, 65 miles southeast of Istanbul. When Muhammad II (1451–1481) seized Istanbul in 1453, he became heir to the (Christian) Byzantine Empire.

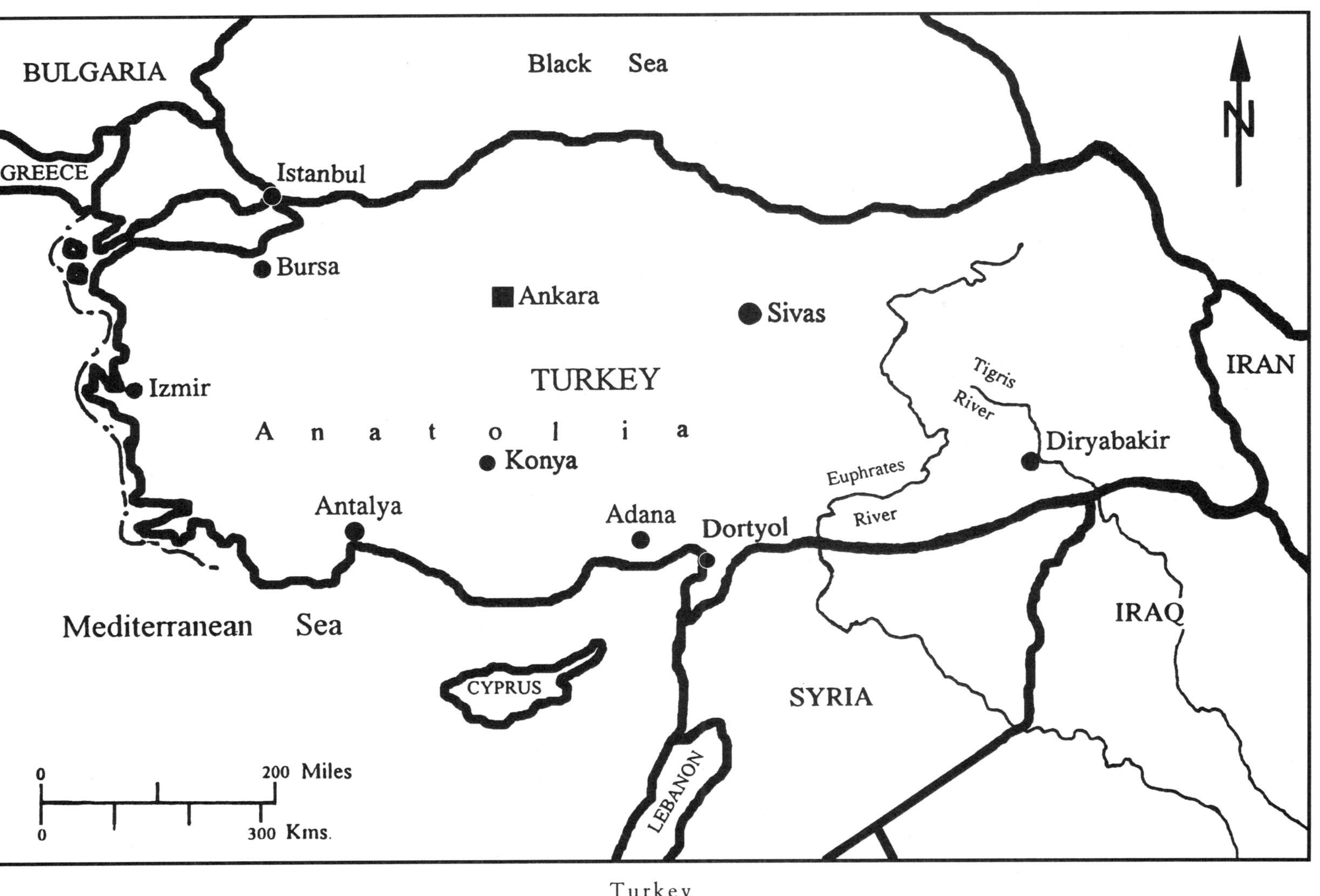
BULGARIA
Black Sea
GREECE
Istanbul
Bursa
Ankara
Sivas
IRAN
TURKEY
Izmir
A n a t o l i a
Tigris River
Diryabakir
Konya
Euphrates River
Antalya
Adana
Dortyol
Mediterranean Sea
IRAQ
CYPRUS
SYRIA
0
200 Miles
0
300 Kms.
LEBANON

Turkey

Under Selim I (1512–1520), the Ottoman Empire acquired Islamic primacy by usurping the caliphate from the Mamlukes in Cairo. The Ottoman ruler thus became the Sultan-Caliph, a secular-religious ruler, even though they did not start using the title of caliph until the eighteenth century. The empire expanded until the late seventeenth century, stretching from the Persian Gulf to Algeria, from Sudan in the south to southern Russia in the northeast, and to just beyond Budapest, Hungary, in the northwest. Like its rivals, Tsarist Russia and Persia, it had Muslim, Christian, and Jewish subjects.

By the early nineteenth century, mainly due to rapid advances made by the European Powers in technology and administration, the military balance began to turn against the Ottoman Empire. Sultan Mahmoud (1808–1839) tried to rectify the situation in 1827 by introducing administrative and military reforms along European lines, called Tanzimat. The European Powers favored Tanzimat, but that did not deter them from attacking the Ottoman Empire. Tsarist Russia was the most aggressive, with the tsars determined to act as protector of the 12 million Orthodox Christians under Ottoman rule.

Before the reign of Sultan Abdul Aziz (1861–1876), the Ottoman Empire, containing the holy cities of Mecca, Medina, and Jerusalem, as well as the leading Islamic cultural centers of Cairo, Damascus, and Baghdad, was the prime embodiment of Islamic civilization and power. But Abdul Aziz, heavily indebted to European Powers, could do little to protect the interests of Muslims outside his empire. In the mid-1870s, at Russia's behest, Bulgaria, Bosnia, Serbia, and Montenegro rebelled against Istanbul. This rebellion paved the way for the overthrow of Abdul Aziz by Midhat Pasha, the leader of the Young Ottomans, a powerful group formed in 1859 with the main objective of securing an elected assembly of believers.

A constitution drafted by Midhat Pasha, including a bill of rights and provision for an elected chamber, was promulgated by Sultan Abdul Hamid II (1876–1909) in December 1876. In April 1877, the Russian army crossed the Ottoman borders with the objective of winning freedom for Christian Slavs. The Russians reached Istanbul and the sultan had to sign the humiliating Treaty of San Stefano in March 1878, which was later revised by the Treaty of Berlin. According to the San Stefano agreement, Cyprus was handed over to Great Britain, Tunis to France, and the districts of Kars, Batum, and Ardahan to Russia.

In February 1878, Abdul Hamid II suspended the constitution and dissolved parliament. He arrested Midhat Pasha and banished the Young Ottomans to different parts of the empire. He turned to traditional Islamic values and thought to motivate the masses and regenerate cohesion in Ottoman society. His strategy succeeded because there had all along been a widespread current of Islamic feeling among the humbler Muslim subjects of the Ottoman Empire.

However, by the early twentieth century, Abdul Hamid II's populist approach to Islam at home and espousal of pan-Islamism abroad had proved inadequate to revitalize the disintegrating empire. In 1908, the army officers of the empire's European territories and a group of young intellectuals, later to be called the Young Turks, compelled the sultan to reinstate the 1876 constitution. They stood for pan-Ottomanism, the concept of forging a single Turkish-speaking nation out of the various peoples of the empire.

Soon after the 1908 coup, Crete announced its union with Greece, Bulgaria proclaimed its independence, and Austria annexed Bosnia and Herzegovina. In April 1909, an unsuccessful attempt was made to overthrow the Young Turks. They in turn deposed Sultan Abdul Hamid II, hoping that would improve the health of the empire. It did not.

The Balkans War of 1912–1913, in which the Ottoman Empire lost its remaining European territories and Libya, once again underlined the empire's weakness. The war destroyed the concept of pan-Ottomanism and made the empire more cohesive in religion by reducing its size. This encouraged the Young Turk triumvirate of Enver Pasha, Jamal Pasha, and Talat Bey to highlight pan-Islamism and pan-Turkism, when they took power in Istanbul in 1913. They were therefore receptive to the German kaiser's suggestion in 1914 to liberate fellow-Turks and fellow-Muslims from Russian bondage in central Asia to compensate the empire for its losses in Europe and North Africa. Thus, the Ottoman Empire fulfilled the kaiser's hopes by siding with Germany in World War I in October 1914.

Sultan-Caliph Mehmet VI (1909–1923) urged Muslims worldwide to mount a jihad, or religious struggle, against their imperial masters—Great Britain, France, and Russia. The response was poor, and the Ottomans did badly in the war. The Young Turk ministers resigned, and the sultan appointed a new cabinet that signed an armistice with the victorious Allies on 30 October 1918, twelve days before the German surrender.

For the next several years, the situation in Turkey, the nucleus of the old Ottoman Empire, remained turbulent. The new regime tried to break with its past as the center of an Islamic empire by creating a new nation-state once full sovereignty had been regained from the occupying Allied forces.

EMERGENCE OF THE TURKISH REPUBLIC: 1918–1923

In a duplicitous move, the Allies permitted Greek forces to occupy the Turkish port of Izmir on 15 May 1920. As the Greeks began marching east with the stated objective of annexing western Anatolia to create a Greater Greece, the Muslims of Anatolia took up arms under the leadership of Mustafa Kemal to wage a war of independence. Because of his brilliant performance on the battlefield in the defense of the Dardenelles and Galipoli against the British offensive during World War I, Mustafa Kemal had emerged as a war hero.

The collaboration of Sultan-Caliph Mehmet VI with the occupying forces accelerated the transformation of Ottoman nationalism, the driving force of the Young Turks, into Turkish nationalism. The Grand National Assembly (GNA) met in Ankara in April 1920 under the chairmanship of Mustafa Kemal. The constitution it adopted contained the following statements: "The government is based on the principle of the people's direct rule over their own destiny" and "the Grand National Assembly is the only real representative of the people . . . the holder of both legislative and executive power."

Kemal's prestige rose sharply when he won a decisive victory over the Greeks at the Sakarya River in August 1921. By July 1923, the Turks had defeated the Greek army and won Allied recognition of Turkey's sovereignty under the Treaty of Lausanne.

Once Turkey, now a nation of 12 million, had secured international recognition of its sovereignty, its parliament amended the constitution in October 1923 to describe the country's governmental form as "a republic," with power to choose the republic's head resting with parliament. Based in Ankara, the first parliament, so empowered, elected Mustafa Kemal president.

Deprived of temporal power, Mehmet VI went into exile. The mantle of the caliphate fell to his cousin, Abdul Majid. The Turkish parliament had to define its relationship with the new caliph, now only a spiritual figure, and the long-established institution of the caliphate. It recognized the need to maintain some sort of continuity with the past. Reflecting its view, the new construction stated: "The religion of the Turkish state is Islam."

HISTORY OF TURKEY SINCE 1923

Mustafa Kemal strengthened the fledgling republic by organizing his supporters as the Republican People's Party (RPP), and eliminating the other center of power in Tur-

The Blue Mosque, Istanbul, Turkey.

key, the caliphate. The latter had the potential to rally opposition to the new order. In March 1924, at Kemal's behest, the 290-member parliament decided, with a lone voice dissenting, to depose Caliph Abdul Majid and abolish the 1,292-year-old caliphate.

In April, the government promulgated an amended constitution that guaranteed equality before the law and freedom of thought, speech, press, and association. The next month saw further secularization with the abolition of the office of the Shaikh al Islam ("Wise Man of Islam"), the ministries of Sharia and *waqf* (religious endowments), the Sharia courts, religious schools, and the lodges and hostels of the Islamic mystics called *sufis*. The government retained control of mosques as well as the education, appointment, and salaries of the *khatibs* (preachers) and *imams* (prayer-leaders). Responsibility for these groups was given to the newly created Directorate-General of Religious Affairs (DGRA) under the prime minister.

With secularization came westernization, starting with dress. In August 1925, President Kemal issued a decree prescribing hats for all men and criminalizing the wearing of the traditional fez. He described the veil for women as "a ridiculous object," but did not ban it. Another crucial step towards westernization was the supplanting, in December 1925, of the Islamic calendar, which began with the flight of Muhammad from Mecca to Medina in 622 A.D., with the Gregorian calendar, which began with the birth of Jesus Christ.

Legal reform came in 1926. The combination of Ottoman statutes and the Sharia gave way to the Swiss Civil Code, the German Commercial Code, and the Italian Penal Code. The Swiss Civil Code changed the legal position of women overnight, ending polygamy and the inequity borne by women under the Islamic rules of inheritance, as well as legalizing civil marriage. However, women had to wait another eight years for the right to vote.

Thus, between 1922 and 1926, Kemal used state authority to effect revolutionary changes, from abolishing the caliphate to the compulsory wearing of hats. Finally, in 1928, the parliament, at Kemal's urging, deleted the constitutional clause that described Islam as the state religion. The same year, the parliament adopted a law introducing a Latin-based alphabet to replace the Arabic script, which was banned. This had the immediate and dramatic effect of cutting off society from its literature, religious and secular. Furthermore, over the years the Roman script would create an ever-widening gap between Turkey and other Muslim countries.

Secularization and westernization continued until Kemal's death in 1938. Educational reform manifested itself in 1930 in compulsory attendance at secular elementary schools. Religious reform in 1932 meant the call to Islamic prayer was now given in Turkish, instead of Arabic, an interference with the public ritual of Islam that caused widespread resentment. Further westernization came in 1935 with the replacement of Friday, the weekly day of rest in public offices, with Sunday, and with the introduction of surnames in the European style. Mustafa Kemal took Ataturk ("Father of Turks") as his surname. More importantly, in 1937, a year before Ataturk's death, the parliament inserted secularism or "laicism" into the constitution as one of the fundamental principles of the state.

The Kemalist revolution was strong because it was thoroughgoing. Besides reforming or enfeebling Islamic institutions, it impinged on the daily existence of citizens in dress, family relations, education, the alphabet, and the calendar. Its primary weakness was its dependence on a single leader.

After Kemal Ataturk

Following the Kemalist dictum of "Peace at home, peace abroad," the Turkish government remained neutral in World War II until January 1945, when it joined the Allies. But Turkey could not insulate itself from the economic hardships caused by the war. The peasantry and the traditional middle classes—artisans, craftsmen, and petty traders—had gained nothing, socially or economically, from the Kemalist revolution. These groups became disenchanted, and remembered fondly the Islamic era of the Ottomans.

Sensing popular restiveness, President Ismet Inonu (1884–1973), the successor to Kemal Ataturk, and the leader of the ruling Republican People's Party (RPP), allowed the formation of opposition groups. Of these, the Democratic Party (DP), constituted mainly of former Republican People's Party members, and led by Celal (pronounced Jelal) Bayar (1884–1986) and Adnan Menderes (1899–1961), was the most important. While committing itself to upholding Kemalism, it diverged slightly from the ruling RPP by calling for less governmental intervention in the economy and religious affairs. Its demand that religious freedom be treated as "a sacred human right" proved popular.

In the 1950 election, the DP won a landslide victory with 408 seats to the RPP's 79, and 55 percent of the popular vote. Bayar was elected president, and Menderes prime minister. The new government's popular first measure was to abrogate the penalty for reciting the prayer call in Arabic. In foreign affairs, the government's single most important achievement came in 1952, when it secured Turkish membership in the North Atlantic Treaty Organization (NATO), the Western defensive alliance against the Soviet Union and its allies. Sharing borders with the Soviet Union, Turkey became an important member of NATO.

In the general election of 1954, the DP improved its popular vote to 58.4 percent. The government now made religious education compulsory at the primary level and optional at the secondary, and recognized khatib-imam schools and colleges. The state-controlled radio began transmitting Koranic recitations and sermons. New mosques were built at the annual rate of 200-plus.

When a series of record harvests ended in 1954, the economic situation suddenly worsened. The resulting inflation hurt urban residents more than rural. Such influential segments of society as military officers, bureaucrats, and the urban middle class had become disaffected with Menderes whom they saw as favoring illiterate peasantry at their cost. The DP's share of the vote at the next election fell, but not enough to deprive it of power. This made the opposition restive.

To counter the challenge, the Menderes government passed repressive laws. But since the root cause of the troubles, the mismanagement of the economy, remained unresolved, the opposition refused to be cowed. In April 1960, at the behest of Premier Menderes, the parliament appointed a commission of inquiry to search and arrest suspects. By combining legislative and executive authority, the government violated the principle of separation of powers specified in the constitution. In late May, the military, headed by General Celal Gursel (1895–1966), seized power to safeguard "Kemalist values." The generals arrested Menderes and banned all political parties. A National Unity Committee of 38 military officers under General Gursel assumed the powers of the parliament. In January 1961, as a newly appointed constituent assembly began drafting a new constitution and electoral law, the military junta lifted the ban on political parties.

Article 2 of the new constitution specified that secularism was "the foundation stone" of the state. Article 19 stated that "No individual can exploit religion with the aim of changing the social, economic, political or legal structure of the state so as to promote religious principle, neither can he use religion to promote his personal or political interests." Article 21 specified that religious education. "should proceed in accordance with the foundations of modern science and education." Article 57 required political parties to conform to the principles of secularism. At the same time, the constitution exempted the following laws from judicial review: unification of education, wearing of a hat, abolition of *sufi* hostels and lodges, the civil code clause permitting civil marriage, and the Latin alphabet.

The constitution specified a two-chamber parliament, with one-third of the 150-member Senate resigning every two years, and the deputies of the 450-strong Grand National Assembly serving for four years. The introduction of proportional representation allowed the rise of small parties.

In the October 1961 election, the RPP secured 36.7 percent of the vote, and the Justice Party (JP), the renamed Democratic Party, led by Suleiman Demirel (1924–), won 34.7 percent. At the military junta's insistence, the two leading parties formed a coalition government under Ismet Inonu. In the next poll, however, the JP emerged as the clear winner, with 43 percent of the vote, to the RPP's 20 percent.

The JP government extended religious education from the lower grades of secondary schools to the upper. By setting up higher Islamic institutes in Istanbul and Konya, an important religious center, it completed an official system to educate and train a new generation of orthodox clerics, collectively called the *ulema*, thus undoing an important element of Kemalist secularism. In the private sphere, charitable associations centered around mosque construction, and Koranic schools approved by the Directorate-General of Religious Affairs became the chief instruments of Islamic revival. Between 1951 and 1967, the number of religious charities rose from 237 to 2,510.

However, backing for the Justice Party waned when its leader, Prime Minister Demirel, acquired for Turkey associate membership in the European Economic Community (EEC), which was committed to lowering tariffs between members. Since such an arrangement was bound to damage the well-being of the traditional middle classes—the artisans, craftsmen, and traders who were the backbone of the JP—these groups accused the party leadership of selling out to big business, the chief beneficiary of the EEC link. Their desertion of the JP led to the formation of several small parties, including the National Order Party (NOP), headed by Necmettin (pronounced Nejmettin) Erbakan.

Erbakan repeatedly attacked Demirel for being pro-American in foreign policy and being pro-big business at the expense of small traders. A member of the Naqshbandi *sufi*, he won the backing of the widespread Nurcu (pronounced Nurju) movement. The first party congress opened in 1970 with the Islamic cry, "Allahu Akbar," something that had not been heard at political gatherings in Turkey for almost half a century.

The military forced Prime Minister Demirel to resign in March 1971 for his failure to contain the rise of leftist activity in urban centers. It then took the NOP to the Constitutional Court, charging the party with violating the constitution by using religion for political purposes. The court upheld the charge and banned the party.

Undeterred, Erbakan formed the National Salvation Party (NSP) in October 1972 when a military-backed government led by Ferit Melen (1906–1988) was in office. Erbakan argued against Turkey's membership in the EEC because it merely perpetuated Turkey's role as an economic underling of "Western-Christian capitalism." Instead, he advocated independent industrial development as had been pursued by Japan.

In the 1973 poll, the NSP emerged as the third largest party, winning 12 percent of the vote and 49 seats, and holding the balance between the left-of-center RPP and the right-of-center JP. Erbakan became deputy premier in the two coalition governments formed between 1974 and 1977. Defying the constitution, Erbakan propagated Islamic ideas, and called for the formation of an Islamic Common Market consisting of Turkey and the Arab Middle East. Although the NSP's vote declined to 8.6 percent in the June 1977 election, Islamization of politics and education did not. The very existence of the NSP forced all major parties to take the existence of the Islamic vote into account and court it more explicitly.

A revived Islam began to compete with fascism and Marxism for the allegiance of disillusioned urban youth. Reflecting an accelerated emigration from villages, the number of youths in city slums grew sharply. Given the economic recession caused by steep oil price increases, and the country's huge foreign debt, the number of jobless shot up. Unemployed youths joined extremist parties of the left and right, which resorted to violence for political purposes. The developments showed the failure of Kemalism. Its main achievement had been to foster Turkish nationalism. But once nationalism had taken root, Kemalism lost its purpose, and the parties of the militant left and right thrived.

As strife in urban areas spilled into villages, it revived old racial and sectarian hatreds, between Turks and Kurds, and between Sunni and Shia, represented in Turkey by a sub-sect called Alavi (also spelled Alawi). A three-day sectarian-political riot in the southeastern town of Kahramanmaras in late 1978 left 117 people dead, most of them Alavis. Premier Bulent Ecevit (pronounced Ejevit) (1925–) put 12 eastern provinces under martial law to reassure the Alawis, but political violence did not subside. By the summer of 1980, it claimed more than 100 people a week.

On 6 September 1980, a rally in Konya by the World Assembly of Islamic Youth for the Liberation of Palestine, sponsored by the NSP, and attended by delegates from 20 Arab countries, drew large crowds. Among other things, the rally called for the founding of an Islamic state in Turkey. This rally triggered a military coup on 12 September and the removal of the coalition government led by Prime Minister Suleiman Demirel. The communique issued by the military leaders, headed by General Kenan Evren (1918–), the chief of the General Staff, described their action as being against "the followers of fascist and communist ideologies as well as religious fanatics." The junta arrested Erbakan and other NSP leaders and prosecuted them under Article 163 of the penal code for attempting to change "the fundamental principles of the state" and for organizing a demonstration against the secular laws of the country. The military suspended not only all political parties but also the leftist trade union movement.

After the 1980 Coup

While the immediate aim of the five-member National Security Council (NSC) led by General Evren was to halt the slide towards a civil war, its medium-term objective was to rid Turkish society of Marxist ideology and parties. It therefore encouraged Islamic ideas and education as an antidote to Marxism, and made the teaching of Islam in secondary schools compulsory.

In early 1982, the NSC appointed a 160-member constituent assembly. While retaining many of the articles of the 1961 constitution, the latest document whittled down certain basic freedoms. For example, it curbed collective bargaining by trade unions, and deprived students of the right to join a political party. The draft constitution was put to a vote in November 1982. The referendum also included the appointment of Kenan Evren, who resigned his military post, as president. Both proposals received massive support. Following the vote, political life revived, but only the parties approved by the military were allowed to function.

Among these were the Motherland Party, established by Turgut Ozal (1927–1993), the economic overlord of the military junta. By late 1982, most of the leaders of the pan-Islamic National Salvation Party had been released. Lacking legal political outlets, many NSP cadres joined the Motherland Party, thus turning the new organization into a coalition. In the 1983 parliamentary poll, held under an electoral law that discriminated against small parties, the Motherland won a slight majority in parliament, and Ozal became prime minister.

Under the presidency of Evren, the son of a prayer-leader, and the premiership of Ozal, a pious man never without his prayer beads, Islamic revival continued. In 1985, there were 72,000 mosques for 51.4 million Turks, or one mosque for 700 people—up from one mosque for 1,000 people in 1945.

In 1984, the Kurdish minority in Turkey launched an armed rebellion. Kurds are members of an ethnic group inhabiting the Zagros and Taurus Mountains of southeastern Turkey, northwestern Iran, northern Iraq and the adjacent areas in Syria, and the Nakhichevan enclave of Azerbaijan. Descendants of Indo-European tribes, they appear in the records of the early empires of Mesopotomia where they are described as "Kardouchoi." They trace their distinct history as mountain people to the seventh century B.C. Some 14 centuries later they embraced Islam. Like the Persians, who also converted to Islam, they retained their language, Kurdish. But unlike the Persians, they remained Sunni. In the twelfth century, the Kurdish general Salah al Din (Saladin) Ayubi overpowered the Shia Fatimid dynasty in Egypt and established the Ayubid dynasty (1169–1250). During the Ottoman and Persian empires there were periodic uprisings by Kurds against the central power. Kurdish nationalism manifested itself in late nineteenth century; the first Kurdish publication appeared in 1897. The 1920 Treaty of Sevres specified an autonomous Kurdistan, but it was not ratified. When the 1923 Treaty of Lausanne made no mention of Kurdistan, the aspirations of Kurdish nationalists remained unfulfilled.

Although the Treaty of Lausanne required Turkey to respect the rights of minorities, it refused to recognize the Kurds as a minority. They were officially called "mountain Turks," even though Turkish was not their mother-tongue. Turkey's parliament passed a law in 1924 banning the use of the Kurdish language. This meant denying nearly a sixth of the republic's citizens the use of their language at school. In 1964, the Political Parties Act forbade political groups from saying that there were different languages or races in Turkey. This act immediately outlawed the Kurdish Democratic Party formed after World War II.

Following the military takeover in 1971, the authorities used the singing of a Kurdish folk-song as a basis for prosecuting the singers.

During the rising conflict between militant left and right in the 1970s, Kurds sided with the leftists. After the military take-over in 1980, political activity ceased. The slow revival of politics that followed after a few years was limited only to those groups that backed military rule. Kurds did not belong to any of these parties. Many Kurds resorted to violence, chiefly through the Parte Krikarne Kurdistan (PKK), the Kurdish Workers Party, a militant leftist organization committed to creating an independent Kurdistan. It was led by Abdullah Ocala (pronounced Ojala).

The Turkish military remained staunchly opposed to any concessions to Kurds. Civilian Premier Ozal was more interested in conciliating Islamic groups and institutions than in tackling the Kurdish problem. He was widely known to be sympathetic to *sufi* brotherhoods, which revived.

With political life returning to normal in the mid-1980s, competition for voter loyalty increased. Aware of this, the parliament tinkered with the electoral law to benefit the Motherland. The result was 36 percent of the vote for the party in the 1987 parliamentary poll, but 64 percent of the seats—a remarkable achievement under a proportional, representative system.

The other parties to emerge from the election were the Social Democratic Populist Party (SDPP), the successor to the Republican People's Party; the right-of-center True Path Party (TPP), the renamed Justice Party, headed by Demirel; and the renamed (pan-Islamic) Welfare Party, led by Erbakan. Since the socio-economic conditions spawning leftist politics in the 1970s persisted, and since the left was virtually outlawed, the role of opposition fell increasingly to the Welfare Party.

Two important developments in the region had an impact on Turkish politics. One was the success of the Islamic forces in 1979 in Iran; they toppled the powerful pro-Western monarch, Muhammad Reza Shah Pahlavi, and showed that Islam was capable of overturning Western influence. Ten years later, by compelling Soviet troops to withdraw from Afghanistan, the Islamic groups there showed that Islam was capable of defeating Marxist socialism. Islam thus established its credentials as an indigenous third way, wedded neither to the East nor the West.

Reflecting the rise in popular interest in Islam, the staff of the Directorate General of Religious Affairs grew 16 percent annually, from 47,000 to 1985 to 84,000 in 1990, including 69,000 full-time clerics operating from mosques in Turkey, and 800 preachers and prayer-leaders attached to 21 Turkish embassies and consulates to serve Turkish expatriates abroad.

To widen the popular base of his party, Ozal continued to court the Islamic constituency. In 1988, he went on pilgrimage to Mecca, and became the first eminent leader to do so in the 65-year history of the republic. Ozal was elevated to the presidency in November 1989, following the end of the term of President Evren. In early 1990, the European Community decided to defer, indefinitely, talks on Turkey's full membership. It justified its decision on economic and political grounds: the high price of integrating the Turkish economy into the EC, and Turkey's failure to bring its adherence to human rights up to European standards. But this explanation did not dispel the popular perception among Turks that their country was being excluded on religious grounds.

With the prospect of economic-political integration into Europe receding, and the Marxist forces at home and abroad in decline, the popular attraction of Islam as a viable social ideology increased. On the eve of the Gulf War between Iraq and the U.S.-led coalition in January 1991, Turkish public opinion was divided. Turkey suffered economic loss due to the termination of its large trade with Iraq by the UN embargo against Baghdad. Many Turks accepted the presentation of the conflict by Iraqi President Saddam Hussein as a struggle between believers and unbelievers.

The government allowed its Incirlik (pronounced Inchurlik) base near Adana to be used by coalition air forces to bomb Iraqi targets.

In 1991, the government revived the Higher Islamic Council (HIC), composed of senior clerics and theologians, which had been disbanded after the 1980 military coup. When the secular press presented this as a precursor of Islamic reform, Hamdi Mert, deputy president of the DGRA, disagreed. "Our religion is an unchanging system. We believe it's the final revealed religion, so reform is out of the question." The repeal of Article 163 of the penal code, dealing with those who challenged secularism, in April 1991, gave a further fillip to Islamist forces.

Two major factors had weakened the Kemalist heritage. One was the unprecedented extension of access to information and personal mobility that television, telephones, and cars gave to ordinary Turks during the decade of economic liberalization and prosperity under Ozal. The other was the equally rapid expansion of higher education during earlier decades; the religious beliefs of a 99 percent Muslim society had by now reached the top layers of a civil administration headed by popularly elected politicians since the return of parliamentary democracy in 1983.

The October 1991 elections showed Islamist forces gaining ground. The alliance led by the Welfare Party won 17 percent of the vote and 62 seats, 40 of these belonging to Welfare. The Motherland, reduced to 115 seats, gave way to a coalition of Suleiman Demirel's True Path Party and Erdal Inonu's Social Democratic Populist Party. The new government, headed by Demirel, and supported by 266 deputies in a house of 450, took office in November. Later, the defection of 22 Kurdish members of the SDPP to form their own New Democratic Party reduced the government's plurality.

The Motherland's lackluster performance was due to poor economic growth, down from 9.2 percent in 1990 to 1.9 percent in 1991 (partly due to the Gulf War), and a lack of the dynamic leadership previously provided by Ozal. As president, he was required to stay away from party politics. During the same period, annual inflation shot up to 74 percent

Demirel's new government repressed the nationalist Kurdish movement by strictly applying Article 8 of the Anti-Terrorism Law, which forbids any activity, including expressing a verbal opinion, that can be interpreted as a "threat to national unity," irrespective of "the thought or purpose behind it." A result of the repression was the break-up of the Kurdish New Democracy Party, and the sentencing of eight of its parliamentarians to up to 15 years in jail. Behind the scene, President Ozal persuaded the government to recognize the existence of the Kurdish language by allowing radio and television broadcasts in Kurdish. But before this promise could be made public and translated into action, Ozal died of a heart attack in April 1993.

Premier Demirel was elevated to president. His True Path Party elected the American-educated minister of economy, Tansu Ciller (pronounced Chiller) (1946–), as its leader. She became the first woman prime minister of Turkey, and led the coalition of the TPT and the SDPP. During her premiership, the Kurdish problem worsened. Repeated attempts by the military to quash the Kurdish insurgency failed. In March 1995, some 35,000 Turkish troops marched into northern Iraq to wipe out the PKK insurgents operating from there. The exercise proved almost futile. By mid-1995, the Kurdish conflict had claimed 19,000 lives, with 2,000 rebels killed in the first half of the year. More than 160 people, including academics and journalists, were in jail, merely for expressing the need for granting cultural and political rights to Kurds. Among them was Yashar Kemal, the country's best known novelist, who received a 20-month jail sentence in March 1996. (He was later released.) The military's iron-fist policy led to the depopulation of many Kurdish villages in southeast Turkey, while the population of the leading Kurdish city of Diryabakir doubled.

On the Islamic front, the March 1994 countrywide local elections revealed rising support for the Welfare Party. By more than doubling its vote since the last such poll to 19 percent, the party now vied with the mainstream True Path (21.5 percent) and Motherland (20 percent) parties. Its capture of the town halls in Ankara and Istanbul surprised many. This was not the only measure of the rising popularity of political Islam. Both the True Path and Motherland parties had Islamic factions.

In the December 1995 parliamentary election, the Welfare Party emerged as the largest group (158 seats) in the 550-member chamber, well ahead of the True Path Party (135 seats) and the Motherland Party (132 seats). But it failed to share power in the coalition government that followed. By the mid-1990s, there was no longer deep hostility to Islamists from the government and the political establishment. Strong opposition to Islamists was now limited to diehard secularists and top military officers.

Yet, in its relations with the Muslim-majority republics in central Asia that formed in December 1991 following the collapse of the Soviet Union, Ankara stressed its secular image. It projected itself as a rival to Iran, which was portrayed as intent on exporting Islamic fundamentalism to these republics.

CHAPTER

Iran

The Islamic Republic of Iran is the most populous country in the region and the most strategic in the world. Its shoreline runs along the eastern side of the oil-rich Persian Gulf and about 300 miles of the Arabian Sea. For all practical purposes, it is a neighbor of the six Gulf states. It has land borders with Pakistan, Afghanistan, Turkmenistan, Azerbaijan, Armenia, Turkey, and Iraq, and it shares its Caspian Sea littoral with Kazakhstan and Russia. Archaeological excavations show Iran's history stretching back some 6,000 years. Its language and culture have influenced not only the regions to its north and west but also the Indian subcontinent to its east. In recent times, it has impinged strongly on the Western public mind as a hotbed of Islamic fundamentalism.

PROFILE

Area & Population: Measuring a maximum of 1,400 miles diagonally from northwest to southeast and an average of 450 miles across from northeast to southwest, Iran covers 636,300 square miles. Its estimated population in 1993 was 61,581,000.

Cities: With a population of 6,475,500, Tehran, the capital, is also the largest metropolis. Next in size are Mashhad 1,759,100, Isfahan 1,127,000, Tabriz 1,089,000, Shiraz 965,100, Ahvaz 724,700, and Qom 543,100.

Constitution: A draft constitution, submitted to the popularly elected Assembly of Experts by the Islamic government in August 1979, was modified, and then approved by a referendum in December of that year. It gave the leadership of the republic to Islamic jurists. Another referendum in July 1989 approved 45 amendments to the constitution. Iran is an Islamic republic, where social, political, and economic affairs are conducted according to the tenets of Islam. The constitution provides for an outstanding Islamic jurisprudent to be the supreme leader. Standing above the executive, legislative, and judicial branches of the state, the supreme leader exercises extensive powers, including the declaration of war and peace. He has the authority to appoint half the members of the Council of the Guardians [of the Constitution], the supreme judge, and the chief of the general staff. He can dismiss the elected president if the supreme court finds him derelict in his duties or the parliament, called the Majlis, declares him politically incompetent. Ayatollah Ruhollah Khomeini, named the first supreme leader, was assigned these powers for life. After Khomeini's death, the supreme leader, or the leadership council of three or five members, must be chosen by a popularly elected Assembly of Experts consisting exclusively of clerics. The president of the republic is the chief executive, and is elected directly for a four-year term. Legislative authority rests with the elected Majlis, which has a four-year tenure. The bills passed by the Majlis are vetted by the Council of the Guardians to see that they are in line with the constitution and Islamic precepts. The constitution specifies Islam of the Twelver Jaafari school, or Twelver Shiaism, as the official religion, with other (Sunni and Shia) Islamic schools accorded full respect. It recognizes Christians, Jews, and Zoroastrians as religious minorities, and entitles them to representation in the Majlis.

Economy: At an estimated national Gross Domestic Product (1992) of $71.2 billion, the per capita GDP was $1,190.

Education: Literacy in the population aged 15 and above (1990) was 54 percent (female 43.3 percent, male 64.5 percent).

Ethnic Composition: Persians 67 percent, Azeris 17 percent, Kurds 9 percent, Baluchis 2.5 percent, Arabs 2 percent, Turkmens 2 percent, and Armenians 0.5 percent.

Geography: Iran can be divided into four geographical regions: the Caspian Sea and its hinterland, the Persian Gulf and its hinterland, the plateau, and the central lowlands. The narrow band between the Caspian Sea and Elburz Mountains is fertile, with mild summers and winters. In contrast, the Persian Gulf hinterland is hot and humid. Between the mountain ranges of Zagros, running from Azerbaijan in the northwest to Baluchistan in the southeast, and Elburz, running from north to northeast, lies a large plateau. In the central area of this region are situated two salt deserts.

Governmental System: Iran is a republic, with a supreme leader chosen by a popularly elected Assembly of Experts.

Military: Iran's total armed forces number 513,000 actives and 350,000 reserves, with 100,000 in the Revolutionary Guard Corps. After examining the nuclear power project in Bushahr in January 1995, the inspectors of the International Atomic Energy Agency said that they saw no evidence of military use of the power plant. Military expenditure as percent of the GDP in 1992 was 5 percent.

Mineral Resources: Iran's mineral resources include chromite, coal, copper, iron ore, lead, magnesite, mica, silica, and zinc. At 92.9 billion barrels, its oil deposits are 9.2 percent of the global total; and at 20,700 billion cubic meters, its gas deposits are the second largest in the world, accounting for 14.6 percent of the aggregate. At the current rates of extraction, Iran's oil will last 70 years, and its gas deposits 360 years.

Religious Composition: Muslim 98.4 percent, of which Shias are 90.4 percent and Sunnis 8 percent; Christian 0.7 percent; Jew 0.1 percent; Zoroastrian 0.1 percent; and others 0.7 percent.

HISTORY BEFORE 1925

For most of its history, Iran has existed as an empire. The earliest Persian empire was ruled by the Achaemenid dynasty; at its peak in the fifth century B.C., the empire stretched from Afghanistan to North Africa. Alexander the Great (336–323 B.C.), overthrew the Achaemenid empire in 331 B.C., and after him Iran was ruled by the Seleucid, Arsacid, Parthian, and Bactrian dynasties. The Sassanians built a new empire during the first half of the third century A.D. They declared

Iran

Zoroastrianism as the state religion, and ruled over a society divided into priests, fighters, bureaucrats, artisans, and peasants. They reached their zenith under Anushirvan, who died in 579 A.D. After their defeat by Muslim Arabs in 637 A.D, their realm became part of the Islamic empire. With Iranians increasingly adopting Islam, their influence in the Islamic empire rose. This continued until 1258, when the Abbasid Empire, based in Baghdad, disintegrated. After several changes of ruler, Iran became part of the vast empire of the Turkish conqueror Tamerlane, who died in 1405. His descendants controlled Iran for about a century.

In the early sixteenth century, a Persian empire emerged under the leadership of Ismail Safavi. Until then, the inhabitants of Iran (called Persia until 1933), were mostly Sunnis. But Shah Ismail (1501–1524), a Shia, made Shiaism the state religion, party because the Turkish Ottoman Empire, which sought to conquer Persia, was Sunni. Under Shah Ismail, the Persian empire expanded to include Afghanistan and Iraq.

Safavid rule ended in 1722. By then, Iran was predominantly Shia. After the rise and fall of the Afshar and Zand dynasties, Muhammad Khan Qajar (1790–1797) set up the Qajar dynasty. In the twentieth century, Iran experienced successful popular agitation for a written constitution. Muzzafar al Din Qajar (1896–1907) introduced a written constitution and an elected parliament, called the Majlis, in 1907. Four years later, he disbanded the Majlis.

By the end of World War I, the financial position of Iran was so dire that only British subsidies could keep it afloat. Even the discovery of oil at Masjid-e Suleiman in southwest Iran in 1908 by British prospector William Knox D'Arcy did not help Iran's financial situation. D'Arcy's firm, which had begun commercial mining of oil in 1912, expanded to become the Anglo-Persian Oil Company (APOC). With the British admiralty's decision in 1913 to switch from coal to oil, the importance of petroleum increased. To ensure supplies, Great Britain acquired a controlling share in APOC, which later became the Anglo-Iranian Oil Company, following the renaming of Persia as Iran, and then British Petroleum.

London concluded a secret agreement with the Iranian government in 1919, which turned Iran into a virtual protectorate of Great Britain. The Majlis refused to ratify the treaty and Great Britain decided to supplant weak Qajar power with a strong authority represented by Colonel Reza Khan, commander of the elite Cossak Brigade. Reza Khan carried out a coup against the government of Fathullah Gilani in February 1921. He became war minister, and later prime minister. By crushing tribal and other revolts, he raised his popular standing. In October 1925, parliament, at his instigation, deposed Ahmad Shah Qajar, and appointed Reza Khan regent. Two months later, a freshly elected constituent assembly proclaimed Reza Khan (who had chosen Pahlavi as his surname) shah of Iran. He thus ascended the throne as Reza Shah Pahlavi (1925–1941).

THE PAHLAVIS: 1925–1979

Reza Shah Pahlavi established a strong, centralized state. In his drive to modernize the state, Reza Shah created a national civil service and police force. He quickened the pace of economic development, fueled by oil revenues. He canceled the economic preference given to European nations over the past century, and increased tariffs on imports. He pressured APOC in 1932 to raise oil royalties, and reduced its concessionary area by 80 percent. To create a national Iranian identity out of many ethnic ones, he required all males, by law, to wear Western-style dress and a round peaked cap. He ordered all public places and educational institutions to admit women. He reduced the powers and scope of the Sharia courts and strengthened secular, state courts. By manipulating elections, he reduced the share of clerics in parliament from 40 percent in the Sixth Majlis (1926–1928) to none in the Eleventh Majlis (1936–1938). He boosted industrialization by building 14,000 miles of roads and the Trans-Iranian Railroad by 1938.

Following the rise of Adolf Hitler in Germany in 1933, Reza Shah tried to play off Berlin against London and Moscow, which dominated Iran politically and commercially. When World War II erupted in September 1939, Germany was Iran's number one trading partner.

Reza Shah declared Iran neutral in the war, but the Allies saw the German invasion of the Soviet Union in June 1942 as one part of a pincer movement with its other arm being the German thrust into North Africa. In late August, Soviet and British troops invaded Iran at five points. Fearing a march of Soviet troops into Tehran, Reza Shah abdicated on 16 September in favor of his eldest son, Muhammad Reza. He left for British-ruled Maritius Island in the Indian Ocean, and then for South Africa.

Muhammad Reza Shah Pahlavi allowed the Allies to use Iran as a conduit for supplies to the Soviet Union to raise its capacity to fight Nazi Germany. This assistance helped turn the tide against Berlin on the Russian front.

Germany surrendered in May 1945. Following the departure of the British and the Soviets after the war, Muhammad Reza Shah Pahlavi faced leftist autonomous governments in Azerbaijan and Kurdistan, inhabited, respectively, by Azeri and Kurdish minorities. Aided by the U.S., he overpowered them.

After a failed assassination attempt in February 1949, Muhammad Reza Shah imposed martial law and consolidated his power. However, in his tussle with the nationalist leader, Premier Muhammad Mussadiq, the shah yielded in 1951 to the parliament's desire to nationalize the British-owned AIOC. Iran set up its own National Iranian Oil Company (NIOC). Great Britain protested, and succeeded in securing a Western boycott of Iranian oil. In August 1952, the parliament gave Mussadiq emergency powers for six months, and renewed them for a year in January 1953. Mussadiq came into conflict with the shah over control of the defense ministry. The ensuing power struggle led to the flight of the shah to Rome on 16 August 1953. But three days later, aided by the U.S. Central Intelligence Agency (CIA) and royalist military officers, the shah staged a come-back.

The U.S. now replaced Great Britain as the dominant Western power in Iran. On Washington's advice, the shah kept the oil nationalization law on the statute books, but downgraded the role of the NIOC. In 1954, it leased the rights to, and management of, Iranian oil for the next 25 years to a Western consortium, with the following share-out: AIOC 40 percent, five major U.S. oil companies (Exxon, Gulf, Mobil, Socal, and Texaco) 8 percent each, Royal Dutch Shell 14 percent, and Compagnie Francaise des Petrole 6 percent.

In 1955, Muhammad Reza Shah took his country into the Western-sponsored Baghdad Pact. At home, he established political police under military officers, later called Savak, a Persian acronym meaning Organization of National Security and Intelligence. Savak had strong ties with the CIA.

Under pressure from President John Kennedy (1917–1963), Muhammad Reza Shah began land reform in 1961. To overcome resistance to reform, he dissolved parliament and ruled by decree, a move that led to increased opposition, including from Ayatollah Ruhollah Khomeini, a Shia cleric based in the holy city of Qom. In January 1963, Muhammad Reza Shah launched a six-point White Revolution, and repressed the groups that called for a boycott of the referendum on it. The White Revolution won 91 percent approval. The shah's conflict with Khomeini reached a climax in June, and led to a nationwide uprising. The shah crushed it, reportedly causing thousands of deaths. Following a general election in September 1963, the shah eased his grip over the nation slightly. But when Khomeini resumed his opposition after his release from prison in April 1964, the shah expelled him from Iran to Turkey.

The shah further strengthened Iran's economic, military, and cultural ties with the West. To persuade the Western oil consortium to raise output, his government gave further concessions. Two ambitious Five Year Plans between 1963 and 1972 accelerated economic development in agriculture and industry, and raised literacy. In October 1971, Muhammad Reza Shah celebrated 2,500 years of "unbroken" monarchy in Iran, a dubious claim, at the ancient capital of Persepolis near Shiraz.

On the tenth anniversary of the White Revolution in January 1973, Muhammad Reza Shah announced nationalization of the Western oil consortium. The NIOC took over all the operations and ownership of the Western oil consortium. Buoyed by a rise in production to 6 million barrels/day in 1974, and the quadrupling of oil prices in 1973–1974, the shah visualized Iran becoming the fifth most powerful nation in the world. In 1977, oil revenue of $19.5 billion provided three-quarters of the government's annual income.

The inflated Five Year Plan of 1973–1977, involving, among other things, high expenditure on Western arms purchases, overheated the economy, causing rapid migration of rural workers to cities, high inflation, and widespread corruption. The discontent of a growing middle class of professionals and businesspersons—which had emerged during a quarter century of repression that destroyed all avenues of opposition except the mosque—combined with the alienation experienced by an underclass of recent rural migrants to create a powerful protest movement that began to stir in the fall of 1977.

With all avenues of secular opposition blocked by the shah's regime, more and more Iranians turned to the mosque and clergy to express their rising discontent. Under pressure from newly elected U.S. President Jimmy Carter, the shah began moderating his repression of the opposition. This move emboldened the dissenters.

Guided by Khomeini, who had been based since 1965 in the Iraqi city of Najaf, religious and secular opposition combined to mount a popular revolutionary movement to demand the shah's deposition. The movement proved influential enough to immobilize the vital oil industry and cause the disintegration of the 413,000-strong military. The strike of oil workers in October 1978, when oil production was at 5.3 million barrels/day and domestic consumption at about 800,000 barrels/day, played a crucial role in weakening the shah's regime. The loss of Iran's supplies to the international oil market pushed the world price from $13 to $20 a barrel.

The shah's last-minute ploy to appoint a dissenter, Shahpour Bakhtiar, as prime minister failed. On 16 January 1979, the Shah left Iran for "holiday" in Aswan, Egypt. This was the end of monarchy in Iran, which dated back to 1501. In its place arose an Islamic republic under Khomeini. During the 15-month revolutionary struggle some 20,000 to 40,000 Iranians were killed. From Egypt, the shah traveled to other countries seeking asylum, and failing. He was allowed to enter the U.S. clandestinely in October 1979 for medical treatment. Iran demanded his extradition on charges of corruption and violation of Iran's 1906–1907 constitution. The U.S. refused. Relations between Iran and the U.S. deteriorated sharply.

THE ISLAMIC REPUBLIC SINCE 1979

The Islamic Republic of Iran was founded by Ayatollah Ruhollah Khomeini following a popular referendum. Born in a religious Shia family in Khomein, he was educated in theology at a religious school run in the nearby city of Arak. At 20, he went to Qom for further theological studies. After graduating in the Sharia, ethics, and spiritual philosophy, he became a theological teacher in Qom. In 1945, he graduated to the clerical rank of *hojatalislam* ("proof of Islam"), which allowed him to collect a circle of disciples who accepted his interpretations of the Sharia. In 1961, following the publication of his book *Clarification of Points of the Sharia*, he was promoted to ayatollah ("Sign of Allah"). This qualified him to become a leader of radical clergy.

In early 1963, he combined criticism of the White Revolution with a personal attack on the shah. His subsequent arrest in June triggered a countrywide uprising. The shah used the army to quash it. Later, pressured by clerics, he transferred Khomeini from a jail to a house under guard in a Tehran suburb. After his release in April 1964, Khomeini resumed his oppositional activities; he soon found himself expelled to Turkey. He spent a year in Bursa, and then moved to Najaf, Iraq, a holy city of Shias. From there, Khomeini kept up his campaign against the shah. In 1971, he published *Islamic Government: Rule of the Faqih* [Jurisprudents]. In it, he argued that instead of prescribing do's and don'ts for the believers and waiting passively for the return of the Hidden Imam (the last Shia religious leader who disappeared in 774 A.D.), the Shia clergy should attempt to oust corrupt officials and repressive regimes, and replace them with ones led by just Islamic jurists.

Following the Algiers Accord of March 1975 between Iraq and Iran, which ended the hostility that had existed between the two countries since the overthrow of the pro-Western Iraqi monarchy in 1958, the number of Iranian Shia pilgrims who came to Najaf rose sharply. Khomeini was able to guide his followers in their anti-shah campaign through tape recordings smuggled into Iran by pilgrims. These audio tapes became all the more important as the revolutionary process, consisting of massive and repeated demonstrations and strikes, gathered momentum from November 1977 to October 1978, when Khomeini was exiled to France. By then, he had shrewdly united various disparate forces along the most radical demand—deposition of the shah. Soon the shah was on the defensive, with the economy, crippled by the stoppage of vital oil exports, in a tailspin.

On 13 January 1979, three days before the shah's final departure from Iran, Khomeini appointed an Islamic Revolutionary Council (IRC) to facilitate the formation of a provisional government to produce a constitution for an Islamic republic in Iran. Following a referendum based on universal suffrage, Khomeini announced the establishment of the Islamic Republic of Iran on 1 April. In August, an elected Assembly of Experts debated the draft constitution, which gave the Islamic jurisprudents leadership of the republic. The final document was approved by a referendum in December.

Khomeini first isolated and then repressed all non-Islamic forces that had backed the revolutionary movement. In the early crisis-ridden years of the Islamic Republic, he ruthlessly crushed all opposition bent on either staging a military coup against the regime (the strategy of monarchists) or triggering a civil war (the strategy of the Mujahedin-e Khalq, a leftist body). Convinced that Iran could never be truly independent until it had removed American influence form all walks of Iranian life, Khomeini kept up his campaign against the U.S. He regarded it as the prime source of moral corruption and imperialist domination in the world, and called it the "Great Satan."

The Seizure of American Hostages

On 4 November 1979, militant Islamist students in Tehran occupied the U.S. embassy and took hostage 67 American diplomats. This was done to secure the extradition of the shah, who had been admitted to the U.S. for medical treatment in October. President Carter immediately froze Iran's large reserves in the U.S., severed diplomatic relations, and together with the European Community imposed economic sanctions against Iran. But the disruption of Iranian oil supplies caused prices to rise sharply; and with the resumption of exports at 3.2 million barrels/day in the spring of 1979, Iran earned more than it had with higher exports before the revolution. The clandestine military attempt to rescue the hostages in April 1980 failed, and its many agents in Iran, including the commander of the Iranian air force, Amir Bahman Bagheri, were exposed.

The hostage-takers dispersed their captives to different locations in Iran. Various secret attempts to resolve the crisis proved futile, even though the shah, whose entry into the U.S. had triggered the crisis, died in July 1980 in Cairo. Carter made release of the American hostages a central issue in his campaign for re-election, which made Khomeini intransigent. Along with the sluggish U.S. economy, the hostage issue was instrumental in Carter's defeat by Ronald Reagan (1911–) in the November 1980 presidential election. It was the first time that the policies of a Third World country had so directly affected American politics.

In line with a secret deal between Iran and the U.S., brokered by Algeria, the American hostages (now reduced to 52 due by earlier, individual releases) were freed in Algiers after 444 days in captivity, the release occurred minutes after President Carter handed over the presidency to Reagan on 20 January 1981. The episode poisoned relations between Tehran and Washington.

Before and after the shah's departure from Iran, tens of thousands of rich and upper middle class Iranians fled to the U.S. and Western Europe. With the exit of the Westernized minority, it became easier for the government to reshape society in an Islamic mould. Alcohol, bars, gambling, and mixed bathing were banned. Later the *hajab*, a scarf, was prescribed by law for all women. Revolu-

Friday prayer congregation in the open air, Tehran, Iran.

tionary courts and revolutionary guards became permanent features of life.

Several attempts were made by the displaced Iranian leaders, operating from France, Iraq, and the U.S., to overthrow the new regime through a military coup. When the last of these failed in July 1980, the scene was set for a frontal attack on Islamic Iran, which had by now alienated not only the U.S. but also the neighboring Gulf states.

The Iran-Iraq War

In September 1980, Iraq invaded Iran. Iraq unilaterally abrogated the 1975 Iran-Iraq Treaty, and claimed full sovereignty over the Shatt al Arab waterway, which the two neighbors had agreed to share. Despite the chaotic state of its military, Iran was able to stop the Iraqi advance. Khomeini was incensed that neither the United Nations nor the Islamic Conference Organization (ICO) condemned the Iraqi action. However, the Iraqi aggression helped him rally Iranians on a patriotic platform, and make his factious supporters sink their differences on how to run the country.

By mid-November, Iraq occupied 10,000 square miles of Iranian territory in the southern and central sectors, including the oil city of Abadan. A wet winter helped cause a military stand-off. Although the much enlarged Iranian military blocked further Iraqi advances, it failed to lift the siege of Abadan. The stalemate continued until April 1982.

In Iran, there was turmoil after the Majlis impeached the first popularly elected president, Abol Hassan Bani-Sadr (1933–), in June 1981. The opposition, led by the Mujahedin-e Khalq, mounted an armed struggle against the regime. It claimed to have killed over 1,200 religious and political leaders by early 1982. In return, the government executed 4,000 guerrillas, most of them belonging to the Mujahedin-e Khalq.

During the spring of 1982, Iran recovered most of the land lost in its war with Iraq. By 30 June, Baghdad claimed to have withdrawn voluntarily from all occupied Iranian territory, a claim disputed by Tehran. In early July, Iran marched into Iraq and tried to conquer Basra, the second city of Iraq. With nine divisions locked in the largest infantry combat since World War II, fierce battles raged for a fortnight. Finally, Iran managed to hold only 32 square miles of Iraqi land.

During April 1983, Iran's offensive in the southern sector to reach the strategic Basra-Baghdad highway failed. Its offensive in the Kurdish north four months later yielded the Iraqi garrison town of Hajj Umran. In February 1984, Iran's second attempt to cut off the Baghdad-Basra highway failed. Following an offensive later the month in the Haur al Hawizeh marshes in the south, Iran seized the oil-rich Majnoon Islands of Iraq.

Aware of the unifying effect of the war in Iran, Khomeini repeatedly rejected offers of mediation and a cease-fire. His attempts to export Islamic revolution to the neighboring countries failed. The Gulf monarchs, all of them Sunni, managed to sideline Khomeini by successfully portraying him as a Shia leader of a non-Arab country.

The war remained stalemated from March 1984 to January 1986. Iraq escalated its attacks on Iranian oil tankers, using French-made Exocet air-to-ship (surface-skimmer) missiles, and intensified air raids on Iran's Kharg oil terminal, which handled most of its petroleum exports. Iran retaliated by hitting ships serving the ports of Kuwait and Saudi Arabia, which were aiding Iraq. In March 1985, an Iranian brigade reached the Baghdad-Basra highway, but was unable to withstand Iraqi counter-attacks, which rolled back the Iranians. Intensified Iraqi attacks on the Khrag oil terminal and Iranian tankers reached a peak in mid-August 1985.

From February 1986 to January 1988 the war of attrition between the combatants escalated, and the U.S. began intervening covertly in the conflict by aiding Iraq. The Iranian assault in February 1986 in the south, which resulted in the capture of 310 square miles of the Fao Peninsula, broke the stalemate. Determined effort by Iraq to regain Fao failed.

In March 1986, following a report by UN experts on poison gases, the UN Security Council combined its condemnation of Iraq for deploying chemical weapons with its disapproval of the prolongation of the conflict by Iran. The next month, Kuwait and Saudi Arabia flooded the oil market and caused the petroleum price to fall below $10 a barrel from $27 in the previous December. This sharply reduced the oil income of Iran and Iraq, but the latter was cushioned by the aid of some $10 billion a year from its Gulf allies, the West, and the Soviet Union.

From July 1986, using covert official American expertise, Iraq began using its air force more aggressively than before, hitting Iran's economic and infrastructral targets, and extending its air strikes to the Iranian oil terminals in the lower Gulf. In January 1987, Iran's offensives in the south brought its forces within seven miles of Basra, but Iran failed to capture the city.

On 20 July 1987, the UN Security Council unanimously passed Resolution 598 calling for a cease-fire and a withdrawal by the warring forces to the international border. The 10-article text included a clause for an impartial commission to determine war responsibility, one of the major demands of Iran. Iraq accepted the resolution on condition that Iran did the same. Four days later, a Kuwaiti supertanker on the first Gulf convoy escorted by U.S. warships hit a mine, believed to have been planted by Iran. The subsequent naval build-up by the U.S., Great Britain, and France brought 60 Western warships to the region.

On the seventh anniversary of the war on 22 September 1987, Iraq had nearly 400 combat aircraft, six times the number of Iran's airworthy warplanes. Baghdad possessed 4,500 tanks, 3,200 armored fighting vehicles, and 2,800 artillery pieces versus Tehran's respective totals of 1,570, 1,800, and 1,750. Iraq had 955,000 regular troops versus Iran's 655,000, and Iraq's Popular Army, at 650,000, was slightly larger than Iran's Revolutionary Guards Corps at 625,000.

Iranian outpost along the Shatt al Arab, January 1989.

In October, the U.S. navy sank three Iranian patrol boats in the Gulf, claiming that Iran had fired on an American patrol helicopter; U.S. warships destroyed two Iranian offshore oil platforms in the lower Gulf in retaliation for an Iranian missile attack on an American-flagged supertanker docked in Kuwaiti waters. Tehran's capacity to mount major offensives was much reduced by shortages of manpower and money, and the damage done to its bridges, factories, and power plants by ceaseless Iraqi bombing.

During this phase of the war, from February to June 1988, Iraq succeeded in hitting Tehran with long-range surface-to-surface missiles, thus demoralizing the population. Iran retaliated by hitting Baghdad, which was much nearer to the international border. In mid-April, the Iraqis recaptured the Fao Peninsula by using chemical weapons, while U.S. warships blew up two Iranian oil rigs, destroyed an Iranian frigate and immobilized another, and sank an Iranian missile boat. During late May, Iraq staged offensives using chemical weapons in the northern and central sectors, and then in the south, regaining territory. Between 19 and 25 June, the Iraqis, using poison gas, retook the Majnoon Islands.

On 3 July, an American cruiser shot down an Iran Air airbus with 290 civilians abroad in the lower Gulf, mistaking it for a combat aircraft. On 18 July, Iran accepted UN Security Council Resolution 598 unconditionally. Two days later, Khomeini stated that acceptance of a truce was "in the interest of the revolution and the system at this juncture." By then, he had realized that further military reverses at Iraqi hands would threaten the future of his regime. Iraq's new offensives to seize Iranian territory failed, and on 20 August 1988 a truce came into effect under UN supervision.

The twentieth century's longest conventional war cost Iran 194,931 dead, and Iraq somewhere between 160,000 and 240,000 dead. The estimated cost of the war to Iran was \$74 to \$91 billion, plus military imports of \$11.6 billion, and to Iraq \$94 to \$112 billion, plus military imports of almost \$42 billion. In July 1990, Iraq's deputy premier, Tariq

Aziz, put military imports during the war at $102 billion.

Neither state lost much territory, nor was there a change of regime in either country. With a million men in its military, Iraq emerged as the most powerful country in the region, outstripping Turkey and Egypt. On the other side, the eight-year conflict enabled Khomeini to consolidate the Islamic revolution.

Khomeini died of cancer in June 1989. He left behind an Iran with its territorial integrity intact, its Islamic regime well-entrenched, but its economy shattered. He also left behind his fatwa on *The Satanic Verses*, a novel by Salman Rushdie, a writer born in India but educated in Great Britain and holding British citizenship.

The Rushdie Affair

In September 1988, a London-based publisher, Viking Penguin, published *The Satanic Verses* in Great Britain. In the second chapter of the book, Salman Rushdie portrayed Prophet Muhammad—thinly disguised as a fictional character called Mahound—as an unscrupulous, lecherous impostor who hoodwinked his followers. Later, the author suggested that Mahound included in the Koran certain verses that turned out to be the work of the devil—the satanic verses. In the fourth chapter of the book, Mahound was portrayed as "spouting rules, rules, rules until the faithful could scarcely bear the prospect of any more revelations." This was seen by Muslims as a symbolic attack on the Sharia, which consists of the Hadith and the divinely revealed Koran. Later, the writer offered a long fantasy about "the Curtain," the most popular brothel of Jahilia (i.e., Mecca). In order to attract clientele, the prostitutes assumed the names of the wives of Muhammad.

Certain Muslim leaders in Great Britain requested Prime Minister Margaret Thatcher to ban the book and prosecute Rushdie for slandering Islam. She replied that the content of the book, a literary work, did not contravene British law, which limits freedom of expression only in such areas as national security, personal libel, and engendering racial hatred. Secondly, slandering Islam was not an offense in law. Irate Muslims began demonstrating against the book and its author. In mid-January 1989, when a copy of the book was burned at a Muslim rally in the city of Bradford, the national media took note of the issue. On 12 February, on the eve of the publication of the American edition of the novel, there was a demonstration in Islamabad, the capital of Pakistan, where the novel had been banned. As the demonstrators marched to the American Center, they were fired upon by the security forces, and six people were killed.

This news was broadcast in Iran, a neighbor of Pakistan. One or two acolytes of Khomeini approached him about delivering a *fatwa*, a religious verdict, on the matter. On 14 February, Khomeini issued the *fatwa*:

> I would like to inform all the fearless Muslims that the author of the book entitled *The Satanic Verses*, which has been compiled, printed and published in opposition to Islam, the Prophet [Muhammad] and the Koran, as well as the publishers, who are aware of the contents, have been sentenced to death. I call on all zealous Muslims to execute them quickly . . . so that no one [would] dare to insult Islamic sanctity.

Hojatalislam Hassan Sanai, head of a religious foundation in Iran, offered a reward of $2.6 million to an Iranian and $1 million to a non-Iranian for the assassination of Rushdie. With this, the issue became international, involving sovereign states, and soured Iran's relations with several Western nations, especially Great Britain. Khomeini's death made no difference to the validity of his *fatwa*, his followers argued. Also, with his demise, there was now no chance of the *fatwa* being revoked or annulled. He was the only one who had the authority and religious standing to do so.

Iran After Khomeini

The succession to Khomeini's office of supreme leader by Ayatollah Ali Khamanei, the erstwhile president, was smooth. So too was the elevation of Ali Akbar Hashemi Rafsanjani (1934–), the erstwhile speaker of parliament, to the presidency by popular vote.

Iran benefited, directly and indirectly, from the 1990–1991 Kuwait crisis and Gulf War. Ten days after invading Kuwait on 2 August 1990, Iraqi President Saddam Hussein unilaterally offered to abide by the 1975 Iran-Iraq Treaty, stipulating an equal sharing of the Shatt al Arab. Iran agreed. Aware of the importance of Iran in making effective the UN embargo against Iraq, President George Bush reassured Iranian president Rafsanjani, through the Swiss embassy in Tehran, which looked after American interests in Iran, that the U.S. would leave the Gulf once Iraq had been expelled from Kuwait.

Tehran observed the UN embargo, but was unhappy to see fellow Muslims in Iraq suffer as a result of the war that erupted in January 1991. Whatever understanding had been established between Rafsanjani and Bush was lost when the latter left the White House in January 1993.

Upon Bill Clinton's assumption of the presidency, and appointment of Warren Christopher as secretary of state, relations between Washington and Tehran reverted to cold hostility. As a senior official in the state department during Carter's presidency, Christopher nurtured a grudge against Iran for taking American diplomats hostage, and making the U.S. appear helpless to its own people and to the world.

Making a break with the immediate past, President Rafsanjani tried to liberalize the Iranian economy, which had a strong public sector. Removing subsidies on essentials and selling oil products at higher prices at home to cut the budget deficit proved unpopular. His vote in the presidential poll declined from 94 percent in 1989 to 63 percent four years later. However, low prices for oil in the world market, fluctuating around $16 a barrel in the mid-1990s, were beyond Rafsanjani's control.

Washington continued to list Iran as a state that supported international terrorism. In 1995, after Iran had signed a contract with Russia to supply nuclear facilities to Iran for its nuclear power plant in Bushahr, Washington alleged that Iran was pursuing a military nuclear program. The inspectors of the International Atomic Energy Agency failed to find evidence to support this charge. Moscow argued that the nuclear reactors they had contracted to sell were of the same type that South Korea would supply North Korea under an agreement devised by Washington.

In March 1995, President Clinton imposed a trade and investment embargo on Iran, and urged the Western allies and Japan to do the same. None of them followed suit. Indeed, the $1 billion contract that Conocon, a subsidiary of an American oil giant, was obliged to cancel was picked up by a French oil company, Total. Canada, the members of the European Union, and Japan argued in favor of "constructive engagement" with Iran to persuade it to moderate its policies. They were aware of Iran's vast oil resources, its (comparatively) large population in the region, and its geostrategic significance. They were conscious too that alone among the eight states in the gulf region, only the Islamic regime in Iran had held regular multi-candidate elections—parliamentary and presidential—and that its Majlis had emerged as the most lively parliament in the region after the Israeli Knesset.

However, the U.S. further hardened its policy towards Tehran. In July 1995, President Clinton ordered the Fifth Fleet to be deployed permanently in the Persian Gulf. Its main, though unstated, task was to police Iran. This was further evidence that the Clinton administration was committed to pursuing the "dual containment" policy it had adopted in early 1993. The basic idea was to treat both Iran and Iraq as pariah states, and work towards weakening them by all means short of war. Until then, the U.S. state department had considered Iran and Iraq part of a "zero sum" equation, that is, gain by one meant loss for the other, and vice versa. Under the zero sum policy, the U.S. sought not to weaken Iran too much, fearing that would make Iraq too powerful, and not to enfeeble Iraq too much so as to make Iran too strong.

As in the case of all other oil-exporting countries, the economy of Iran is suffering due to low petroleum prices. This is creating disaffection among ordinary Iranians. But there is no sign as yet that it has reached such proportions that it is destabilizing the regime. Since Muslim clerics, the backbone of the Islamic state, are in daily touch with the masses, the present system has a built-in feedback mechanism. Therefore, a popular, sustained uprising on a national scale, such as the one which overthrew the Pahlavi dynasty, is unlikely. Also, since elections to parliament and the presidency are held regularly on a multicandidate (though not multi-party) basis, the voters know they have a chance to change their law-makers and their chief executive. That in turn ensures that popular disaffection does not build up to revolutionary proportions.

Within this general framework, Iran is set to continue as an Islamic state even if the U.S. increases the economic and diplomatic pressure against it in the coming years.

CHAPTER 11

Iraq

The Republic of Iraq consists largely of the fertile plain of Mesopotamia and the mountainous region of Kurdistan. Mesopotamia, a cradle of ancient civilization, is irrigated by the Euphrates and Tigris rivers. Known in the biblical era as Perath, the Euphrates rises in east Turkey, passes through Syria and Iraq, and merges with the Tigris (called Hiddekil in ancient times), which also originates in the mountains of eastern Turkey, to form the 120-mile Shatt al Arab, which flows into the Persian Gulf.

PROFILE

Area & Population: Roughly triangular, Iraq measures 170,600 square miles. Its estimated population in 1992 was 18,838,000.

Cities: With a population of 4,217,000, Baghdad, the capital, is also the largest metropolis. Next in size are Basra 1,634,000, Mosul 1,282,000, Irbil 850,000, and Najaf 550,000.

Constitution: Following a coup by the Arab Baath Socialist Party military officers in July 1968, an interim constitution was promulgated in September. Amended about a year later, it was replaced by another provisional version in July 1970. The latter document was amended in 1973 and 1974. A draft of the permanent constitution was submitted in March 1989 to the National Assembly, which had been established in 1980. Although the Assembly endorsed it in July 1990, it remains to be approved by referendum before it can be enforced. The September 1968 constitution described Iraq as "democratic and sovereign," and Islam as the state religion. The highest authority in the country is the Revolutionary Command Council (RCC), which takes decisions by two-thirds majority, and which was authorized to issue laws until the establishment of a parliament. The size of the RCC has varied from 5 to 17 members; it had 8 members in 1995. The 1969 amendments made the chairman of the RCC president of the republic and the supreme commander of the military. The peace agreement between the Iraqi government and the Kurdish insurgents in March 1970 stipulated an official promise to amend the present constitution to declare that the people of Iraq consist of two principal nationalities, the Arabs and the Kurds; to confirm the national rights of Kurds within the framework of Iraqi unity; and to appoint a Kurd as a vice-president of Iraq. The July 1970 interim constitution required that the president and vice-president(s) should be elected by a two-thirds majority of the RCC, and that cabinet ministers should report to the president. The National Charter promulgated by the president three years later mentioned the creation of a National Assembly. The Law for Autonomy in Kurdistan, issued in March 1974, provided for a Legislative Council there. Following an RCC decree in March 1989, elections to the National Assembly and the Legislative Council (for Kurdistan) were held, respectively, in June and September.

Economy: At the national Gross Domestic Product (1992)of $17 billion, the per capital GDP was $902.

Education: In 1974–1975, the government made education free at all levels, and abolished all private schools and colleges. Literacy in the population aged 15 and above (1990) was 59.7 percent (female 49.3 percent, male 69.8 percent).

Ethnic Composition: Arabs 79 percent; Kurds 17 percent, Turkmens 1.5 percent, Persians 1 percent, and others 1.5 percent. One of the two vice-presidents of the republic has been a Kurd since 1974.

Geography: Iraq is divided roughly into three geographical regions: the Mesopotamian plain, the Kurdish highlands, and the western and southwestern desert. The Mesopotamian plain, formed by the Euphrates and Tigris rivers, is the heartland of Iraq. The Kurdish highlands, lying between the Tigris River and the Iranian frontier, occupy northeastern Iraq. Southern and southwestern Iraq, bounded by the Euphrates River and the Saudi Arabian and Syrian frontiers, is desert.

Governmental System: Iraq is a republic, with a president elected by the Revolutionary Command Council.

Military: Iraq's total armed forces number 382,000 actives and 650,000 reserves. Military expenditure as percent of the GDP in 1992 was 14.7 percent. Production of biological warfare agents started in 1989 and continued for a year. In the course of enforcement of United Nations Security Council Resolution 687 of April 1991 concerning the Gulf War cease-fire, the research facilities were demolished by UN inspectors, and Iraq claimed to have destroyed all the stored agents in October 1990. Iraq began using chemical weapons—mustard and nervous gases—in the 1980–1988 Iran-Iraq War from 1981 onwards, culminating in large-scale deployment in the last months of the war in 1988. During that year, the government also used chemical arms against Kurdish insurgents and civilians in the Kurdistan Autonomous Region. As a result of the implementation of UN Security Council Resolution 687, these facilities were destroyed by UN inspectors by 1993. Research and development in the nuclear weapons program was well advanced at the time of the 1991 Gulf War. In the course of enforcing UN Security Council Resolution 687, the UN Special Commission (Unscom) on Iraq and the International Atomic Energy Agency (IAEA) examined 25,000 pages of documents, 700 rolls of film, and 19 hours of videotape to assess the Iraqi Atomic Energy Commission's personnel and procurement of materials. The conclusion was that Iraq had not produced a detonator for an atom bomb, and had not accumulated enough enriched uranium on its own. All military nuclear research and development facilities were destroyed by UN inspectors by 1993.

Mineral Resources: Iraq is rich in sulfur. At 100 billion barrels, its oil deposits are 9.9 percent of the global aggregate; at 3,100 billion cubic meters, its gas reserves amount to 2.2 percent of the world total. At its 1989 (pre-Gulf War) rate of 3 million barrels/day, Iraq's oil reserves will last until 2080. At the 1989 rate of extraction of 29.2 million cubic meters/day, Iraq's gas deposits will be exhausted by 2095.

Religious Composition: Muslim 95.5 percent, of which Shias are 61.5 percent and Sunnis 34 percent; Christian 3.7 percent; and others 0.8 percent.

HISTORY BEFORE 1918

Archaeological excavations, conducted over the past century and a half, have provided evidence of civilization in Mesopotamia dating back to about 10,000 B.C. The earliest settled agrarian society, with irrigation systems, crafts, and clay-brick buildings, evolved in Mesopotamia. The first city was built here around 4,000 B.C., and writing was invented in about 3,000 B.C. The ancient cities of Ur, Babylon, and Nineveh arose in the region. Babylon was the capital of Babylonia nearly four millenia ago during the reign of Hammurabai (1792-1750 B.C.), and retained that position for about a thousand years. At the height of the city's prosperity under King Nebuchadezzar (605–562 B.C.), it measured 2,500 acres and was the planet's largest settlement. After it fell to the Persians under Cyrus the Great in 538 B.C., it continued to be the leading city of the world. It surrendered to Alexander the Great in 331 B.C. Alexander died in Babylon, his planned capital, in Nebuchadezzar's palace in 323 B.C.

Incorporated into the Parthian empire (250 B.C.–226 A.D) in the second century B.C., Mesopotamia declined steadily. After 38 B.C., it became a buffer between the Parthian and then the Sassanian (226–640 A.D.) empires in the east and the Roman (27 B.C.–395 A.D.) and then Byzantine (395 A.D.–1453) empires in the west. It fell to Muslim Arabs in 637 A.D., and its history became the history of Iraq.

Baghdad became the seat of the Abbasid caliphate (750 A.D.–1258) in 763 A.D. From here, the caliphs ruled an Islamic domain that extended from Persia across the Arabian Peninsula to Egypt and North Africa, and then through Spain to the French border. Baghdad reached the pinnacle of prosperity as a commercial center under Caliph Haroun al Rashid (786–809 A.D.), a state well-captured in many episodes of *Thousand and One Nights*. Baghdad suffered heavily during the invasion of the Mongols in 1258, which ended Abbasid rule. It faced a similar fate again in 1400 under Tamerlane and in 1524 under Shah Ismail of Persia. When Mesopotamia came under Ottoman suzerainty in 1638, Baghdad's population was below 15,000. During the Ottoman period, the region was divided into the provinces of Basra and Baghdad.

HISTORY: 1918–1958

After the dissolution of the Ottoman Empire in 1918, the League of Nations gave the mandate over Basra and Baghdad provinces to the British. They called the new entity Iraq, and placed it under the authority of King Faisal I ibn Hussein al Hashem (1921–1933) in 1921. Four years later, a League of Nations arbitration committee ruled against the Republic of Turkey, and awarded the predominantly Kurdish province of Mosul to Iraq. By amalgamating Mosul with Baghdad and Basra provinces, the British unwittingly created a Kurdish problem for the enlarged Iraq.

The efforts of the Turkish Petroleum Company (TPC), owned largely by the Anglo-Persian Oil Company (APOC) after World War I, bore fruit in 1927 when it struck oil in commercial quantities in the Kirkuk area of Mosul. Under pressure from Washington, the TPC was reconstituted in 1931 as the Iraq Petroleum Company (IPC). Government-owned British, French, and Dutch companies and two private American corporations each owned a 23.5 percent share in the IPC. The remaining 5 percent was held by a Portuguese businessman.

Before granting independence to Iraq in 1932, Great Britain signed a treaty with King Faisal I which required him to coordinate his foreign policy with London, and allow the posting of British troops on Iraqi soil. Iraq then joined the League of Nations. Most Iraqis considered their independence incomplete so long as British forces remained in their country.

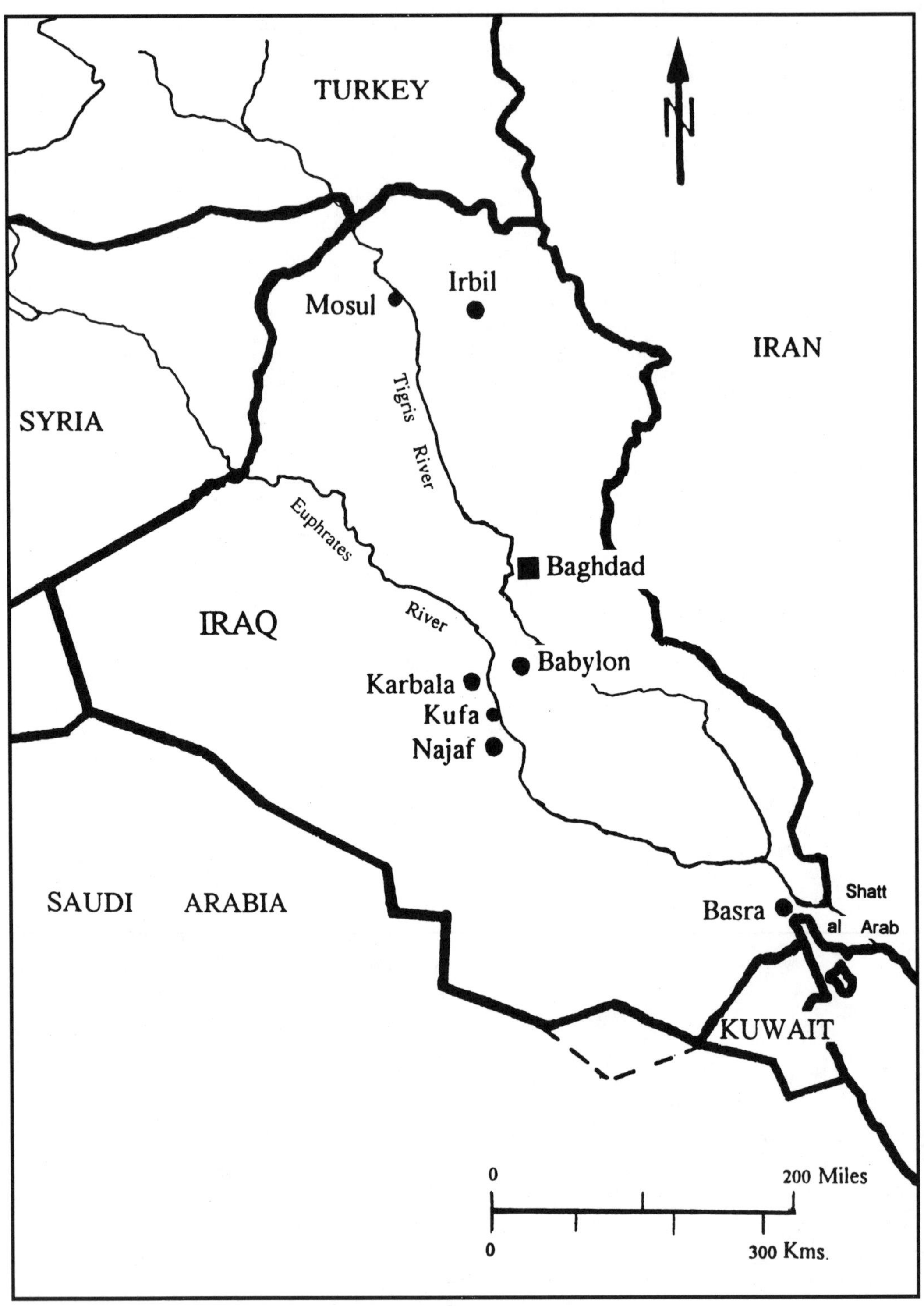
TURKEY
N
IRAN
SYRIA
Irbil
Mosul
Tigris River
Euphrates River
Baghdad
IRAQ
Babylon
Karbala
Kufa
Najaf
SAUDI ARABIA
Basra
Shatt al Arab
KUWAIT
0
200 Miles
0
300 Kms.

Iraq

In April 1941, during World War II, Premier Rashid Ali Gailani led a successful coup against the British and the Iraqi royal family. By then, petroleum output in Iraq had reached such proportions that Great Britain was unwilling to relinquish this source of such a vital commodity. The British struck back next month, defeated Gailani, and restored Faisal II, then a minor, to his throne. Later in the war, Mustafa Barzani led a failed Kurdish rebellion. He fled to Iran, and from there to the Soviet Union.

Following the Arab defeat in the 1948-1949 Arab-Israeli War, in which Iraq was one of the participants, national sentiment turned strongly anti-Western and anti-Zionist. But Premier Nuri al Said, a pro-Western strongman, ignored it. Defying the rising tide of Arab nationalism at home and in the region, he led Iraq in 1955 into the Western-sponsored regional military alliance, often called the Baghdad Pact. He refused to condemn the Anglo-French-Israeli aggression in the Suez War of 1956. This refusal angered large sections of the population. The more he tried to suppress opposition the stronger it became. In this context, pan-Arabist Free Officers led by Brigadier General Abdul Karim Qasim carried out a coup against King Faisal II ibn Ghazi on 14 July 1958. They executed Nuri al Said and the royal family, and declared a republic.

REPUBLICAN IRAQ SINCE 1958

Abdul Karim Qasim, who became the prime minister, was popularly known as the "Sole Leader." He withdrew Iraq from the Baghdad Pact, and carried out wide-ranging socio-economic reform. Mustafa Barzani, the Kurdish leader, returned home from the Soviet Union, and backed the new regime. In exchange, Baghdad legalized the Kurdistan Democratic Party (KDP) and promulgated a constitution which stated that "Arabs and Kurds are associated in this nation." Two-thirds of the Kurds, forming one-sixth of the national population, lived in the three northern provinces of Dohak, Irbil, and Sulemainiya. When Barzani advanced an autonomy plan, Qasim rejected it. Fighting broke out between the two sides in September 1961 and continued for five years.

In 1961, Qasim issued a decree that deprived the IPC of 99.5 percent of the 160,000 square miles originally allocated to it for petroleum prospecting, covering almost the whole country and including oil-rich Rumeila in the south. The government set up its own Iraq National Oil Company (INOC). The IPC challenged the law and a practical compromise was reached in 1969. Qasim had been overthrown in 1963 by a group of military officers belonging to the Arab Baath Socialist Party, popularly known as the Baath.

Due to the divisions among the Baathist officers, power passed to non-Baathist Abdul Salam Arif, and after his death in April 1966 to his brother Abdul Rahman Arif. In June 1966, he signed an agreement with the KDP, the Kurdish party. It granted official recognition to the Kurdish language and a proportional representation of Kurds in the civil service. But the agreement failed to dissipate mutual mistrust. In 1967, President Arif gave wider powers to the INOC, and an exclusive right to develop the Rumeila oil field. Arif was overthrown in mid-1968 by a Baathist coup led by Ahmad Hassan Bakr.

Born into the Tikriti clan from Tikrit, north of Baghdad, Bakr allied with Saddam Hussein, a close relative, to widen his power base in the officer corps. He reached an accord in 1970 with the KDP, which had resumed its armed struggle against the central government in March 1969. The constitution of July 1970 recognized Kurds as one of the two nationalities of Iraq, and Kurdish as one of the two languages in the Kurdish region. But once again the agreement failed to hold. Ignoring the non-cooperation of the KDP, the Baghdad government enforced the Kurdish autonomy law in March 1974. The law included the appointment of a Kurdish diplomat, Taha Muhyi al-Din Maruf, as a vice-president of the republic; the formation of the Kurdistan

Autonomous Region (KAR), with its capital in Irbil, from the provinces of Dohak, Irbil, and Suleimaniya; and the establishment of the Kurdistan Legislative Council. Despite these moves, fighting erupted again.

This time, the KDP had the active backing of Iran's Muhammad Reza Shah Pahlavi, who wanted to weaken the pro-Moscow regime in Baghdad. At one point, the KDP controlled a third of the KAR, and its 45,000 guerrillas pinned down four-fifths of Iraq's 100,000 troops and nearly half of its 1,390 tanks. The conflict resulted in 60,000 civilian and military casualties, the destruction of 40,000 homes in 700 villages, and 300,000 refugees. To prevent the conflict from escalating into a full-scale war between Iran and Iraq, the two countries signed an accord in Algiers, Algeria, in March 1975, which resulted in Iran cutting off military and logistical aid to the KDP. Barzani escaped to Iran, and then to the U.S.

On the oil front, to pressure Baghdad to reverse its hard-line policy, the IPC reduced output from the Kirkuk oilfileds by half in March 1972. In mid-May 1972, Iraq warned the IPC that it would end talks if its demands were not met within a fortnight. They were not, and the government nationalized the IPC in June. It nationalized the American and Dutch interests in the Basrah Petroleum Company, which operated in the south, during the October 1973 Arab-Israeli War. The quadrupling of oil prices in the mid-1970s benefited the populace at large and enabled the governing Baath Party to consolidate its regime.

With the emergence in early 1979 of an Islamic republic in Iran, a predominantly Shia country, the Iraqi regime found Islamic militancy rising among its Shias, a majority of the population. Bakr's strategy for countering this problem by conciliating Shia dissidents and accommodating the party ideology to the rising wave of religious revival was overruled by Saddam Hussein. Hussein turned against Bakr in June 1979. He secured Bakr's resignation from all his governmental and party posts on "health grounds" a month later.

Born in Auja, a village near Tikrit, into the family of a landless peasant who died before his birth, Saddam Hussein was raised by his maternal uncle, Khairallah Talfa. After his arrival in Baghdad in 1955 for further education, he joined the Arab Baath Socialist Party. Following the 1958 republican coup, he engaged in fights between the Baathists and the followers of Premier Abdul Karim Qasim. In late 1959, he escaped to Syria and then to Egypt, where he studied law at Cairo University. After the Baathist seizure of power in 1963, he returned to Iraq. When Abdul Salam Arif usurped power from the Baathists, Saddam Hussein got involved in an abortive attempt to overthrow Arif. He was imprisoned but managed to escape in July 1966. He spent the next two years reorganizing the party. He was 31 when the Baath recaptured power in 1968.

In late 1969, Hussein secured a place on the ruling Revolutionary Command Council (RCC), chaired by Bakr. Thereafter, the Bakr-Hussein duo came to dominate the Baath as a result mainly of their cunning decimation of their RCC colleagues. By the mid-1970s, Saddam Hussein had outstripped Bakr in leadership, cunning, ruthlessness, and organizational ability. It was he who signed the Iran-Iraq Accord with the shah of Iran in 1975.

The Hussein Regime

Two weeks after assuming power, in late July 1979, Saddam Hussein discovered a major "anti-state conspiracy" involving 68 top Baathist civilian and military leaders. All were tired summarily, and 21 were executed. While generously funding the improvement of Shia shrines, and being conciliatory towards senior Shia clergy, he severely repressed such militant Shia bodies as al Daawa. Funds for palliating Shias came from the burgeoning petroleum income. In 1979 and 1980, with output at over 3.5 million barrels/day and exports at 3.3 million barrels/day, the oil revenue was, respectively, \$21.3 billion and \$26.3 billion.

The Iraqi government's promise, contained in the National Charter of 1973, to convene a popularly elected parliament was kept in June 1980 when elections to the 250-member National Assembly were held on the basis of universal suffrage. The Baath Party won 188 seats. In the poll for the second 294-member National Assembly in October 1984, the Baath Party's share declined to 183.

In September 1980, Hussein invaded Iran to recover the eastern half of the Shatt al Arab that he had conceded to Tehran in the 1975 Algiers Accord. The subsequent war lasted until August 1988. (A full narrative of this conflict appears in Chapter 10.)

Baghdad's oil output declined to 800,000 barrels/day in 1982 before rising to 1.75 million in 1986, when the price fell to below $10 a barrel, and the Iraqi oil income to $7 billion. Baghdad was able to withstand the price crash because of the large grants and loans it received from Saudi Arabia and Kuwait. Later, Iraq built a pipeline to connect with a Saudi pipeline leading to the Red Sea port of Yanbu, thus supplementing its earlier pipeline running to the Turkish port of Dortyol. Demanding parity with Iran in its export quota, Iraq ignored the output agreements made by the Organization of Petroleum Exporting Countries (OPEC) from October 1986 to May 1988. In that month, OPEC assigned Iraq parity with Iran, which Iran accepted under protest.

Initially, as Iraqi troops made inroads into Iran, Saddam Hussein raised his war aim to incorporating the captured area into Iraq because the majority of its inhabitants were ethnic Arabs. By mid-1982, when the Iranians had expelled the Iraqis from their territory, two outcomes were possible: a draw or an Iranian triumph. Afraid that Iran's victory would destabilize the region, including the oil-rich Gulf states, the U.S. and the Soviet Union, as well as France, enhanced their military, economic, and intelligence aid to Iraq.

During the war, the activities of the Kurdish insurgents, now allied with Tehran, compelled Iraq to deploy army divisions in the north to the detriment of its war effort elsewhere. Taking advantage of the pressure of war on Baghdad, the KDP, now led by Masoud Barzani, a son of Mustafa, as well as the Patriotic Union of Kurdistan (PUK), headed by Jalal Talabani, set up liberated zones along the borders with Iran and Turkey.

On the other hand, by extending the fight into the Gulf from 1984 onwards, Saddam Hussein succeeded in getting the U.S. involved in the conflict to protect oil shipping lanes from Iran. By mid-1987, Tehran found itself facing the U.S. navy in the Gulf.

In February 1988, Saddam Hussein unleased a seven-month campaign of vengeance against KDP strongholds that involved the use of chemical weapons, affected 3,800 villages, and reclaimed the area lost to the insurgents. The defeated Kurdish leaders escaped to Iran or Syria.

In the course of the Iran-Iraq War, Saddam Hussein enlarged his military from a quarter million to over one million, vastly expanded the industrial-military complex, and made much progress in developing or producing chemical, biological, and nuclear arms. In the political sphere, he held regular elections to the National Assembly and Legislative Council of Kurdistan. In the poll for the Third National Assembly, held in April 1989, the Baath won 150 seats, a narrow majority. The elections to the Third Legislative Council of Kurdistan followed in September.

After the end of the Iran-Iraq War, Baghdad returned to OPEC's quota system. OPEC put Iraq on a par with Iran: 2.64 million barrels/day each. In 1989, Iraq's production reached 2.83 million barrels/day and exports 2.4 million barrels/day, with foreign earnings from oil at $12 billion. In the first half of 1990, production rose to 3.1 million barrels/day, but flooding of the market by Kuwait and the United Arab Emirates depressed the price from $18 to $12 a barrel, making Iraq lose about $20 million daily.

In August 1990, determined to make his weight felt in the region, Saddam Hussein invaded and occupied Kuwait, an emirate to

Iraqi soldiers tearing up an Iranian flag near the frontline of the Iran-Iraq War, 1988.

which Iraq had in the past laid claim. U.S. President George Bush rallied the international community to reverse the Iraqi aggression. He cobbled together an alliance of 29 Western and Arab and Muslim nations. The United Nations imposed a military and economic embargo on Iraq. When Saddam Hussein refused to withdraw Iraqi troops from Kuwait by the UN deadline of 15 January 1991, the U.S.-led coalition began an air campaign against Iraq and Iraqi-occupied Kuwait, thus initiating the Gulf War. A description of the Gulf War, which ended in late February 1991, appears in Chapter 5.

Iraq Since the Gulf War

In April 1991, Saddam Hussein accepted a humiliating UN Security Council resolution which outlined the cease-fire, war reparations, and the conditions for lifting economic sanctions against Iraq. These conditions included destruction of Iraq's medium- and long-range ground-to-ground missiles as well as non-conventional arms and manufacturing facilities.

Also as a result of the Gulf War, Baghdad lost control of the Kurdish areas in the north. During the crisis created by Iraq's occupation of Kuwait in August 1990, which had drawn most of the troops away from the Kurdistan Autonomous Region, KDP leaders returned to the region. Following Iraq's defeat in the Gulf War, the Kurdish nationalists persuaded the 100,000-strong local Iraqi army auxiliary force, made up of Kurds, to change sides. Within a week, the rebels controlled the KAR and large parts of the oil-rich province of Tamin, including its capital, Kirkuk. In late March, a government counterattack reversed the situation, causing an exodus of 1.5 million Kurdish refugees into Iran and Turkey. Having fully regained the region, Baghdad signed a truce with the insurgents in mid-April. In the subsequent talks with the central government, Barzani, acting as the leader of the Iraqi Kurdistan Front (IKF), a coalition of seven Kurdish groups, reached a draft agreement in June. It conceded to Kurds the predominant military and political authority over the KAR, with joint control of the army and policy by the Kurdish authorities and Baghdad. In return, Kurds had to surrender their heavy weapons and cut all links with outside powers. Despite further clarifications from Baghdad, Barzani failed to win the approval of the majority of IKF leaders for the agreement.

With 16,000 Western troops deployed in the 3,600 square mile security zone created by the U.S.-led coalition in the Iraqi-Turkish border reign, Baghdad was forced to withdraw its forces from the KAR by late October. Although the U.S., Great Britain, and France, the three permanent Western members of the UN Security Council, pulled their troops out of the area by late 1991, they continued their air surveillance of northern Iraq above the 36th parallel from the Turkish air base of Incirlik. Thus protected, the Kurds conducted their own elections for parliament in May 1992, and chose their own government. Among other things, the parliament adopted a flag and established an army. Kurds thus acquired a semi-independent administrative-political entity.

Despite repeated efforts by the leading Western powers, Israel, and Saudi Arabia to assassinate Saddam Hussein or overthrow his regime through a coup, he survived. His military and intelligence apparatus remained effective. However, the Western powers' imposition of a "no fly" restriction above the 36th parallel virtually ended his control over the Kurdish region in October 1991. In August 1992, the Western allies also declared the predominantly Shia area of Iraq below the 32nd parallel a "no fly" zone for Baghdad.

While economic sanctions caused high inflation and a dramatic drop in Iraqi living standards, there were no signs that popular discontent against the regime had reached such proportions as to destabilize it. However, Saddam Hussein's elation at Bush's defeat in the U.S. presidential election in November 1992 proved premature. President Bill Clinton continued Bush's hardline policy towards Saddam Hussein. A denouement came in late June 1993 when the U.S. navy hit the Iraqi intelligence complex in Baghdad with missiles because Saddam Hussein had planned Bush's assassination during the former president's trip to Kuwait in April.

The experiment of creating an autonomous, democratic Kurdish region turned sour in the spring of 1994 when the KDP and the PUK began fighting each other. Despite repeated efforts by the Western powers, especially the U.S., violence continued for more than a year, claiming more than 2,000 lives. The conflict severely jeopardized Washington's clandestine plans to undermine Saddam Hussein's regime by actively backing its opponents.

By October 1994, having complied with all the conditions of UN Security Council Resolution 687 and Resolution 715 (concerning long-term monitoring of Iraq's military industry), Saddam Hussein felt that it was time for the UN to lift economic sanctions, as provided in Resolution 687. To force the issue, he moved Iraqi troops southwards. The U.S. construed this as a plan by Baghdad to invade Kuwait again, and dispatched its troops and warships to the region. Iraq withdrew the troops to their pre-crisis positions. At the Security Council, Russia called for lifting the sanctions by the spring of 1995, but did not press its proposal to a vote.

Due to the UN embargo, Iraq's GDP decreased from $58.54 billion in 1989 to $17 billion four years later. The value of the Iraqi dinar fell from $3.23 to 0.2 cents, a 1,600-fold depreciation. Although there was no ban on importing food and medicine, Iraq lacked foreign currencies to do so. This caused untold misery to millions of ordinary citizens.

To alleviate the situation, the UN Security Council, at the behest of Washington and London, adopted Resolution 986 in April 1995 which allowed Baghdad to export $2 billion worth of oil over the next six months, on a renewable basis. Iraq had to ship petroleum under UN supervision, deposit its funds in a UN account, and only use part of the money to import food and medicine. The government and parliament in Baghdad rejected the offer, arguing that it violated Iraqi sovereignty. The Iraqi regime worried that once it accepted and implemented such a resolution the U.S. would renew it and bypass paragraph 22 of Security Council Resolution 687, which specified "reducing or lifting" the embargo once Iraqi disarmament had been achieved and monitoring equipment had been installed in factories and elsewhere to ensure that Baghdad did not resume the banned activity.

By 1995, the head of the UN commission on disarming Iraq, Rolf Ekeus, had cleared Iraq in the fields of chemical and nuclear arms and missile projects, stating that it had cooperated fully with the UN. The exception was Iraq's past military biological program. In July 1995, Iraq admitted that it had produced the germ warfare agents clostridium botulinum and bacillus anthracis during 1989-1990, and claimed that all stored stocks had been destroyed before the start of the Gulf War in January 1991. These statements had to be checked by Ekeus before the Security Council could decide its next step.

Meanwhile, the five permanent members of the Security Council had become divided on the issue. China, France, and Russia wanted to reward Iraq for its cooperation, and ease, if not lift, the economic sanctions, as Clause 22 in Resolution 687 specified. The U.S. and (to a lesser extent) Great Britain were opposed to making any concessions to Baghdad.

Indeed, the U.S. began adding further conditions for Iraq to meet. These included the repatriation of unaccounted-for Kuwaiti civilians and prisoners of war, the handing over of Kuwaiti property and payment of war reparations, and the ending of "the repression of Iraqi civilian population in many parts of Iraq" as stated in Security Council Resolution 688. Although the conditions pertaining to Kuwait were mentioned in Security Council Resolution 687, they were not part of the disarmament of Iraq to which the UN embargo was directly linked. As for ending repression of Iraqi citizens, specifically Kurds, this separate resolution was again not tied to disarming Iraq.

Washington was trying to use the Security Council to pursue its national policy of "dual containment" regarding Iraq and Iran. The general aim was to ostracize both states, and thus enfeeble them. In the process, it was unwittingly bringing the two countries together.

In the region, the Gulf monarch were divided in their policy towards Baghdad. Qatar re-established links with Baghdad. Both the United Arab Emirates and Qatar expressed their concern about the continued suffering of the Iraqi people. Their top officials highlighted the report published by the UN Food and Agricultural Organization (FAO) in late 1995. It stated that malnutrition caused by UN sanctions against Iraq had resulted in the deaths of more than 560,000 children since the Gulf War, and that infant mortality in the country had doubled. This had little impact on the rulers of Saudi Arabia and Kuwait, who wanted the economic embargo to continue until Saddam Hussein's regime collapsed.

If FAO's prediction of a poor harvest in 1996, followed by large-scale deaths, comes to pass, then it will be hard for the international community to ignore the human tragedy. Any humanitarian aid will have to be channeled through the authorities. This will have the indirect effect of strengthening Saddam Hussein's government. It is most unlikely that starving Iraqis will rise up against it.

Part of the reason why many Iraqis are backing the present regime is their fear that were it to fall, the country would slide into civil war along ethnic—Arab and Kurd—and sectarian—Shia and Sunni—lines. This would turn Iraq into a bloodier, and more entangled, version of Bosnia.

In the absence of a dramatic turn for the worse, a weak and chastened Iraq is likely to flounder along under the leadership of Saddam Hussein and his long-time Baathist colleagues.

CHAPTER 12

Kuwait

Kuwait, a tiny state in the Persian Gulf region, grabbed Western public attention in August 1990 as the victim of Iraqi aggression. However, this crisis was the third in a century to involve Kuwait; the first had occurred in 1897, and the second in 1961 soon after Kuwaiti independence. Each of these crises centered on Kuwait's relations with Iraq, its powerful neighbor.

PROFILE

Area & Population: Squarish in shape, with a triangular appendage, Kuwait measures 6,880 square miles, including the Kuwaiti share of the Kuwait-Saudi Arabia Neutral Zone, and the Bubiyan and Warba offshore Islands, which account for 348 square miles. Its estimated population in 1993 was 1,650,000, of whom only 660,000 are Kuwaiti nationals.

Cities: With a population of 265,600, Kuwait City, the capital, is also the largest settlement. Next in size are Salimiya 118,800, Hawalli 71,000, and Ahmadi 23,000.

Constitution: Following Kuwait's independence in June 1961, the ruler, called the emir, appointed a constituent assembly. The constitution drafted by it was promulgated in November 1962. Kuwait is a hereditary emirate, or principality, under the control of the descendants of Shaikh Mubarak I al Sabah (1896–1915). A National Assembly of 50 members is elected for a four-year term by those literate, male Kuwaiti citizens who can prove their family domicile to 1921. The ruler has the right to dissolve the Assembly provided new elections are held within two months. Executive authority rests with the emir who exercises it through a council of ministers. He appoints or dismisses the prime minister. After consulting the prime minister, the emir appoints or dismisses ministers. Nonparliamentarian ministers become ex-officio members of the National Assembly. Ministers are responsible to the Assembly, which must approve bills before the emir promulgates them as laws. If dissatisfied with the prime minister, the National Assembly can convey its lack of confidence in him to the emir, who must then dismiss him or dissolve the Assembly. The emir is the supreme commander of the military, and is authorized to declare war and peace and sign treaties.

Economy: At the national Gross Domestic Product of $21.7 billion (1992), the per capita GDP was $15,500.

Education: Education is free for all Kuwaiti nationals. Literacy in the population aged 15 and over (1990) was 73 percent (male 77.1 percent, female 66.7 percent).

Ethnic Composition: Arabs 75 percent, including Kuwaiti nationals 40 percent; South Asians 9 percent; Persians 4 percent; and others 12 percent.

Geography: Kuwait is a desert with a few oases, but enormous reserves of oil. Located in the northwestern corner of the Persian Gulf, its settlements are dotted along the coastline of the Gulf or the Bay of Kuwait.

Governmental System: Kuwait is a monarchy; the emir is head of state and chief executive.

Military: Kuwait's total armed forces number 15,000 actives and 23,500 reserves. Military expenditure as percent of the GDP in 1992 was 13.4 percent.

Mineral Resources: At 96.5 billion barrels, Kuwait's oil deposits are 9.6 percent of the global aggregate; and at 1,500 billion cubic meters, its gas reserves amount to 1.1 percent of the world total. At the current rate of extraction of 2 million barrels/day, its oil deposits will last until 2126; and at 43.8 million cubic meters/day, its gas reserves will run out by 2085.

Religious Composition: Muslim 89 percent, of which 62 percent are Sunni, 27 percent are Shia; Christian 8 percent; and Hindu 3 percent.

HISTORY BEFORE 1918

Originally based in the Arabian hinterland, the Anaiza tribal federation migrated to the northern shores of the Persian Gulf after a severe drought in 1710, and settled along the sea at Kuwait. The federation developed trading facilities there, and accepted the overlordship of the Ottoman Turks who dominated the region. Over the decades, pearling and sea-trading brought prosperity to the community.

The al Sabahs, belonging to the Amarat tribe, were one of the three leading families. They conducted administration and provided defense. In 1752, the dynastic rule of the al Sabahs began. The first ruler was Shaikh Sabah I al Sabah, and the second Shaikh Abdullah I al Sabah (1756–1814). He allowed the British East India Company to set up a base in Kuwait in 1776. The base became an important link in the communications system between India and Great Britain.

Because of its strategic position at the top of the Persian Gulf on the land route to the Mediterranean Sea, Kuwait became a center of rivalry between the Ottoman Empire, the British Empire, the Russian Empire, and Germany in the late nineteenth century. The British disapproved of Shaikh Abdullah II al Sabah's (1866–1892) policy of strengthening ties with the Ottomans.

Matters came to a head during the reign of Shaikh Muhammad I al Sabah (1892–1896). Encouraged by the British, the ruler's half-brother, Mubarak, assassinated Muhammad in 1896. In the following year, the Ottoman sultan recognized the official status of Shaikh Mubarak I by appointing him provincial sub-governor of Kuwait within the province of Basra. To deter the Ottomans from imposing direct rule over Kuwait, the British made a show of their naval power along the shoreline. The Ottomans let the matter rest. This encouraged Shaikh Mubarak I to sign a secret treaty with the British in 1899. In exchange for an annual subsidy of $6,000, the Kuwaiti ruler accorded Great Britain the exclusive right of presence in Kuwait and control of its foreign policy.

The Anglo-Ottoman Convention of 1913, which recognized Kuwait as an autonomous *caza* or district of the Ottoman Empire under Shaikh Mubarak I, became invalid when the

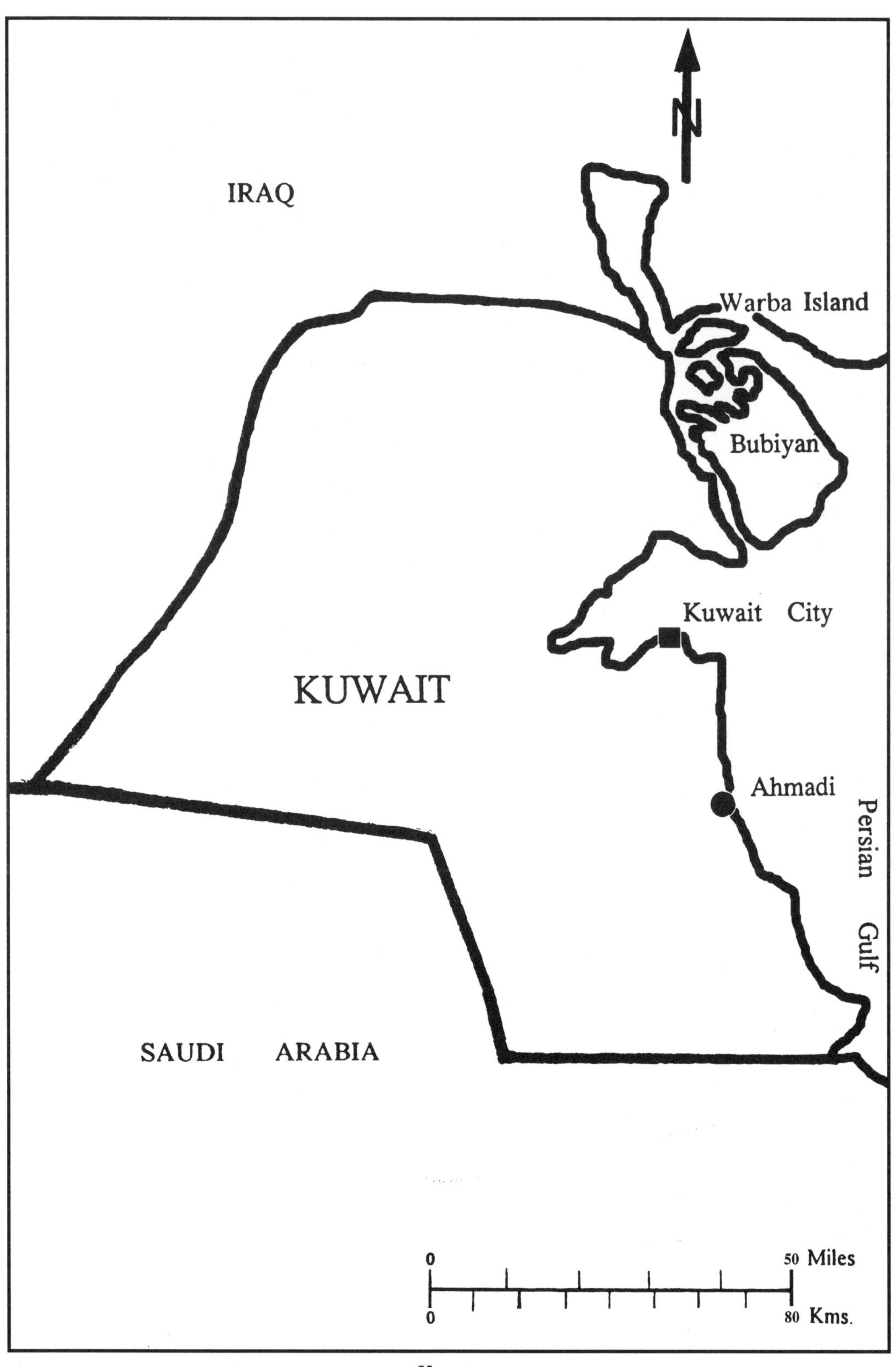
N
IRAQ
Warba Island
Bubiyan
Kuwait City
KUWAIT
Ahmadi
Persian Gulf
SAUDI ARABIA
0
50 Miles
0
80 Kms.

Kuwait

Ottomans joined the Germans in World War I. London now publicly declared Kuwait to be "an independent shaikhdom under British protectorate."

HISTORY: 1918–1961

Until 1921, Kuwait City was surrounded by a mud wall, and its residents lived by fishing, pearling, and trading with India and East Africa. In 1922, the Protocol of Uqair, signed by Kuwait and Najd (later part of Saudi Arabia), defined Kuwait's borders and created the Kuwait-Najd Neutral Zone. The development of an oil industry in Iraq and Iran improved the trading economy of Kuwait. The Kuwait Oil Company, owned equally by the Anglo-Iranian Oil Company (now British Petroleum) and Gulf Oil Company, obtained oil concessions in Kuwait in 1934 for 74 years. The company's exploration for petroleum succeeded in 1938 at Burgan, the largest oil reserve in the world. But all the oil wells were plugged during World War II.

In the post-war years, petroleum extraction and exports reached commercial proportions. Kuwait City and its environs grew dramatically. The Western boycott of the nationalized oil company in Iran in 1951 caused the output of Kuwaiti petroleum to rise sharply. Kuwait became the leading oil exporter in the Persian Gulf region in 1956, with a total output of 1.1 million barrels/day, a position it maintained for a decade. The razing of the mud wall in 1957 accelerated the development of Kuwait City as a prosperous administrative, commercial, and financial center with tree-lined roads, parks, and gardens.

The republican revolution in Iraq in 1958, which ended the pro-Western monarchy, affected British-protected Kuwait. Popular pressure grew on the Kuwaiti ruler, Shaikh Abdullah III (1950-1965), to abrogate the 1899 Anglo-Kuwaiti Treaty. The subsequent Anglo-Kuwaiti talks led to an agreement. The two countries replaced the 1899 treaty with a treaty of friendship that recognized Kuwait's independence and sovereignty. The treaty came into force on 19 June 1961.

INDEPENDENT KUWAIT SINCE 1961

On 25 June 1961, the Iraqi leader, Abdul Karim Qasim, denounced the new Anglo-Kuwaiti agreement and demanded that Kuwait be returned to the southern Iraqi province of Basra of which it had been part in the past. Kuwait appealed to Great Britain for military assistance, and lodged a complaint with the United Nations as well as the Arab League. At the UN, the Soviet Union vetoed Kuwait's membership in the organization. London dispatched 6,000 troops to Kuwait, and the Arab League sent a multi-national force of 2,000 soldiers. This defused the crisis in public, but in private Kuwait agreed to pay Iraq $65 million in grants, a substantial sum in those days.

Shaikh Abdullah III al Sabah appointed a constituent assembly in December 1961 to draft a constitution. He promulgated the resulting document a year later. It specified an elected National Assembly. Having conceded an elected parliament, Shaikh Abdullah III and his successors tried to fix its composition by manipulating the electoral system. They limited the franchise to about 10 percent of the male citizens. The election of 1967, during the reign of Shaikh Sabah III al Sabah (1965–1977), was rigged. The opposition protested, and vainly demanded a re-run. But the experience chastened the ruler. His administration refrained from indulging in electoral malpractices at the polling booths in the 1971 parliamentary election. But as before, pro-government candidates bribed voters on a large scale, leading most observers to conclude that the election was free but hardly fair. Despite these limitations, the National Assembly over the years established itself as a fairly independent forum. It voiced popular views on many internal and external matters.

Pursuing the self-reliance policy of the Organization of Petroleum Exporting Countries (OPEC), Kuwait, one of OPEC's founder-members, acquired a 25 percent share of the Kuwait Oil Company (KOC) in October 1972, with a provision for further annual increases of 2.5 percent in shareholding over the next decade. But after the October 1973 Arab-Israeli War, and a dramatic jump in oil prices, the government acquired a majority holding in KOC immediately, buying the rest of the shares in March 1975. It also responded positively to the parliament's demand that oil output be limited to a maximum of 2 million barrels/day. Due to growing prosperity, stemming from rising oil revenue, there was an ever greater need for labor, which was supplied by foreigners. Their number also rose sharply because of the reluctance of native Kuwaitis to do menial or semi-skilled work. In the 1970s, Kuwaiti citizens became a minority. Among foreigners, Arabs from other countries, particularly Palestinians, became the dominant group, followed by South Asians.

After the 1975 election, parliamentary debates became strident, which was reported in the local press. In August 1976, the ruler suspended four constitutional articles concerning the National Assembly as well as the Assembly itself, accusing it of "malicious behavior" and wasting time on legislation. He dissolved it a year later. Due to the steep rise in oil prices in the mid-1970s, Kuwait became prosperous, and the state set up a national fund for future generations.

When the Iran-Iraq War started in September 1980, Kuwait declared itself neutral, but was so only in name. It helped Iraq financially and logistically. Following the disruption of Iraqi oil supplies because of the war, Kuwait volunteered to meet Iraq's obligations. In early 1986, it used the oil weapon in alliance with Saudi Arabia to flood the market to depress the price from $28 to $10 a barrel within four months, thus severely damaging Iran's ability to prosecute the war. The negative impact on Iraq was compensated by subventions given to it by Kuwait and Saudi Arabia.

At home, Shaikh Jabar III al Sabah (1977–) yielded to popular pressure and reinstated the National Assembly with depleted powers in early 1981. The new parliament proved to be a handmaiden of the ruler. The parliament elected in early 1985 contained five nationalist-leftists and 11 Islamic fundamentalists. By offering a combined opposition, and demanding an official inquiry in the disastrous collapse of the unofficial stock exchange in 1982, which involved $97 billion in paper debts, the opposition made the al Sabah dynasty uneasy. In July 1986, Shikh Jabar III dissolved the Assembly again.

Once the Iran-Iraq War ended in August 1988, agitation for the restoration of the National Assembly resumed. When the ruler conceded a 75-member National Council (with one-third of the members nominated) with powers only to make recommendations, protest continued. The opposition boycotted the June 1990 National Council election. This unrest was a major factor behind Iraqi President Saddam Hussein's decision to invade Kuwait in August 1990. He felt that the regime was unpopular and that Kuwaitis would welcome the Iraqi troops as liberators.

After the Iran-Iraq War, Kuwait insisted that Iraq repay the $12–$14 billion it had loaned Baghdad by supplying oil to Iraq's customers during the conflict. When Baghdad refused, Kuwait began flooding the petroleum market by exceeding its OPEC quota of 1.5 billion barrels/day by 40 percent, thus depressing the price and hurting Iraq.

In mid-July 1990, Iraq complained to the Arab League that the oil glut caused by Kuwait and the United Arab Emirates (UAE) had caused the price to fall to $11 to $13 a barrel—far below the reference price of $18 set by OPEC. A drop of $1 a barrel reduced Iraq's annual revenue by $1 billion. On 31 July, Iraqi and Kuwaiti officials met in Jiddah, Saudi Arabia, against the background of some 100,000 Iraqi troops massed along the Kuwaiti border. The next day the talks failed. According to the Kuwaitis, they refused to accept Iraqi demands to write off the $12–$14 billion in wartime loans, to relinquish some Kuwaiti territory along the Iraqi border, and to lease its Bubiyan and Warba Islands to Baghdad to enable Iraq to lengthen its shoreline along the Persian Gulf and become a proper Gulf power. According to the Iraqis, they saw no sign of Kuwait's willingness to repair the economic damage it had inflicted on Iraq by depressing oil prices.

This was the background to the Iraqi invasion and occupation of Kuwait in early August 1990. A full description of the Kuwait crisis and the Gulf War appears in Chapter 5.

Just before retreating in the Gulf War, the Iraqi troops set ablaze 640 of the more than 800 Kuwaiti oil wells. During the seven months of Iraqi occupation, Kuwait suffered wanton damage, and Kuwaitis suffered exile and unprecedented brutality, including rape, summary executions, and arbitrary confiscation of property. All the foreign residents, a majority of the population, left Kuwait. After the expulsion of Iraq from Kuwait in February 1991, the emirate was restored to Shaikh Jabar III.

The first priority for the Kuwaiti government was to extinguish the fires burning at hundreds of oil wells. By hiring teams of foreign experts, it succeeded in this task fairly rapidly. Shaikh Jabar III held elections to the restored National Assembly in October 1992. Of the 50 members, 31 belonged to the opposition, despite the government's success in rebuilding the country's shattered oil economy. Although political groups are not permitted in Kuwait, several semi-political organizations are known to exist. In the 1992 election, the factions that won Assembly seats included the Islamic Constitutional Movement, a moderate Sunni group; the Salafin, a Sunni fundamentalist group; and the Kuwait Democratic Forum, a secular organization.

Kuwait spurned third-party efforts to normalize relations with Iraq. It fortified its frontier with Iraq, using more than 1.25 million Iraqi land mines it had recovered after the Gulf War. Part of the reason why the Kuwaiti emir was firmly against a rapprochement with Iraq was that the subsequent resumption of Iraqi oil exports would lower already weak oil prices.

In 1992, OPEC gave a special dispensation to Kuwait to produce without a fixed quota. In early 1993, OPEC fixed Kuwait's share at 1.6 million barrels/day, which was a fifth lower than what Kuwait was then producing. Although OPEC raised its quota to 1.7 million barrels/day later in the year, Kuwait insisted on 2 million barrels/day, and produced 2.1 million barrels/day. This, and a shrewd policy of investing past national savings in foreign assets, enabled the emirate to return the annual per capita GDP to over $15,000, one of the highest in the world, and provide its nationals with free education and health services.

The Iraqi invasion in 1990 left both the ruler and the ruled deeply scarred. Ordinary Kuwaitis were more affected than officials. They had seen their political and military leaders flee like cowards rather than stay and resist the invader in order to slow down his advance. This meant that the restored Sabah clan could never regain the respect it enjoyed before the Iraqi occupation.

Overall, given the puny size of their emirate compared to its neighbors—Saudi Arabia, Iraq, and Iran—Kuwaitis were in an unenvious position. Since they were apprehensive of both Iraq and Iran, their long-term salvation lay with Saudi Arabia. They needed to seriously consider some sort of confederation between Kuwait and Saudi Arabia. But there were no signs in the mid-1990s that such a plan was under consideration either in Riyadh or Kuwait.

CHAPTER

Bahrain, Qatar, and the United Arab Emirates

BAHRAIN

The smallest country under study, Bahrain consists of 33 islands, of which only two—Bahrain and Muharraq—are inhabited. Endowed with sweet water wells and springs, these islands have attracted human settlement as well as maritime traffic over the past several millennia. This and its central position in the Persian Gulf have given Bahrain strategic importance far beyond its size. On the other hand, alone among the states of the region, its petroleum and gas reserves are niggardly.

Profile

Area & Population: Altogether, the main island and 32 smaller ones add up to 268 square miles. The estimated population in 1992 was 531,000, of which 361,000 were Bahraini nationals.

Cities: With a population of 154,000, Manama, the capital, is also the largest city. Muharraq has 75,000 inhabitants.

Constitution: The ruler of Bahrain, called emir, became sovereign in August 1971 with the abrogation of the 1892 Anglo-Bahraini treaty. The constitution, drafted by a partly elected constituent assembly, specified a National Assembly of 42, with 30 deputies to be elected on a limited franchise. The first Assembly elected in December 1973 was dissolved in August 1975 and the constitution was suspended. Legislative powers reverted to the emir, who also holds executive authority. As head of a council of ministers appointed by the ruler, the prime minister is in charge of running the day-to-day administration. A consultative council called the Majlis al Shura is a 30-member advisory council that was inaugurated in January 1993. Nominated by the ruler, the Majlis al Shura lacks legislative powers.

Economy: At the national Gross Domestic Product (1992) of $4.2 billion, the per capital GDP was $7,910.

Education: Literacy in the population aged 15 and over (1990) was 77.4 percent (female 69.3 percent, male 82.1 percent).

Ethnic Composition: Arabs 77 percent, South Asians 13 percent, Persians 8 percent, Europeans 1 percent, and others 1 percent.

Geography: About 20 miles offshore from the Qatari and Saudi Arabian coastline, the archipelago of the Bahraini islands is located in the shallow waters of the Persian Gulf. A causeway, built in 1986 with Saudi funds, connects Bahrain with Saudi Arabia.

Governmental System: Bahrain is a monarchy, with the ruler as head of state and chief executive.

Military: Bahrain's total armed forces number 8,100 actives. Military expenditure as percent of GDP in 1992 was 15.8 percent.

Mineral Resources: At 70 million barrels of petroleum, 0.07 percent of the global aggregate, and at 200 billion cubic meters of gas, 0.15 percent of the world total, Bahrain's reserves are puny. With the current oil production rate of 42,000 barrels/day, its reserves will last until the late 1990s, and at the gas extraction rate of 20 million cubic meters a day, its deposits will be exhausted by 2017.

Religious Composition: Muslim 85 percent, of which 51 percent are Shia and 34 percent Sunni; Christian 7 percent; and others 8 percent. All non-Muslims are alien residents. The ruling Khalifa dynasty is Sunni.

History Before 1971

Following the migration of the al Khalifa clan of the Utaiba tribe of the Anaiza tribal federation from the Arabian Peninsula to the offshore islands of Bahrain, the clan succeeded in 1783 in wresting control of the islands from Iran. The al Khalifas consolidated their hold by signing a series of treaties with Great Britain (1861, 1880, and 1892), turning the island archipelago of Bahrain into a British protectorate. Bahrain was the base of the British resident for the Persian Gulf region. The local economy centered around fishing, pearling, and trade.

The Anglo-Bahraini Agreement of 1914 barred Bahrain from giving petroleum concessions to non-British companies without London's permission. After Shaikh Isa I ibn Ali was deposed by the British in 1923, his son Hamad al Khalifa (1923–1942) became the ruler. During his reign, to get around the 1914 treaty, the Standard Oil Company of California combined with the Texas Company to form the Bahrain Petroleum Company (Bapco) in 1929, and registered it in Canada, a British dominion. Bapco commenced commercial production in 1932. With this, Bahrain became the first territory in the Persian Gulf to yield oil. Output reached 19,000 barrels/day in 1940. While using the petroleum income to expand public services, the emir maintained tight control over his subjects, refusing trade union rights to workers despite a strike in the oil industry in 1938.

Shaikh Hamad was succeeded by his son Shaikh Salman II al Khalifa (1942–1961). During World War II, he continued his father's policy of cooperation with the Allies, and afterwards he allowed the British navy to use Bahrain's docking and other facilities, later extending this privilege to the U.S. Middle East Force. His close ties with Great Britain became a point of contention during the 1956 Suez War when an Anglo-French-Israeli alliance invaded Egypt, and his subjects mounted massive pro-Egyptian demonstrations. Economic progress continued, with Manama, already a thriving commercial and financial center, becoming a free port in 1958.

Named heir apparent at 24, Isa II ibn Salman II al Khalifa (1961–) succeeded his father three years later. During his reign, Manama acquired deep-water shipping facilities. With its modern harbor and ship-repairing facilities, it emerged as one of the leading ports of the Gulf; it also contained two-fifths of the national population.

Shaikh Isa II faced increasing agitation by his subjects, including a strike by oil workers in 1965, for political reform. But it was not until January 1970 that he appointed an advisory 12-member Council of State. He did so because Great Britain had declared its intention to withdraw from the region.

Independent Bahrain Since 1971

As Great Britain prepared to leave in 1971, Shaikh Isa II transformed the Council of State into a cabinet, and charged it with framing a constitution. Bahrain became independent in August 1971. Severe rioting and strikes in March and September 1972 led the emir to concede a 42-member constituent assembly, half-elected and half-nominated, to draft a constitution. It did so in mid-1973, and Shaikh Isa II approved the document. It provided for a National Assembly with a four-year tenure. The elections to the Assembly were held on a limited franchise in December 1973. The emir dissolved the parliament and suspended the constitution in August 1975.

With 60 percent of its nationals being Shia, Bahrain was most affected by the Islamic revolution in Shia-dominated Iran in 1979. When the Islamic opposition demanded that Bahrain be declared an Islamic republic, Shaikh Isa II, a Sunni, reacted with a heavy hand. In May 1981, he took Bahrain into the Gulf Cooperation Council composed of the six regional monarchies. In January 1982, his government arrested 60 residents for plotting an Iranian-instigated coup. He sided with Baghdad in the 1980–1988 Iran-Iraq War. During the Kuwait crisis in 1990–1991, he took a firm pro-Kuwaiti line and contributed troops and warplanes to the war against Iraq.

Although Islam is the official religion of Bahrain, alcohol is not banned. The Bahraini-Saudi causeway has made it easy for Saudi citizens to travel from the mainland to Bahrain and drink legally. The Bahraini capital, Manama, has acquired a worldwide reputation as an offshore banking center.

To meet a rising demand for reform, Shaikh Isa II appointed a 30-member Consultative Council in 1993, but kept the 1973 constitution suspended. His gesture proved insufficient. In December 1994, widespread anti-regime demonstrations broke out, with protesters calling for the restoration of the parliament dissolved in 1975. Government repression followed. Violent protest, inspired partly by the Islamic Liberation Front of Bahrain, revived in March, leading in turn to large-scale arrests and curfews. By April 1995, the disturbances had claimed the lives of 16 people, and led to scores of injuries and 1,600 arrests.

The popular struggle for democracy and human rights, which revived in early 1996, received no approval from the Western capitals, including Washington, which has maintained close ties with Bahrain since 1949. After independence, Bahrain leased its docking facilities to the U.S. This proved useful to Washington, especially in times of crisis, such as the rescue mission for the American hostages in Tehran in April 1980. With the permanent stationing of the U.S. Fifth Fleet from mid-1995 onward, the significance of U.S.-Bahraini military links rose sharply.

QATAR

Qatar sticks out like a thumb along the western coast of the Persian Gulf. Qatar's physical shape helped the al Thani clan consolidate its rule in the area after migrating there in the eighteenth century. In mid-1995, Qatar hit the headlines when Crown prince Hamad ibn Khalifa al Thani deposed his father Shaikh Khalifa ibn Hamad (1972–1995) in an bloodless coup—a repeat of what Shaikh Khalifa had done in 1972 when he overthrew his cousin Shaikh Ahmad ibn Ali (1960–1972).

Profile

Area & Population: Roughly rectangular in shape, the peninsular state of Qatar measures 4,412 square miles. Its estimated population in 1992 was 530,000, of which only 124,000 were Qatari nationals.

Cities: With a population of 277,000, Doha, the capital, is also the largest city, followed by Umm Said at 64,000.

Constitution: An interim constitution, promulgated in 1970 by Shaikh Ahmad ibn Ali al Thani, named the al Thanis the hereditary ruling family and invested the ruler, called emir, with supreme power. It specified a 10-member cabinet, appointed and led by the emir. The cabinet ministers were to be the additional members of the 23-person Consultative Council, with 20 of its members chosen from the 40 popularly elected representatives. Such a council has not yet materialized. After ascending the throne in 1972, Shaikh Khalifa ibn Hamad al Thani appointed a fully nominated Advisory Council of 20 members, with powers to advise the cabinet only on the matters referred to it by him. It was expanded to 30 members in 1975 and 35 in 1988. Since its formation, its four-year tenure has been extended repeatedly.

Economy: At the national Gross Domestic Product (1992) of $7.1 billion, the per capital GDP was $13,395.

Education: Literacy in the population aged 15 and over (1990) was 75.7 percent (female 72.5 percent, male 76.8 percent).

Ethnic Composition: Arabs 46 percent, South Asians 36 percent, Persians 12 percent, and others 6 percent.

Geography: A peninsula located midway along the western coast of the Persian Gulf, Qatar is a low lying, oil-rich desert surrounded by shallow waters. Inland wells are the chief source of drinking water.

Governmental System: Qatar is a monarchy, with the ruler as head of state and chief executive.

Military: Qatar's total armed forces number 10,000 actives. Military budget as percent of the GDP in 1992 was 4.9 percent.

Mineral Resources: At 3.7 billion barrels of petroleum, Qatar's reserves are 0.4 percent of the global aggregate; and at 7,100 billion cubic meters of gas, its deposits amount to 5 percent of the world total. Qatar's offshore North Field is the world's largest single deposit of (unassociated) natural gas. At its current pumping rate of 500,000 barrels/day, Qatar's oil wells will be exhausted by 2014. At the present extraction rate of 55 million cubic meters/day, its gas reserves will last 360 years.

Religious Composition: Muslim 92 percent, with Sunnis 84 percent and Shias 8 percent; Christian 6 percent; and others 2 percent.

History Before 1971

The progenitor of the al Thani dynasty was Shaikh Thani ibn Muhammad, a member of the Mudari tribe of the Bani Tamin tribal federation based in the central Arabian Peninsula. The al Thanis, belonging to the puritanical Wahhabi sect of Islam, migrated to Qatar in the eighteenth century.

By intervening in the Qatari-Bahraini battles of 1867–1868, Great Britain became the dominant foreign influence in the politics of Qatar. During the brief Ottoman suzerainty of Qatar between 1872 and 1916, the al Thanis retained their pre-eminence. The end of the Ottoman authority brought Abdullah ibn Qasim al Thani (1916–1948) and the British closer, a relationship formalized in the 1916 Anglo-Qatari Treaty. Great Britain guaranteed Qatar's territorial integrity against external aggression while Qatar promised not to cede any rights, including mineral rights, to a third party without British consent. London maintained a political agent in Doha. The local inhabitants made their living by fishing, pearling, and trading.

The concession given in 1925 to the Anglo-Persian Oil Company, which yielded nothing, was transferred in 1935 to an Iraq Petroleum Company subsidiary, Petroleum Development (Qatar)—later renamed Qatar National Petroleum Company (QNPC). It struck oil in 1939, but large-scale extraction was interrupted by World War II and did not resume until 1948. After oil was found in the Dukhan area in 1939, and commercially exploited after World War II, Doha prospered, and underwent dramatic change.

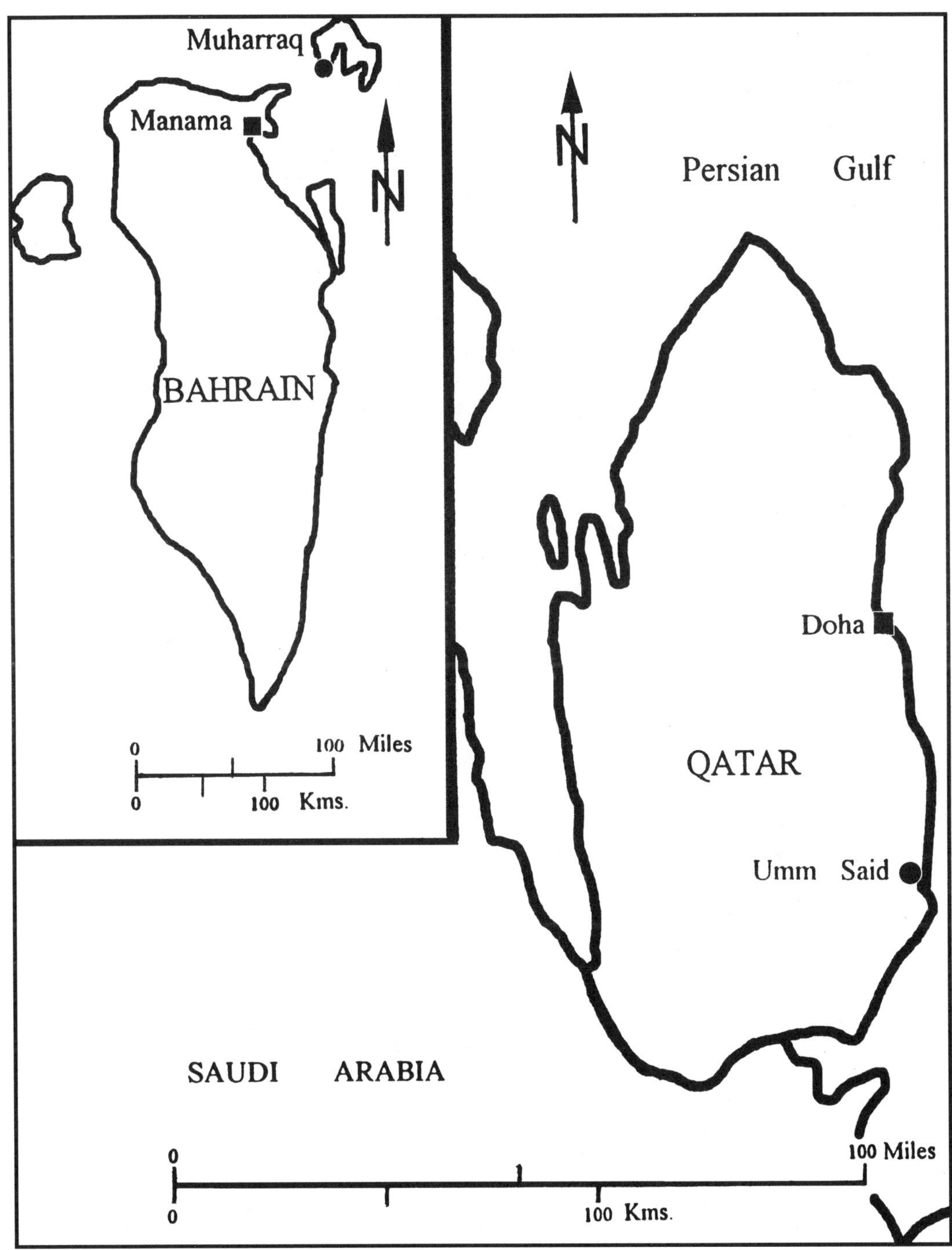

Bahrain and Qatar

Shaikh Abdullah was succeeded by his son, Shaikh Ali ibn Abdullah al Thani (1948–1960). His accession coincided with the extraction of oil on a commercial scale. This allowed him to develop public services and build up economic infrastructure. Being a Wahhabi, he moved cautiously in the economic and political spheres; he based the legitimacy of his rule on Islam and refused to share power. This policy was unsatisfactory to the British, who made him abdicate in 1960 in favor of his son, Ahmad.

Although installed on the throne by the British, Shaikh Ahmad ibn Ali al Thani tried to show some independence. He took Qatar into the Organization of Petroleum Exporting Countries (OPEC) in 1961, and into the Organization of Arab Petroleum Exporting Countries (OAPEC) in 1970. In 1964, he yielded to pressure by Great Britain and the opposition National Unity Front and appointed an Advisory Council with authority to issue laws and decrees for "the fundamental principles and basic rules of overall policy." He promulgated an interim constitution in April 1970 and introduced the infrastructure of a modern state. But he left untouched the "rule of four quarters": The first quarter for administration, the second to the princes, the third to the reserves controlled by the royal clan of some 1,000 male adult al Thanis, and the remainder for economic development. Shaikh Ahmad negotiated the ending of the 1916 Anglo-Qatari Treaty with Great Britain and declared Qatar independent in September 1971.

Independent Qatar Since 1971

As oil output soared to 600,000 barrels/day, it brought in funds on a large scale. Shaikh Ahmad's extravagance reached unprecedented proportions. The Shaikh's lavishness, and his refusal to establish a Consultative Council specified by the 1970 constitution, paved the way for a bloodless coup by his cousin and prime minister, Khalifa ibn Hamad al Thani, in February 1972.

On his accession, Shaikh Khalifa appointed a fully nominated Advisory Council of 20 members with powers to advise the cabinet only on matters referred to it by him. He abolished the practice of allocating a quarter of the state's revenue to the personal account of the ruler. But, by giving 10 of the 15 ministries to his brothers and sons, he consolidated his powers.

He tried to direct the process of modernization stimulated by the boom in oil output. He also pursued self-reliant policies. A dramatic increase in oil revenue due to a sharp price rise in 1973–1974 enabled his government to buy the Western-owned Qatar National Petroleum Company in two stages in 1974 and 1976. Doha expanded rapidly, and by the mid-1980s accounted for three-fifths of the national population. Qatar's oil revenue soared to $5.4 billion in 1980, when its population was less than a quarter million, making it one of the richest countries in the world.

Shaikh Khalifa backed Iraq financially in the 1980–1988 Iran-Iraq War. He was a cofounder of the Gulf Cooperation Council in 1981. While continuing to rule by decree, he periodically expanded the Advisory Council to keep pace with the rise in population. He backed Kuwait after it had been occupied by Iraq in August 1990, and joined the U.S.-led coalition against Iraq in the 1991 Gulf War. By then, most of the important decisions were being taken by his son, Shaikh Hamad ibn Khalifa, whom he had named crown prince and defense minister in 1977.

Among other things, Shaikh Hamad was determined to underline Qatar's independence, especially in its relations with its powerful neighbor, Saudi Arabia. While King Fahd of Saudi Arabia was implacably opposed to reconciliation with Iraq, Shaikh Hamad took a different view. At his initiative, Qatar reestablished diplomatic ties with Baghdad.

Assured of the loyalty of Qatar's armed forces, which he had commanded since 1977, Shaikh Hamad mounted a coup against his father, Shaikh Khalifa, in June 1995 when the latter was on a visit to Geneva, Switzerland. Within days, all the Western powers, including the U.S., recognized the new regime.

UNITED ARAB EMIRATES

The United Arab Emirates (UAE) is a federation of seven emirates: Abu Dhabi, Ajman, Dubai, Ras al Khaima, Sharjah, and Umm al

Qaiwain. Each principality is ruled by a hereditary emir. The UAE, which came into existence in 1971, is abundantly endowed with oil and gas.

Profile

Area & Population: Occupying the southern end of the Persian Gulf, called the Lower Gulf, the United Arab Emirates measures 30,000 square miles. Of these, 26,000 square miles belong to the Abu Dhabi emirate, and another 1,510 square miles to the Dubai emirate. The estimated population of the UAE in 1992 was 2,160,000, with 900,000 living in the Abu Dhabi emirate, 566,000 in the Dubai emirate, and 355,000 in the Sharjah emirate. Only 520,000 inhabitants are UAE nationals.

Cities: With a population of 500,000, Abu Dhabi, the capital, is also the largest city. Next in size are Dubai 430,000, Sharjah 125,000, al Ain 102,000, and Ras al Khaima 90,000.

Constitution: The interim constitution, which came into effect in December 1971, specified a federal system for the constituent emirates. The seven-member Supreme Council of Emirs (SCE) is the highest federal body, which elects the president and vice president of the UAE from among its members. The president appoints the prime minister and the cabinet. The SCE's decisions must be approved by five emirs, including those of Abu Dhabi, and Dubai. The legislative authority lies with the Federal National Council, a fully nominated consultative assembly of 40 members, with a two-year tenure. The membership is made up of eight each from Abu Dhabi and Dubai; six each from Ras al Khaima and Sharjah; and four each from Ajman, Fujaira, and Umm al Qaiwain. It debates legislation proposed by the cabinet, and has the authority to amend or reject. The provisional constitution has been extended every five years since its promulgation, the last extension being in 1991. The Supreme Council of emirs currently consists of Shaikh Zaid ibn Sultan al Nahyan (1966–) of Abu Dhabi, Shaikh Maktum ibn Rashid al Maktum (1990–) of Dubai, Shaikh Saqr ibn Muhammad al Qasimi (1948–) of Ras al Khaima, Shaikh Sultan ibn Muhammad al Qasimi (1972–) of Sharjah, Shaikh Humaid ibn Rashid al Nuaimi (1981–) of Ajman, Shaikh Hamad ibn Muhammad al Sharqi (1975–) of Fujaira, and Shaikh Rashid ibn Ahmad al Mualla (1981–) of Umm al Qaiwan.

Economy: At the national Gross Domestic Product of $34.9 billion, the per capital GDP was $16,065.

Education: Literacy among the population aged 15 and over was 73 percent (female 68.4, male 74.5 percent).

Ethnic Composition: Arabs 36 percent, South Asians 58 percent, Persians 2 percent, Europeans 1 percent; and others 3 percent.

Geography: The Persian Gulf coast between Qatar and the Ras Musandam at the Hormuz Straits has shallow waters, a fringe of sandbars and coral reefs, and stretches of saline mudflats. Human settlements grew either around creeks, which provided sheltered anchorage's for seacraft, or on firm sandbars and islands with ground water. The interior is sand desert with occasional oases fed by shallow ground water, such as at Liwa in Abu Dhabi. There is a narrow strip of silts and gravel topped with soil, and possessing pockets of ground water, between the desert and the Omani Mountains. This strip allows irrigated cultivation between Ras al Khaima in the north and al Ain in the south.

Governmental System: The UAE is a federation of monarchies, with a president, elected by the rulers of the constituent emirates, as head of state and chief executive.

Military: The UAE's total armed forces number 61,500 actives. Military expenditure as percent of GDP in 1992 was 6 percent.

Mineral Resources: At 98.1 billion barrels, the UAE's oil deposits are 9.7 percent of the global aggregate; and at 5,800 billion cubic meters, its gas reserves amount to 4.1 percent of the world total. At the production rate of 2.4 million barrels/day, the UAE's petroleum will last 112 years. At the extraction rate of 64 million cubic meters/day, it will take 249 years to exhaust its gas reserves.

Religious Composition: Muslim 81 percent, Christian 9 percent, Hindu 8 percent, and others 2 percent.

History Before 1971

By 1892, having signed Exclusive Agreements with London, the rulers of the six emirates of the Lower Gulf—Abu Dhabi, Ajman, Dubai, Ras al Khaima, Sharjah, and Umm al Qaiwain—conducted their foreign affairs through Great Britain, which appointed political officers at the capitals of each of the emirates. In 1939, the Trucial Coast Development Oil company, later the Abu Dhabi Petroleum Company (ADPC), a subsidiary of the Iraq Petroleum Company (IPC), obtained exploration rights in Abu Dhabi.

In 1952, after upgrading the province of Fujaira to an emirate, Great Britain established the Trucial States Council (TSC), consisting of the rulers of the seven emirates; the TSC's development office (funded by London), based in Sharjah, acted as its executive. The next year, Great Britain replaced seven local political officers with a political agent based in Sharjah, and set up the Trucial Oman Scouts, a central military force, to maintain peace in the emirates. The TSC met regularly to discuss common problems. In 1954, the Abu Dhabi Marines Area (ADMA), formed by British Petroleum and Compagnie Francaise des Petroles, secured oil concessions in Abu Dhabi. Following successful exploration, oil production started in 1960 on a modest scale.

Since Abu Dhabi and Dubai account for most of the UAE's area and population, the history of the UAE is largely their history. Located on the offshore island of the same name, Abu Dhabi was founded by members of the aal Bu Falah clan of the Bani Yas tribe in 1761. A quarter century later, they transferred their main base from the Liwa oasis in the interior to Abu Dhabi. In the early twentieth century, Abu Dhabi's 6,000-odd inhabitants were dependent on pearl fishing and petty trading for their livelihood. In 1946, the emir of Abu Dhabi, Shaikh Shakbut ibn Sultan (1928–1966), appointed his younger brother, Zaid, governor of the eastern province, with its capital in al Ain. Zaid became popular by ruling as a Bedouin chief, consulting tribal notables and being accessible to ordinary people. When, after 1960, Shaikh Shakbut refused to spend the revenue accruing from oil production on economic development, he lost the backing of the British. They conspired successfully with Shaikh Zaid ibn Sultan to depose Shaikh Shakbut in 1966. Shaikh Zaid succeeded his elder brother. He appointed highly trained advisers and administrators to handle the emirate's burgeoning government revenues and activities.

Established in 1799, Dubai became an important pearling center in the early twentieth century. With traders from the Indian subcontinent and Iran settling there, it developed as a trading port. Dubai was ruled by the al Maktum family of the aal Bu Falasa section of the Bani Yas tribe. Dubai's commercial and political significance grew to the extent that in 1954 London transferred its political agent for the Trucial States from Sharjah to Dubai.

Shaikh Rashid ibn Said al Maktum (1958–1990), who in 1958 succeeded his father, proved to be a good administrator and economist. He turned Dubai into a leading entrepot of eastern Arabia, basing its commercial prosperity initially on the import and export of gold. Its gold supply sources were banks in Switzerland and its export destinations were India or Pakistan.

Oil was discovered offshore in Dubai in 1966 by the Dubai Petroleum Company (DPC), which had taken over from the IPC

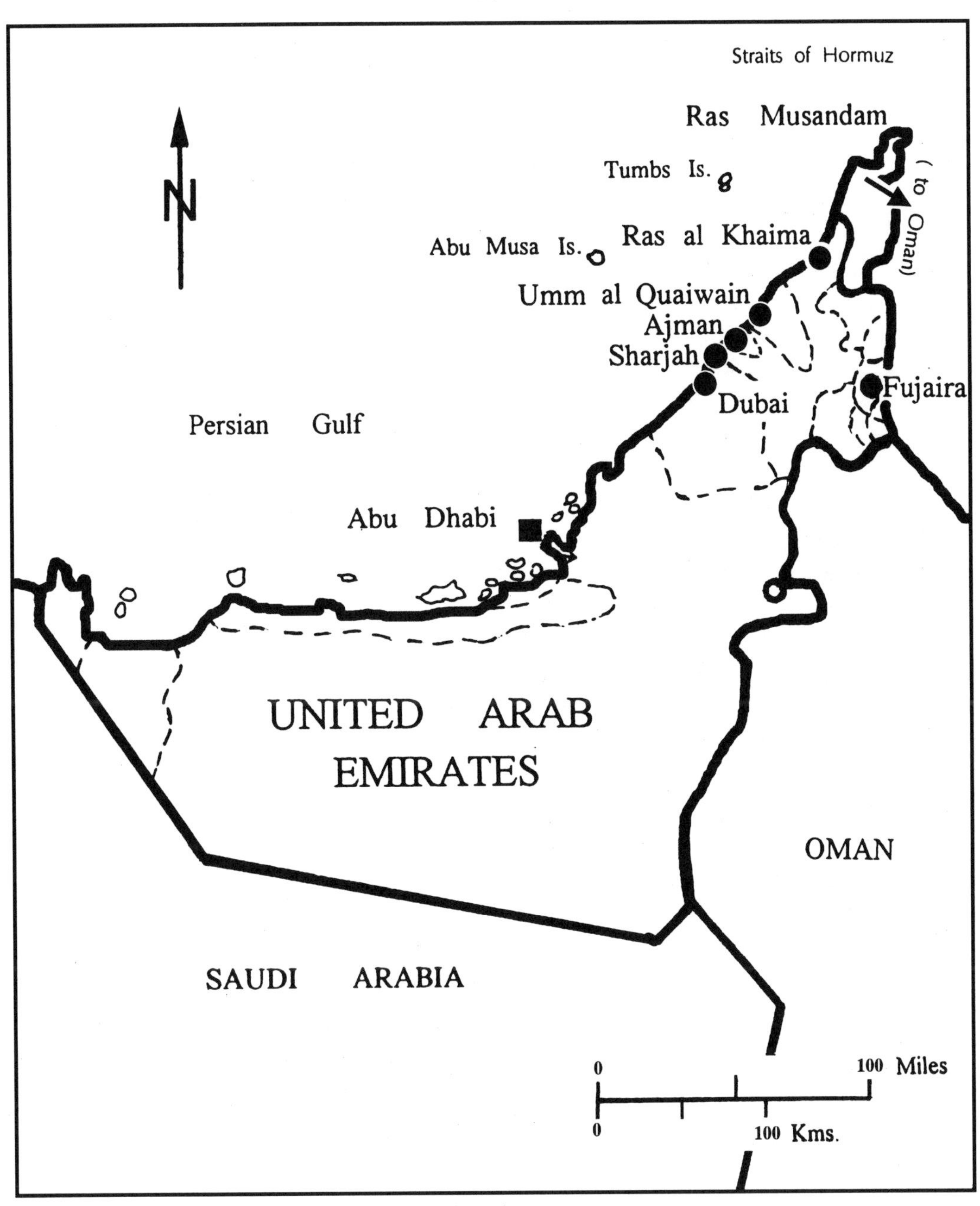

United Arab Emirates

in 1961 after it surrendered the concession it had held since 1937. Commercial production, which began in 1969, rose to 420,000 barrels/day two decades later.

In 1968, Great Britain initiated talks about the formation of an Arab Gulf Federation to come into being after its withdrawal from the Persian Gulf region by December 1971. At the TSC meeting in July 1971, it was announced that all of them, except Ras al Khaima, had agreed to form a federation, to be called the United Arab Emirates, on the eve of the British departure. Ras al Khaima then joined the UAE in 1972. It was primarily Abu Dhabi's booming oil revenue that encouraged the small neighboring emirates to agree to form the federation. A Supreme Council of Emirs was established, with Shaikh Zaid al Nahyan of Abu Dhabi as its president, and Shaikh Rashid al Maktum as its vice-president.

Independent UAE Since 1971

Although both Shaikh Zaid and Shaikh Rashid realized the importance of cooperation to make a success of the fledgling federation, personal rivalry and incompatibility intervened. Shaikh Rashid was a sophisticated entrepreneur whereas Shaikh Zaid was a bedouin chief. When a single federal council of ministers came into being in December 1973, Shaikh Zaid abolished the Abu Dhabi cabinet, and appointed a 50-member Consultative Council. To the detriment of the UAE, rivalry between him and Shaikh Rashid persisted for many years.

During the period 1966–1975, ambitious plans to modernize Abu Dhabi city were implemented, and it was turned into a modern settlement with offices, hotels, light industry, and an international airport. Following the independence of the Dubai emirate in 1971, the city of Dubai became its capital. It acquired a modern port and dry docks in the 1970s.

By 1978, the ADPC and ADMA had been restructured into the Abu Dhabi Company for Onshore Oil (ADCO) and ADMA-OPCO for offshore work. These companies accounted for 93 percent of Abu Dhabi's oil output, which amounted to 1.8 million barrels/day on the eve of the Iraqi invasion of Kuwait in 1990. Two sharp rises in oil price, in the mid- and the late-1970s, made the UAE, with less than a million people, one of the five richest countries in the world.

Following the Islamic revolution in Iran in early 1979, the nominated Federal National Council and the federal cabinet demanded parliamentary democracy and a unitary state. This alarmed Shaikh Zaid and Shaikh Rashid, who sank their differences. In July 1979, at the behest of Shaikh Zaid, the Supreme Council of Emirs called on Shaikh Rashid to become the UAE's prime minister. He agreed, taking over from his eldest son Maktum ibn Rashid, and applying his considerable administrative and financial skills to the running of the UAE for the next decade.

During the early phase of the 1980–1988 Iran-Iraq War, Shaikh Zaid sided with Baghdad. But as the conflict dragged on, with Iran in a stronger position, he took an increasingly neutral position. During the war, the importance of Dubai as a center for re-exporting Western goods to Iran rose dramatically. A cosmopolitan metropolis with excellent financial facilities, Dubai thrived. A large majority of Dubai's residents are expatriates from South Asia (India, Pakistan, and Bangladesh), Iran, and Europe.

In 1981, the UAE became a founding member of the Gulf Cooperation Council (GCC), a regional body of six Gulf monarchies that aimed to coordinate internal security, procurement of arms, and the national economies of member-states. But formation of the GCC did not rule out bilateral cooperation with a view to achieving a specific objective.

For instance, during the spring of 1990 Shaikh Zaid cooperated with the Kuwaiti emir in the latter's plan to hurt the Iraqi economy by flooding the oil market and lowering prices. In July 1990, the UAE's output soared to 2.3 million barrels/day, more than twice the quota fixed by the Organization of Petroleum Exporting Countries (OPEC), of which it had been a member since 1971. The price fell to $12 a barrel, a third below the $18 reference price fixed by OPEC. The UAE ignored Iraqi President Saddam Hussein's warning, but, unlike Kuwait, did not suffer at the hands of Iraq.

In the 1991 Gulf War, the UAE joined the U.S.-led coalition against Baghdad. It contributed troops and military hardware to the coalition forces as well as $5 billion to the war chest. In this, Shaikh Zaid had the backing of his new vice-president, Shaikh Maktum ibn

Downtown Abu Dhabi, United Arab Emirates. Photo: Courtesy of the Embassy of the United Arab Emirates in London.

Rashid, who succeeded his father, Shaikh Rashid ibn Said, as the emir of Dubai in October 1990. He also took over the premiership of the UAE. As a Western-educated royal, he got along well with the substantial community of Western oil and financial experts in the UAE. Under the stewardship of Shaikh Zaid and Shaikh Maktum, the UAE continued its close ties with Washington, and was reassured by the permanent stationing of the U.S. Fifth Fleet in 1995.

CHAPTER 14

Oman

Of the six states on the western side of the Persian Gulf, the sultanate of Oman has the longest established identity even though until 1970 it was officially called the Sultanate of Muscat and Oman. It has also been an imperial power, exercising authority far from its shores. Its pivotal position at the mouth of the strategic Hormuz Straits, through which pass the world's busiest oil shipping lanes, enhances it geopolitical importance.

PROFILE

Area & Population: Since Oman's borders with the neighboring states are not delineated, its area of 118,150 square miles is an estimate. Its estimated population in 1992 was 1,790,000, of which 1,310,000 were Omani nationals.

Cities: With a population of 120,000, Muscat, the capital, is also the largest city. Next in size are Nizwa 63,000, Sumail 45,000, and Salalah 20,000.

Constitution: There is no written constitution. An absolute monarchy, Oman lacks legislature, political parties, or trade unions. The ruler, called sultan, is both head of state and prime minister. He governs by decree and heads a nominated council of ministers. In 1991, the sultan set up a 60-member Consultative Council with a three-year tenure. The deputy premier for legal affairs selects a member from a list of three submitted by the governor of each of the 59 provinces. The sultan appoints the speaker. The Council drafts legislation only on socio-economic affairs for submission to the appropriate ministry.

Economy: At the national Gross Domestic Product of $11.2 billion, the per capita GDP was $6,257.

Education: Literacy in the population aged six and above was 41 percent (female 24 percent, male 58 percent).

Ethnic Composition: Arabs 73 percent, South Asians 22 percent, and others 5 percent.

Geography: Situated in the southeast of the Arabian Peninsula, Oman is bordered by the Gulf of Oman, the Arabian Sea, Yemen, and the Empty Quarter region of Saudi Arabia. Its enclave at the tip of Ras Musandam stands at the narrowest point in the Hormuz Straits. The coastal plain of Batina lies between the shoreline along the Gulf of Oman and the Oman Mountains. Beyond the mountains, in the interior of the country, gravel and silt plains change into stony flats and desert sands. The southern Dhofar region, occupying a third of Oman, consists of a narrow coastal plain along the Arabian Sea near Salalah against the background of high plateaus which turn into desert sands and flats in the north.

Governmental System: Oman is an absolute monarchy, with the sultan as head of state, chief executive, and sole legislator.

Military: Oman's total armed forces number 42,500 actives. Military expenditure as percent of the GDP in 1990 was 15.7 percent.

Mineral Resources: At 4.7 billion barrels, Oman's oil reserves amount to 0.5 percent of the global total; and at 510 billion cubic meters, its gas deposits are 0.3 percent of the world aggregate. At the current production rate of 780,000 barrels/day, the country's petroleum reserves would be exhausted by 2010; and at the present extraction rate of 16 million cubic meters/day, its gas deposits would last until 2079.

Religious Composition: Muslim 85 percent, Hindu 14 percent, and others 1 percent.

HISTORY OF MUSCAT AND OMAN BEFORE 1970

The history of the land of Oman is interlinked with that of the port of Muscat. By the thirteenth century, Muscat was an important center for trade with the Persian Gulf and East Africa. The Hormuzi clan, which then administered it, held supreme for three centuries until it was overpowered by the Portuguese in 1508. They in turn were defeated in 1650 by native Arabs. By 1730, the Arabs had taken over the Portuguese colonies in East Africa. Following internal fighting, the aal Bu Said clan emerged on top. In 1741, Muscat became the capital of Oman. The aal Bu Said dynasty reached its peak in the 1850s when its empire extended to the eastern shores of Africa and Zanzibar Island. In 1861, the two surviving sons of the sultan divided his territories. Zanzibar and the East African colonies formed one sultanate, and Muscat and Oman the other. But infighting so weakened the dynasty that the ruling family, based in Muscat, was overpowered by tribes from the interior. In 1871, the British—involved in the region by the activities of the East India Company—attacked Muscat, and restored the aal Bu Saids to power. Oman thus became a *de facto* colony of Great Britain.

In 1915, the traditional rivalry between the coast and the hinterland resurfaced, with the leader of the tribes of the interior, who bore the title iman, attacking Muscat. Great Britain intervened on behalf of the temporal ruler, the sultan. The subsequent uneasy peace was formalized in 1920 in the Treaty of Sib between Sultan Taimur ibn Faisal (1920–1932) and the tribal leaders, who recognized the sultan's authority in external affairs. The treaty guaranteed freedom of movement to the tribes and urban dwellers, with the sultan agreeing not to raise taxes above 5 percent of the value of trade in coastal towns. The signing of a treaty with the iman implied autonomy for the interior. On the economic development front, the exploration for petroleum by the Anglo-Iranian Oil Company (AIOC), which obtained concessions in 1925, yielded nothing.

When the British deposed Sultan Taimur for fiscal mismanagement in 1932, and replaced him with his son, Said ibn Taimur (1932–1970), the later continued to honor the 1920 Treaty of Sib. Reacting to his father's extravagance, Said took parsimony to extremes. He also monopolized power. Opposed to progress, he prevented his subjects from using, for instance, patent medicines, trousers, radios, books, and even spectacles.

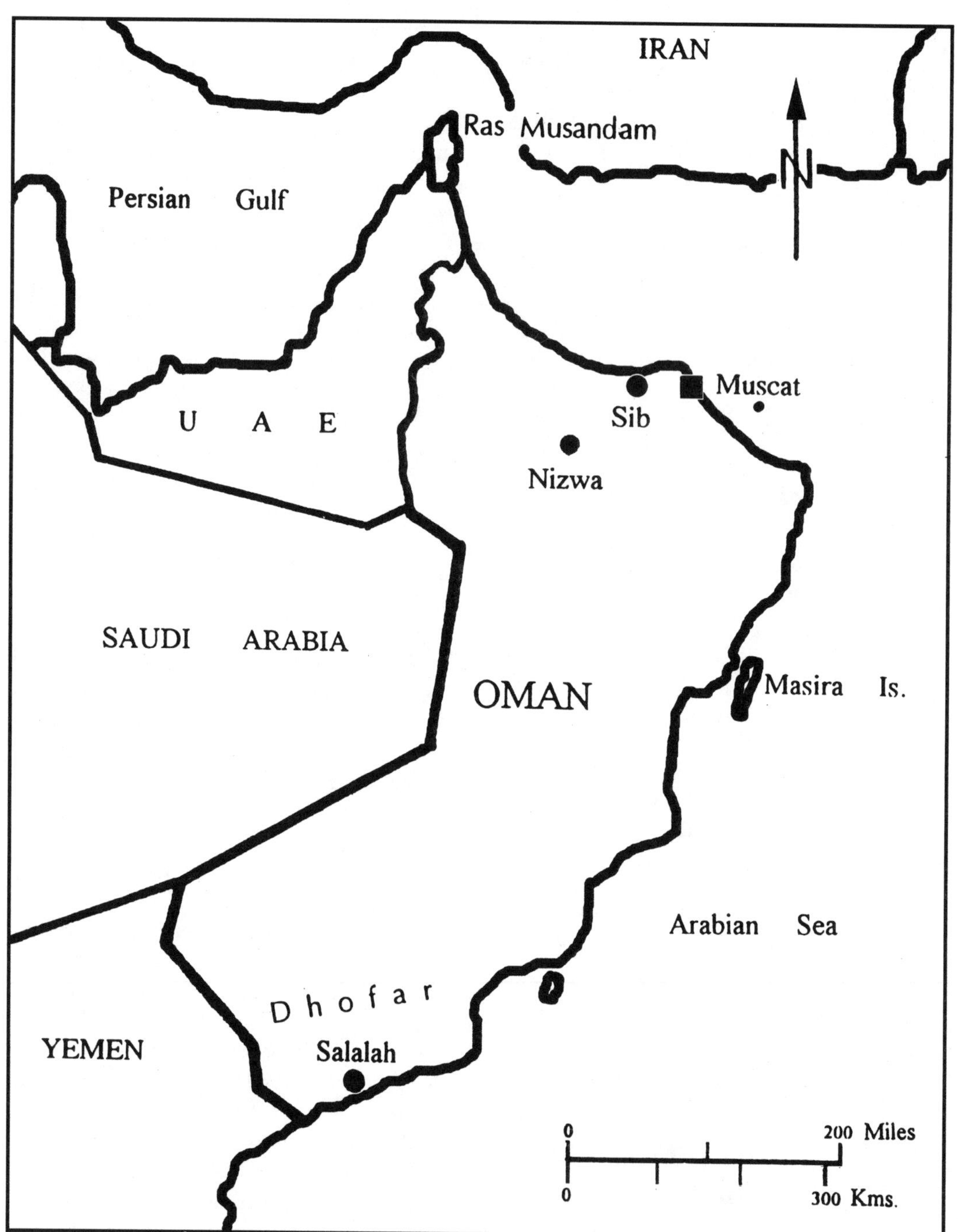
IRAN
Ras Musandam
Persian Gulf
N
Muscat
Sib
U A E
Nizwa
SAUDI ARABIA
OMAN
Masira Is.
Arabian Sea
Dhofar
YEMEN
Salalah
0
200 Miles
0
300 Kms.

Oman

However, in 1937 he gave a 75-year oil concession for the whole country, except Dhofar province, where a separate concession was granted in 1953 to Dhofar Cities Service Petroleum Corporation, to a subsidiary of the Iraq Petroleum Company (IPC), called Petroleum Concessions (Oman). After World War II, it began exploring in the interior, controlled by Iman Ghalib ibn Ali. Problems ensued when its exploration around the Buraimi oasis in 1951 upset Saudi Arabia, which claimed and occupied part of the oasis.

Sultan Said was also challenged by Imam Ghalib ibn Ali, who proclaimed the independent Imamate of Oman in 1954, and applied for membership in the Arab League, to which the Sultanate of Muscat and Oman was not affiliated. Sultan Said maintained that the treaty recognized the Imamate as autonomous only in local and socio-religious affairs. His forces, armed and led by the British, crushed the challenge from the imam by the end of 1955. Acting in collusion with the forces of the Abu Dhabi emirate, Omani forces also recovered the area of Buraimi oasis occupied by the Saudis.

In 1957, Imam Ghalib's brother, Talib ibn Ali, instigated by the Saudis and Egyptians, mounted a rebellion in the interior. Sultan Said called on the British to provide him with military assistance according to the Anglo-Omani Treaty of 1920. The British intervention caused the armed uprising to dwindle into guerrilla actions. Egypt and other Arab states charged that the British had committed armed aggression against the Imamate of Oman, and placed the matter before the United Nations. While the UN commission of inquiry failed to uphold the claim of popular opposition to Sultan Said, several Arab countries succeeded in getting the UN General Assembly to adopt a resolution demanding the end of the British colonial presence in Oman. In 1958, after Sultan Said had withdrawn to his palace in Salalah, 600 miles southwest of Muscat, administrative control of the country passed almost totally into the hands of British civil servants, with London providing funds for all development projects.

In 1962, Petroleum Development Oman, the successor to Petroleum Concessions (Oman), struck oil in commercial quantities. Oil income rose from $21 million in 1967 to $117 million three years later, but Sultan Said left the money untouched. He showed no sign of using it to build the infrastructure of a modern state. By 1963, he faced a challenge to his authority from the inhabitants of Dhofar province. The victory of leftist forces in adjoining South Yemen on the eve of British withdrawal in November 1967 boosted the moral of the Dhofari revolutionaries. This, and the total inflexibility of Sultan Said, made the British apprehensive; they therefore engineered a coup on 23 July 1970 and replaced him with his only son, Qaboos.

SULTANATE OF OMAN SINCE 1970

Among the first acts of Sultan Qaboos ibn Said (1970–) was to rename his country the Sultanate of Oman. Unlike his father, Sultan Qaboos was educated in Great Britain, where he graduated from the Royal Military Academy at Sandhurst. After being called home in 1965, he found himself put under surveillance at the Salalah royal palace by his father. Among his visitors were British expatriates whom Sultan Said trusted. Some of them were used by London to plot Said's deposition.

After becoming the ruler as well as prime minister and defense and foreign minister, Sultan Qaboos ended Oman's isolation by securing it membership in the Arab League and the United Nations. Aided by subventions from Kuwait and the United Arab Emirates, and rising oil output, which reached a peak of 400,000 barrels/day in the mid-1970s, he built or expanded the economic infrastructure, and provided social services to Omani nationals.

He also intensified the campaign against the leftist insurgency in Dhofar. He expanded the army with a large intake of foreign mercenaries, especially Pakistanis. In 1973, he turned to Iran, then ruled by the shah, for extra troops. With British, Saudi, Egyptian, Jordanian, and Iranian backing, he crushed the Dhofari rebellion by late 1975.

Improved income from oil enabled his government in 1975 to acquire a 60 percent share of the PDO, leaving the rest with Royal Dutch Shell and the Compagnie Francaise des Petrole. Muscat became a thriving port and cosmopolitan city, with residents drawn not only from other Arab countries, but also from Iran, India, Pakistan, and East Africa.

Alone among the Arab Gulf states, Oman showed a willingness to allow U.S. forces to use its military facilities, especially the ones on Masirah Island, from which Great Britain had withdrawn its forces in 1977. Sultan Qaboos was also alone in the Arab world in endorsing Egypt's Camp David Accords with Israel in 1978, and did not cut ties with Cairo after the signing of a peace treaty between Egypt and Israel. He was the only Gulf leader to sign a military accord with Washington in June 1980, allowing the U.S. to use Oman's harbors and airports, and to stockpile arms and ammunition on its soil. The commercial extraction of oil in Dhofar, which began in 1989, boosted both state revenue and the ruler's morale.

The outbreak of the Iran-Iraq War in September 1980 enabled Sultan Qaboos to end Oman's regional isolation. Like other Gulf rulers, he took a pro-Iraqi position. He joined his fellow monarchs in 1981 in establishing the Gulf Cooperation Council. As the Iran-Iraq conflict dragged on, making the strategic importance of the Hormuz Straits even more obvious, Sultan Qaboos realized that the territorial waters of Oman at Ras Musandam, extending 12 miles from the coast, overlapped those of Iran in the Straits. This made him adopt an increasingly neutral stand in the conflict, which ended in August 1988.

Along with other GCC rulers, Sultan Qaboos backed Kuwait after it had been occupied by Iraq in August 1990. He joined the U.S.-led coalition against Iraq. Later that year, while refusing to provide his subjects with a written constitution or abandon any of his arbitrary powers, he nominated a Consultative Council with advisory powers on socio-economic matters.

On the Middle East peace process, which began in October 1991, he took a moderate line. He endorsed the Israeli-Palestine Liberation Organization (PLO) Accord signed in September 1993. Later he hosted one of the multilateral conferences, sponsored as part of the regional peace process, in Muscat. Oman's links with the U.S., already strong, became stronger after Washington announced its decision to station the U.S. Fifth Fleet in the Persian Gulf in 1995.

CHAPTER 15

Saudi Arabia

Occupying three-quarters of the vast Arabian Peninsula, and possessing a quarter of the planet's oil reserves, the Kingdom of Saudi Arabia is a powerful state, regionally and globally. Because it contains the holy Muslim cities of Mecca and Medina—the respective birth- and death-places of Prophet Muhammad—Saudi Arabia has a special place in the hearts of more than a billion Muslims all over the world. The country is named after the ruling dynasty, the House of Saud (aal Saud, in Arabic).

PROFILE

Area & Population: Roughly rectangular, Saudi Arabia, including parts of the Saudi-Iraqi and Saudi-Kuwaiti Neutral Zones, measures 865,000 square miles. Its estimated population in 1992 was 16,929,000, of which 11,850,000 were Saudi nationals.

Cities: With a population of 1,308,000, Riyadh, the capital, is the second largest city, next to Jiddah, with 1,500,000. Then follow Mecca 890,000, Medina 485,000, and Taif 300,000.

Constitution: In March 1992, six decades after the founding of the kingdom, King Fahd ibn Abdul Aziz al Saud (1982–) issued a decree that stipulated the introduction of a basic law of government, and the appointment of a Consultative Council of 60 members to be chaired by the monarch. Council members were to sit for four-year terms. It was authorized to question the government and refer any official action it disputed to the monarch. An absolute monarchy, Saudi Arabia lacks legislature, political parties, or trade unions. Executive authority rests with the king who rules through a council of ministers responsible to him.

Economy: At the national Gross Domestic Product of $122.3 billion, its per capita GDP was $7,224.

Education: Literacy in the population aged 15 and above (1990) was 62.4 percent (female 48.1 percent, male 73.1 percent).

Ethnic Composition: Arabs 78 percent, Asians 20 percent, Africans 2 percent, and Europeans 1 percent.

Geography: Saudi Arabia occupies most of the Arabian peninsula. The peninsula is formed by a platform of ancient rock tilting eastwards, so that the land rises sharply from the Red Sea rift to the edges of the mountains that run southwards from the Hijaz region to Aden. In these highlands lie the oases of Medina, Mecca, and Taif. The tilted rock platform slides downwards to the coast of the Persian Gulf. The central zone is mainly desert with scattered oases, such as Riyadh and Hail. The south is a vast, uncharted desert, called the Empty Quarter. Saudi Arabia's huge oil reserves are found mainly in the eastern sector, under limestones and sandstones in shallow waters.

Governmental System: Saudi Arabia is an absolute monarchy, with the king, called malik, as head of state, chief executive, and sole legislator.

Military: Saudi Arabia's total armed forces number 161,000 actives and 20,000 reserves. Military expenditure as percent of the GDP is 12.8 percent.

Mineral Resources: Saudi Arabia's mineral resources include bauxite, copper, gold, gypsum, iron ore, lead, magnesite, marble, rock salt, silver, uranium, and zinc. At 261.2 billion barrels, its oil reserves are 25.9 percent of the world aggregate; and at 5,300 billion cubic meters, its gas deposits are 3.7 percent of the global total. At the present production rate of 8.8 million barrels/day, Saudi Arabia will exhaust its oil deposits by 2077; and at the current extraction rate of 177 million cubic meters/day, its gas reserves will last until 2073.

Religious Composition: Muslim 98 percent, with Sunni 89 percent and Shia 9 percent; Christian 1.5 percent; and others 0.5 percent.

HISTORY BEFORE 1932

The House of Saud was established by Muhammad ibn Saud, the ruler of Najd, the central region of the Arabian Peninsula, in 1745 after he had allied with Muhammad ibn Abdul Wahhab, the founder of Wahhabism, a puritanical Islamic sect also known as *Muwahidun* (Unitarians). Abdul Wahhab condemned the medieval superstitions that had gathered around the pristine teachings of Islam. He was especially opposed to the cult of saints who were often beseeched by believers to intercede on their behalf with God. He and his followers began destroying the tombs of saints.

Once Muhammad ibn Saud, a Wahhabi, became ruler, Wahhabis mounted a campaign against idolatry, corruption, and adultery. They banned music, dancing, and even poetry, integral parts of Arab life. They prohibited the use of silk, gold, ornaments, and jewelry. Regarding themselves as true believers, Wahhabis launched a *jihad*, or holy war, against all others, whom they described as apostates.

Under Saud ibn Abdul Aziz (1803–1814), Wahhabi rule spread to the Iraqi and Syrian borders, and included the Hijaz region, containing the holy Muslim cities of Mecca and Medina. This development led the Ottoman sultan to order the governor of Egypt, Muhammad Ali, to quell the movement. The result was the defeat and execution of Abdullah ibn Saud (1814–1818). However, the power of the Wahhabi House of Saud waxed and waned until 1891 when it was expelled from the area of the Riyadh oasis.

With Abdul Aziz ibn Abdul Rahman al Saud (1902–1953), Wahhabism rose again in the Arabian peninsula. He propagated the creed using military and state power, and fostered the Ikhwan movement. Considering themselves as "the truly guided Islamic community," Wahhabis attacked polytheists, unbelievers, and hypocrites (i.e., those who claimed to be Muslim but whose behavior was unIslamic). They labeled any deviation from the Sharia as innovation, and therefore unIslamic.

In 1902, Abdul Aziz al Saud regained Diraiya and neighboring Riyadh from the rival Rashid clan, which was allied with the

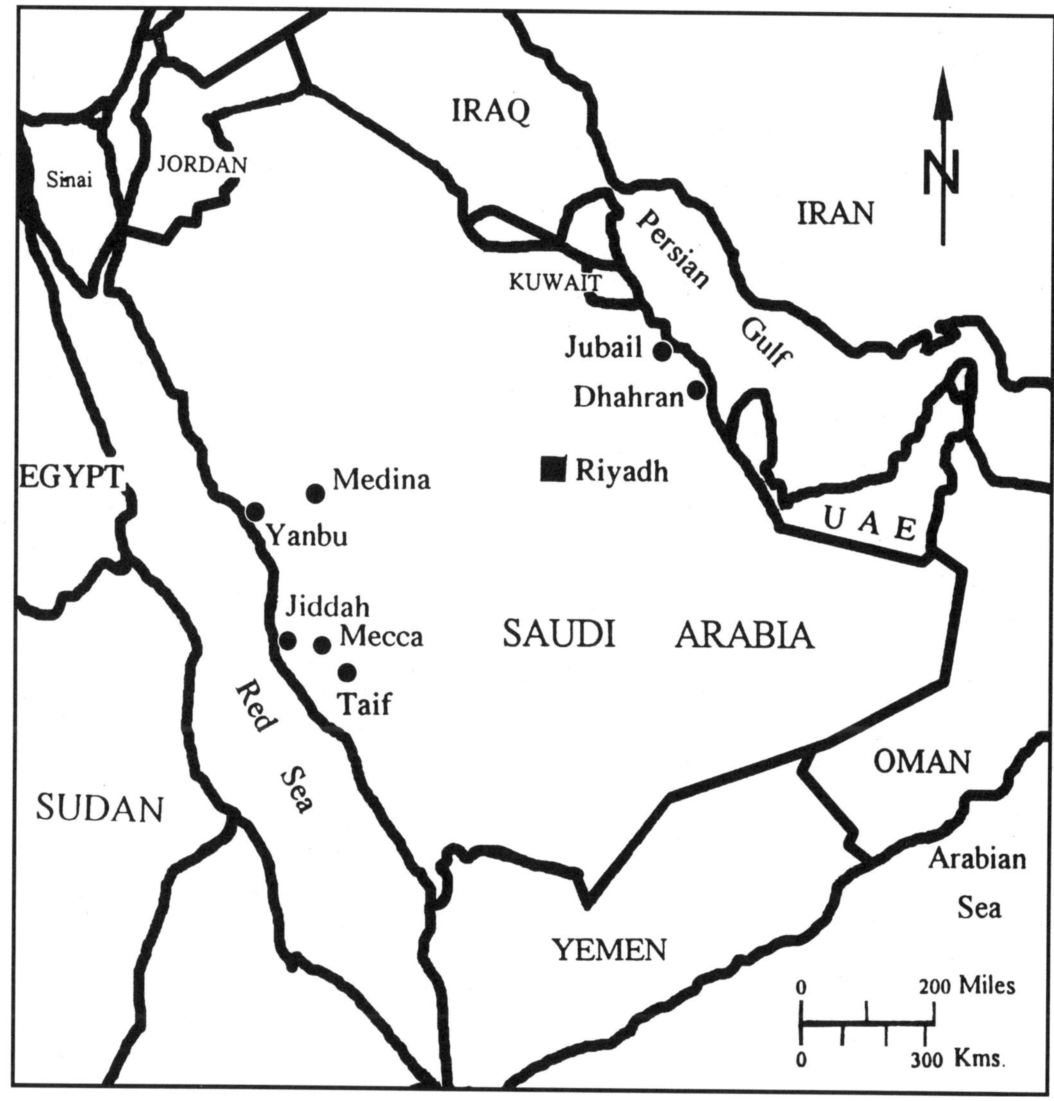

Saudi Arabia

Ottoman Empire. After consolidating his domain, he captured the eastern Hasa region in 1913. Following the downfall of the Ottoman Empire, he conquered the Asir region on the Red Sea in 1920. The next year, he defeated his rival, Muhammad ibn Rashid, who was based in the Shammar region. After he had added more territories to his domain in 1922, he called himself the Sultan of Najd and its Dependencies. He couched his campaigns in Islamic terms, as a struggle to punish either religious dissenters or those who had strayed from true Islam as represented by Wahhabism. In 1924, he defeated Hussein ibn Ali al Hashem, the ruler of Hijaz, and deposed him. Having declared himself King of Hijaz and Sultan of Najd and its Dependencies in January 1926, Abdul Aziz al Saud sought international recognition.

The following year, Great Britain recognized him as king of Hijaz and Najd and its Dependencies by signing the Treaty of Jiddah with him. In 1929, he fell out with the militant section of the Ikhwan (Brethren), the armed wing of the Wahhabis, which had so far been his fighting force. Assisted by the

British, then controlling Kuwait and Iraq, he quelled the Ikhwan rebellion. In September 1932, he combined his two domains, comprising 77 percent of the Arabian Peninsula, into the Kingdom of Saudi Arabia, and called himself king of Saudi Arabia.

KINGDOM OF SAUDI ARABIA SINCE 1932

Within months of assuming the title of king of Saudi Arabia, Abdul Aziz al Saud granted an oil concession to Standard Oil Company of California (Socal). By so doing, he deviated from the policy of other regional rulers who, having signed restrictive treaties with London, had given such concessions to companies based in Great Britain or the British Commonwealth. The special relationship between Saudi Arabia and the United States thus forged has continued to this day.

In 1936, Socal invited Texaco to form a joint corporation, Caltex, which struck oil in 1938. Modest commercial extraction, which started in that year, was interrupted by World War II, in which King Abdul Aziz remained neutral. Oil exports resumed in 1946. Two years later, Caltex expanded into a consortium of four American corporations–Social (later Chevron) 30 percent, Texaco 30 percent, Standard Oil Company of New Jersey (later Esso, then Exxon) 30 percent, and Mobil Oil 10 percent. The consortium was called the Arabian American Oil Company (Aramco). Output rose so sharply that Aramco's earnings jumped from $2.8 million in 1944 to $115 million five years later. The Saudi monarch now required Aramco to pay half of its profit as tax.

As a domineering and militarily successful tribal chief, he behaved as an autocrat. The dramatic increase in oil output caused an economic boom that undermined the traditional, spartan Wahhabi lifestyle of the House of Saud. It also overstretched the rudimentary institutions of the state, supervised by King Abdul Aziz and some of his close aides. Yet, it was not until October 1953, a month before his death, that he appointed a council of ministers, chaired by his eldest son, Saud, as an advisory body.

When Saud ibn Abdul Aziz (1953–1964) became king, he retained the premiership. He proved incapable of handling the fiscal and administrative complexities arising from the increased demand for Saudi oil caused by the 1951–1953 oil nationalization crisis in Iran. The resulting chaos, compounded by Saud's extravagance and mismanagement, created a crisis, and led to a power struggle between him and his brother, Crown Prince Faisal. The struggle was finally settled against Saud, who was forced to abdicate in 1964. In the course of administrative and fiscal reform in 1962, the government set up the General Petroleum and Mineral Organization, known as Petromin, to increase state participation in the oil and gas industry.

On ascending the throne, Faisal ibn Abdul Aziz (1964–1975) reneged on the promise for political reform he had made as crown prince in 1962. Instead, he suppressed the opposition harshly. He increased support to the royalist camp in North Yemen's civil war, in which the republicans were being aided by Egyptian President Gamal Abdul Nasser. But, following the Arab defeat in the 1967 Arab-Israeli War, he buried his differences with Nasser. King Faisal's efforts to establish a transnational organization of Muslim states succeeded in 1969, in the wake of an arson attempt on the al Aqsa mosque in Jerusalem, which resulted in the formation of the Islamic Conference Organization, based in Jiddah.

Petroleum output shot up from 1.3 million barrels/day in 1940 to 8 million barrels/day in 1973 before the Arab-Israeli War in October. During the conflict, King Faisal led the Arab oil embargo against the Western allies of Israel, and backed the quadrupling of oil prices in 1973–1974. Due to increased output, and a sharp rise in price in those years, Saudi oil income reached $22.57 billion in 1974, a 36-fold rise in a decade. Among other things, this allowed Riyadh to pursue the self-reliance policy advocated by the Organization of Petroleum Exporting Countries (OPEC), of which it was a founder-member. It acquired a 25 percent share of Aramco, with a provision for further 2.5 percent annual increases in shareholding until the total reached 51 percent.

Although King Faisal got the oil embargo against Israel's Western allies lifted in March 1974, he disapproved of the pro-Israeli tilt of the U.S. But his stand was not considered sufficiently independent-minded by the pan-Arabist minority within the royal family. One of the king's young nephews, Prince Faisal ibn Musaid, who had become radicalized during his university education in the U.S., assassinated the monarch on 25 March 1975.

On becoming king, Khalid ibn Abdul Aziz (1975–1982) freed political prisoners, and appointed a cabinet in which 15 of the 25 ministers were commoners, but the crucial foreign, defense, interior, and National Guard ministries stayed with the House of Saud. He tried to end the civil war in Lebanon, which broke out in April 1975, gave grants to the Palestine Liberation Organization (PLO), and opposed the Camp David Accords between Egypt and Israel. He cut all links with Egypt after it signed a peace treaty with Israel in March 1979. In domestic affairs, he represented the nationalist trend, committed to greater respect for tradition and slower economic development, which was in conflict with the pro-American trend, stressing rapid economic development. When faced with an armed uprising at the Grand Mosque of Mecca in November 1979, he prevaricated, and took a fortnight to quell it.

To fill the gap created by the stoppage of oil exports from Iran in late 1978 because of the revolutionary turmoil there, Saudi Arabia increased its output to 9.5 million barrels/day in 1979 and 10 million barrels/day a year later. Political turbulence in Iran after the Islamic revolution raised the price from $13 a barrel in early 1979 to $28 a barrel in May 1980, increasing Saudi Arabia's oil income to an unprecedented $106 billion in 1980. This increase enabled Riyadh to buy up the remaining shares of Aramco, and take over the corporation completely. The outbreak of war between Iran and Iraq in September 1980, resulting in extensive damage to both countries' oil industries and a drop in their exports, led to higher prices during 1981, reaching a spot price peak of $41 a barrel. With Saudi production steady at 10 million barrels/day during 1981, the last full year of Khalid's reign, the kingdom earned a record oil revenue of $110 billion.

Responding to the rise of a revolutionary Islamic regime in Iran, King Khalid, a pious Muslim, opted for stricter implementation of Islamic injunctions in his country. The religious police, called *mutaween*, became harsher in enforcing such injunctions as abstinence from alcohol, stopping of work during the five daily prayers, and women's dress, which had to cover not only hair and arms, but also ankles. The ban on non-Muslim religious worship in public as well as non-Muslim places of worship was also rigorously applied.

Nonetheless, Khalid felt threatened by the official Iranian argument that there is no place for hereditary power in Islam, and that only the believer who is judged to be "the best Muslim" by fellow Muslims is entitled to rule an Islamic state. In short, the Muslim ruling dynasties in the Gulf and elsewhere were unIslamic. Therefore, while professing neutrality in public, King Khalid backed Iraqi President Saddam Hussein when the latter invaded Iran in September 1980. King Khalid died of heart attack in June 1982 shortly after Israel invaded and occupied large parts of Lebanon. He was succeeded by his younger brother, Fahd ibn Abdul Aziz (1982–).

Of the two trends that had emerged among senior Saudi princes during Khalid's reign, Fahd belonged to the pro-American school, favoring rapid economic progress. He was also active in regional politics. In September 1982, the Arab League summit accepted his Middle East peace plan: In exchange for the peaceful co-existence of all states in the region there should be an Israeli evacuation of all Arab territories occupied in 1967, a dismantling of

Jewish settlements in these areas, and the founding of a Palestinian state. This remained the common Arab position on a comprehensive settlement until the Middle East peace conference in Madrid, Spain, nine years later.

To aid Iraq in its war against Iran, Saudi Arabia volunteered to honor Baghdad's oil contracts. When high prices caused demand for oil to decline worldwide, Saudi Arabia cut its output sharply to stabilize the price at $29 a barrel. It thus underlined its role as the swing producer within OPEC—the one who, by adjusting its output, could stabilize the price and keep overall OPEC production within agreed limits. However, in the process, its oil income, at 3.5 million barrels/day, fell to $27 billion in 1985.

Yet Saudi Arabia then embarked upon a policy of flooding the market. It did so to increase OPEC's overall share of the world market in the face of price-cutting by non-OPEC producers, and to depress the oil income of Iran and thus damage its capacity to prolong its war with Iraq. Saudi Arabia raised its output by an average of 50 percent over the previous year. The price plummeted from $28 a barrel in December 1985 to below $10 a barrel in June. This price drop hurt not only Iran but also Saudi Arabia itself. King Fahd decided to act, and made a scapegoat of Ahmad Zaki Yamani, the oil minister since 1962. He sacked Yamani in October 1986. He also decided to limit output to raise prices. This policy prevailed at the next OPEC meeting. OPEC cut its total production by 7.5 percent to 15.8 million barrels/day for the first half of 1987. The Saudi share was fixed at 4.1 million barrels/day. As a result, the price stabilized at a little over $18 a barrel, the OPEC reference level. This figure more or less held until the spring of 1990, when flooding by Kuwait and the United Arab Emirates depressed the price to $12 a barrel. The Iraqi invasion and occupation of Kuwait in August caused the spot price of oil to reach $28 a barrel.

In keeping with his vacillating manner, King Fahd took a whole week before making public his position on Iraq's invasion of Kuwait on 2 August 1990. He called on the U.S. and other Arab countries to send troops to help protect Saudi Arabia, and end the Iraqi occupation of Kuwait.

An emergency meeting of OPEC in August 1990 allowed OPEC members to increase output beyond the allocated quota due to the loss of 4 million barrels/day of oil previously exported by Iraq and Kuwait. With an average output of 6.84 million barrels/day, Saudi Arabia ended 1990 with an oil income of $40.7 billion, more than double the average figure for the past four years.

King Fahd played a pivotal role in the resolution of the Kuwait crisis. But for his invitation to foreign troops and his decision to let them set up bases on Saudi soil, it would not have been possible for the U.S.-led coalition to eject the Iraqis from Kuwait as speedily as it did. Had the coalition been confined to launching air raids and missiles from warships, it would have been extremely difficult to expel the well-entrenched Iraqis from Kuwait. In the process, Saudi Arabia paid a hefty price. At $45 billion, the direct and indirect expenses incurred by it before and during the Gulf War totaled 57.3 percent of its annual GDP. In contrast, the $17.9 billion spent by the U.S. on the war amounted to 0.34 percent of its annual GDP.

The presence of more than 500,000 mainly American troops on Saudi soil had an impact on the domestic system, which could be summarized as royal autocracy. For instance, capital punishment (by beheading with a single stroke of a sword) was carried out only on 27 people in 1991. This figure went up fourfold next year. King Fahd was slow in reducing his monopoly of power. He took a year after the Gulf War to offer a fully nominated Consultative Council, which had been promised in 1962, and a further 17 months to fulfill the promise.

This reform came against the background of mounting discontent in the kingdom. Due to the rearming program that followed the Gulf War, and the drop in oil prices to

$15–$17 a barrel, the government began cutting the generous social services and subsidies it provided its nationals. On the other hand, there was no lessening in the corruption rampant among the royals, who monopolized political and economic power. In August 1992, more than a 100 leading Islamic scholars, clerics, judges, and academics submitted an "advisory memorandum" to King Fahd. It criticized the current state of Saudi society—the fawning role of clerics, legislation, the judiciary, the media, citizens' rights, financial assistance to the poor, public administration, the economy, and the military and foreign affairs. It was critical of Saudi Arabia's intimate ties with the U.S. and the repressive nature of its regime. More specifically, it condemned the widespread practice of paying 30 percent kickbacks as commissions to senior princes and their cronies on business transactions with the government and public sector undertakings. The memorandum angered King Fahd, who tried to discredit the signatories.

He took another year before naming the members of the Consultative Council, which had a strictly advisory role. Meanwhile, the opposition remained active. Encouraged by the holding of the first multi-party general election in neighboring Yemen in April 1993, six Saudi human rights activists—professors, lawyers, and civil servants—established the Committee for the Defense of Legitimate Rights (CDLR). Aiming to eliminate injustice and defend the legitimate rights of citizens, the CDLR called on Saudi citizens to report official acts of injustice to it, and demanded political reform, including elections based on universal suffrage. The government arrested the CDLR's head, Professor Muhammad al Masaari, and sacked the remaining founders from their jobs.

After his release, Masaari escaped to Yemen, and from there to Great Britain. The CDLR, banned in Saudi Arabia, began operating from London. It made extensive use of faxes to receive information from Saudi Arabia and communicate with its supporters there. In September 1994, it revealed that large-scale arrests had followed demonstrations against the detention of two militant clergymen. Unprecedently, this was later confirmed by the Saudi government, which was believed to be holding up to 300 protesters in jail by the end of the year. A further setback for the government in 1994 was its failed attempt to undo the unification of the Republic of Yemen, consummated in 1990, by encouraging South Yemen to rebel against North Yemen.

CHAPTER

Yemen

In 1990, the unification of North Yemen and South Yemen resulted in the founding of the Republic of Yemen. The republic was a re-creation of the Yemen of ancient times, the southeastern part of Arabia Felix, which also included southern Hijaz and the rest of the Arabian Peninsula south of Arabia Deserta. Saba (or Sheba or Sabu), its best known kingdom, left behind a recorded history from 950 B.C. to 110 B.C. The concept and reality of a Greater Yemen in ancient times was a powerful incentive for the regimes in North Yemen and South Yemen to unify their countries.

PROFILE

Area & Population: Shaped like a thick check mark, Yemen measures 182,280 square miles, excluding 23,070 square miles claimed by North Yemen along its undemarcated eastern frontier with Saudi Arabia. Its estimated population in 1992 was 12,592,000.

Cities: With a population of 427,200, the capital, Sanaa, is the largest city. Next in size come Aden 318,000, Taiz 178,000, Hodeida 155,000, and Mukalla 59,000.

Constitution: The constitution, based on the document endorsed by North Yemen and South Yemen in 1981, was approved by a referendum in May 1991, a year after the proclamation of the united Republic of Yemen. Describing the republic as "an independent, indivisible state," it specifies Islam and Arabic as state religion and language, respectively. The Sharia is to be the primary source of legislation. Power rests with the people, who exercise it through elections and referendums. The republic's economy is to be founded on protecting private property and assuring Islamic social justice while striving to develop the state sector as the main means of production. Executive authority rests with the president, who is appointed by parliament. The House of Representatives, provisionally made up of the 159-member Consultative Council of North Yemen, the 111-member Supreme People's Council of South Yemen, and 31 new members appointed by President Ali Abdullah Salih (1942–), functioned from May 1990 to April 1993, when new elections, based on universal suffrage, were held to the 301-member chamber.

Economy: At the national Gross Domestic Product of $7.57 billion, the per capita GDP was $601.

Education: Literacy in the population aged 15 and over (1990) was 38.5 percent (females 26.3 percent, Males 53.3 percent).

Ethnic Composition: Arabs 99 percent, others 1 percent.

Geography: North Yemen has the narrow, arid coastal strip of Tihama along the Red Sea, next to barren hills that rise to the Jahal Mountains. The inland highlands, relatively well watered with an annual 30-40 inches of monsoon rainfall, support rain-fed and irrigated agriculture. Further to the east, the land grades downward into the southern deserts of Arabia. In South Yemen, the narrow, arid, and discontinuous coastal plains along the Arabian Sea rise to the highland edge of the Arabian massif, which rises to 10,000 feet in the west and falls to 1,000 feet in the east. The Hadramaut Valley is one of the few distinctive features. In the highlands bordering North Yemen, relatively high monsoon rainfall supports agriculture.

Governmental System: Yemen is a republic, with a president elected by parliament.

Military: Yemen's total armed forces number 66,000 actives and 85,000 reserves. Military expenditure as percent of GDP is 5.3 percent.

Mineral Resources: Yemen's mineral resources include gold, granite, lead, marble, and zinc. At 4 billion barrels, its oil deposits are 0.4 percent of the global aggregate; and at 420 billion cubic meters, its gas deposits amount to 0.3 percent of the world total. At the production rate of 220,000 barrels/day, its petroleum reserves will last until 2045; and at the extraction rate of 174 million cubic meters/day, its gas deposits will be exhausted by 2057.

Religious Composition: Muslim 99.8 percent, with Sunni 53 percent and Shia 46.8 percent; and others 0.2 percent.

NORTH YEMEN BEFORE 1962

In ancient times, Yemen's citizens profited from trading in incense which was grown in India and was then shipped to the Mediterranean region. They eventually lost out to alternate trade routes through Iraq and Syria, and then to the Roman exploitation of the sea route from the Persian Gulf and the Arabian Sea through the Red Sea to Egypt and Europe. Christian missionaries were at work in Yemen in the fourth century A.D. Jewish tribes were also present. Persian rule, imposed in 575 A.D., gave way to Islam in the 630s. While the moderate Zaidi school of Shia Islam established itself in the highlands, the coastal plain of Tihama came under the influence of the Shafii school of Sunni Islam. In 898 A.D, the Zaidi iman, Yahya al Hadi il aal Haqq, founded the al Rassid dynasty of Yemen, which survived, with some interruptions, until 1962.

At the turn of the twentieth century, historic (Greater) Yemen, stretching over some 1,200 miles of shoreline along the Red Sea (400 miles) and the Arabian Sea (800 miles) and its hinterland, was divided into northern and southern parts. Its Arabian Sea section, known in Western capitals as South Yemen, was sub-divided into the Aden Colony and the Aden Protectorate, consisting of 23 provinces. The Colony was ruled directly by the British, and the Protectorate indirectly. Historic Yemen's Red Sea section, known among Western diplomats as North Yemen, was under the nominal suzerainty of the Ottoman Turks, and was ruled by Iman Yahya Hamad al Din (1908–1948).

By rebelling against the Ottoman Empire in 1911, Iman Yahya obtained wider powers. During World War I, he was loyal to the Ottomans. With the collapse of the Ottoman Empire in 1918, North Yemen became fully independent. Imam Yahya aspired to re-create the Yemen of the ancient past. In 1925, he regained the port of Hodeida, which had been occupied in 1921 by the ruler of the neighboring Asir region with British conniv-

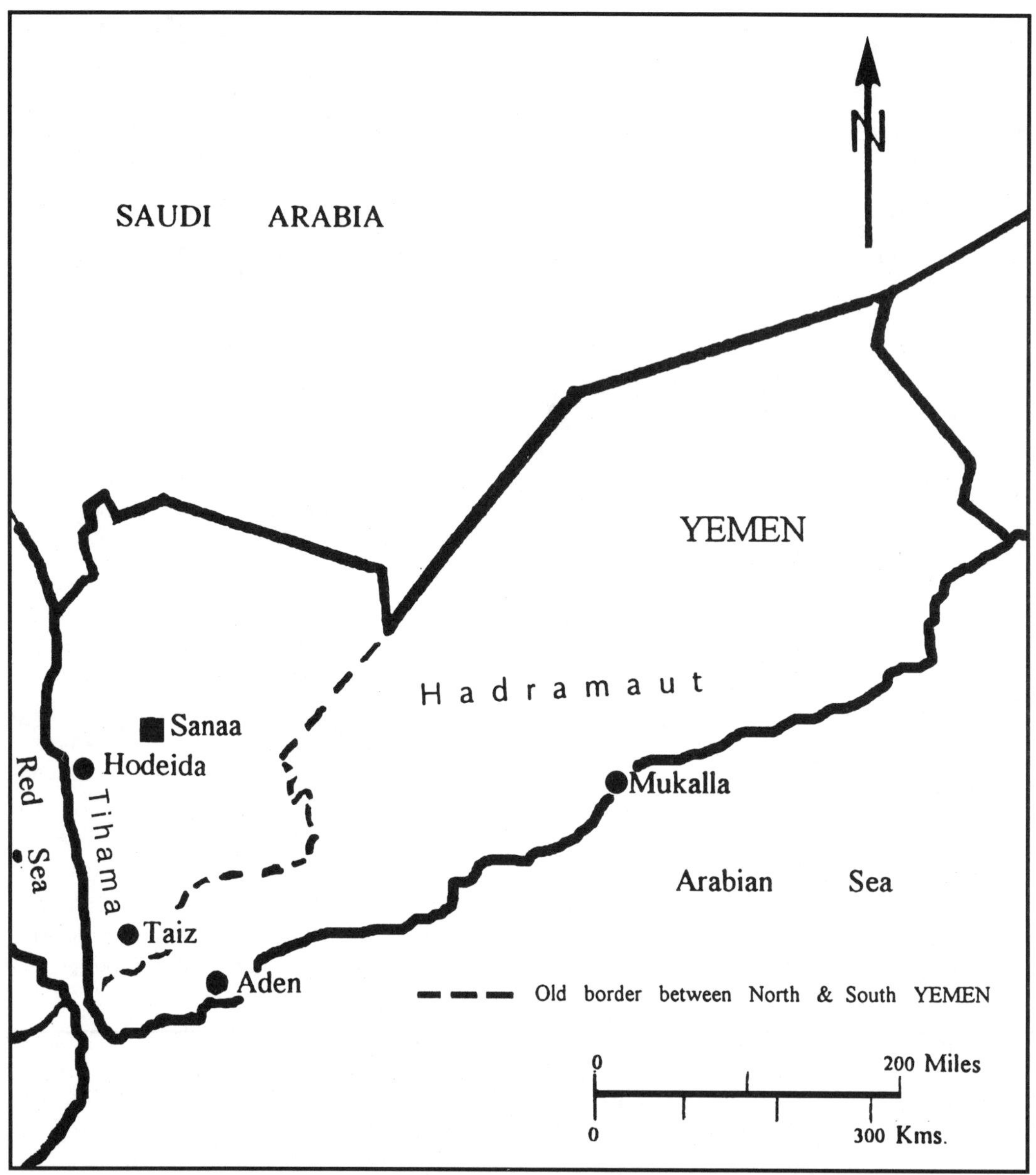

Yemen

ance. The resulting dispute over Asir culminated in a war in 1934 between North Yemen and Saudi Arabia, which was started by the latter. Having overpowered the North Yemenis, and captured Hodeida, the Saudis accepted a cease-fire mainly because British, French, and Italian warships rushed to Hodeida, intent on curbing Saudi expansionism. The Treaty of Muslim Friendship and Arab Fraternity returned to Imam Yahya nearly half the area he had lost in the war, including the southern part of the Tihama coastal plain. The treaty left the upland Najran and Asir in Saudi hands.

Following an abortive coup in February 1948, which resulted in the murder of his father, Ahmad ibn Yahya (1948–1962) assumed supreme power. When his ambition to re-create Greater Yemen at the expense of the British Protectorate of Aden was frustrated by London, he signed a mutual defense pact in 1956 with Egypt, then ruled by President Gamal Abdul Nasser. Two years later, Imam Ahmad formed a loose federation of North Yemen with the United Arab Republic (UAR), called the Union of Arab States. By then, he had concluded friendship treaties with Moscow, Peking, and other communist capitals. After the breakup of the UAR in September 1961, he cut his ties with Egypt, and began attacking Nasser, who reciprocated. Soon after Imam Ahmad's death in September 1962, a military coup, led by General Abdullah Sallal (1917–), deposed his son, Imam Muhammad al Badr (1962), and ended the 1,064-year rule of the al Rassid dynasty.

REPUBLICAN NORTH YEMEN: 1962–1990

The overthrow of Imam al Badr led to a bitter civil war. The republicans, deriving their major support from the Shafii (Sunni) tribes inhabiting the coastal plain and southern hills, were aided by Egypt, while the royalists, with a solid base among the Zaidi tribes in the north, were helped by Saudi Arabia. In 1967, Sallal tried to regain the area lost to the monarchists in the war, but failed partly because of the June 1967 Arab-Israeli War, which diverted Egypt's resources. Cairo decided to withdraw its forces from North Yemen, which weakened the position of Sallal. He was overthrown in November 1967 during his visit to Moscow by the forces led by Abdul Rahman al Iryani (1908–). In March 1970, following complex negotiations, the civil war ended; a governmental system based on a presidential council and a nominated consultative council emerged. The eight-year conflict consumed some 200,000 lives.

The first post-civil war president, al Iryani, was deposed in 1974; the second and third, Ibrahim Hamdi (1943–1977) and Ahmad Hussein Ghashmi (1938–1978), were assassinated in October 1977 and June 1978, respectively. Ali Abdullah Salih, deputy commander-in-chief, succeeded Ghashmi.

Salih legitimized his power by gaining the backing of the Constituent People's Assembly (CPA). In October 1980, Salih replaced Premier Abdul Aziz Abdul Ghani with Abdul Karim Iryani to placate leftist opposition at home. In October 1981, he established a 1,000-member General People's Congress (GPC), partly by appointment and partly by indirect elections, and two months later he signed an agreement with South Yemen on unity.

In North Yemen, the state-owned oil company's efforts since the 1970s failed to discover petroleum. But in 1984, the Yemeni subsidiary of the U.S.-based Hunt Oil Company discovered oil in commercial quantities. Production picked up rapidly and reached 200,000 barrels/day on the eve of the merger of North and South Yemen in 1990.

Salih maintained friendly relations with Saudi Arabia, the chief paymaster of North Yemen, while cultivating the leftist South Yemen by periodically renewing the 1981 agreement on eventual unity between the two Yemens. Following his re-election as president in 1988, he responded positively to the idea of an alliance of North Yemen with Egypt, Iraq, and Jordan, which materialized as the Arab Cooperation Council in early 1989.

SOUTH YEMEN BEFORE 1990

At the turn of twentieth century, Great Britain ruled the Aden Colony through a governor attached to the India Office in London, and the Aden Protectorate through local provincial rulers. After World War I, London frustrated Imam Yahya's attempt to annex parts of the Aden Protectorate, and severed the Protectorate from the India Office in 1927 and the Aden Colony 10 years later. In 1947, Great Britain introduced a fully nominated legislative assembly into the Aden Colony.

In 1962, London offered a plan to knit together the colony and the Protectorate into the Federation of South Arabia. This plan was opposed, among others, by the National Front for the Liberation of South Yemen, popularly called the NLF. The NLF achieved power in late 1967 by launching a successful armed campaign against the British. The NLF's increasingly leftist stance led to the founding of the People's Republic of South Yemen. Differences between moderate and radical elements within the NLF came to the fore in June 1969 and resulted in the victory of hardliners who were committed Marxist-Leninists. A new radical constitution was promulgated in November 1970. By the time the sixth congress of the NLF was held in March 1975, the regime felt secure. In October, the NLF decided to widen its base by forming the United Political Organization-National Front (UPO-NF).

Following the assassination of North Yemeni President Ahmad Ghashmi in June 1978, in which South Yemeni agents were allegedly involved, fighting began in Aden. President Salim Rubai Ali (1935–) lost. In October 1978, the UPO-NF was transformed into the Yemen Socialist Party (YSP). The radical policies of Abdul Fattah Ismail (1936–1986) as chairman of the Presidential Council did not suit his erstwhile ally, Ali Nasser Muhammad (1939–). In April 1980, Ismail was forced to resign and go into exile in Moscow, leaving Muhammad as the sole leader. But South Yemen's close ties with the Soviet Union remained intact.

Five years later, Ismail returned home as a result of mediation by the Communist Party of the Soviet Union. He was appointed secretary-general of the YSP's central committee, a position without power. In January 1986, the internal rapproachement broke down. In the subsequent fighting, Ismail lost his life but his radical side won, and Ali Salim al Beidh (1938–) became the leader of the YSP.

The presidency went to a technocrat, Haidar al Attas (1939–), and al Beidh emerged as the real power. He began to moderate his radical stance, and introduced economic and political reform—especially after Moscow cut its aid from $400 million in 1988 to $50 million in 1989. In South Yemen, oil was struck in commercial quantities in 1987, and output remained at 10,000 barrels/day until the merger of the two Yemens in 1990. A dramatic fall in Soviet aid accelerated the drive toward unification with North Yemen.

REPUBLIC OF YEMEN SINCE 1990

Unification came on 22 May 1990 when Ali Abdullah Salih became president and Ali Salim al Beidh vice-president of the Republic of Yemen. The five-member presidential council consisted of three North Yemeni and two South Yemeni leaders. However, the new republic's constituents, North Yemen and South Yemen, maintained separate armed forces and broadcasting facilities.

By September, more than 30 new political factions were licensed, with the Yemeni Islah Group, an Islamic party, being the most important. Since Yemen—the only Arab country on the United Nations Security Council—refused to follow Saudi Arabia into the U.S.-led coalition against Iraq after its occupation of Kuwait in August 1990, Riyadh retaliated by withdrawing the speical treatment accorded to Yemeni nationals. The resulting exodus of 900,000 Yemenis (out of 1.5 million) from Saudi Arabia depressed the already troubled Yemeni economy. But the government refused to change its policy. In November 1990, Yemen voted against Security Council Resolution 678, which allowed member states to use "all necessary means" to reverse Iraq's invasion of Kuwait. Yemen's position displeased Washington. In early January 1991, Yemen's peace plan to avert a war against Iraq failed to win approval of the contending parties.

At home, voters endorsed the new constitution in May 1991. But the multi-party general election based on universal suffrage, promised within a year, did not take place until April 1993. Yemen became the first country in the Arabian Peninsula to hold such an election. Out of 301 parliamentary seats; the General People's Congress, now turned into a political party, won 123 seats; the Yemeni Islah Group (YIG) won 62; and the Yemen Socialist Party 56. Ali Salim al Beidh, the leader of the YSP, which had so far shared power with the GPC, objected to President Salih also co-opting the YIG into the new coalition government.

Blaming lack of progress in unification on Salih, al Beidh left Sanaa for Aden, the capital of South Yemen, in August, setting the scene for a conflict which escalated into a civil war in April 1994. Saudi Arabia aided al Beidh in his campaign. In May, he declared South Yemen independent, but this declaration was not recognized by any other country, not even Saudi Arabia. This demoralized al Beidh's side, which lost the war by July. There were 35,000 casualties, including 10,000 deaths. The victorious Salih and the GPC consolidated their power and Yemeni unity.

A year later, King Fahd received President Salih in Riyadh, thus normalizing relations with Yemen. He also resumed aid to the republic. But Salih expressed his opposition to the contunied UN embargo against Iraq, which was backed by Riyadh. This position summed up well the general attitude of Yemenis toward mighty Saudi Arabia. Even though they are the poorest people in the Arab world, Yemenis are proud of their independence and long history.

CHAPTER 17

Egypt

Since time immemorial, Egyptian society and civilization have revolved around the Nile. The world's longest river, the Nile rises in the highlands south of the equator and flows through northeast Africa into the Mediterranean Sea, draining 1,294,000 square miles, an area as large as one-third of the U.S. In the Arab world, Egypt is the most populous and strategic state. The Suez Canal divides its mainland from the Sinai Peninsula. It has played an important role in the history of Islam; from 1250 to 1517 Cairo was the capital of the Islamic empire of the Mamlukes. Its al Azhar University, founded in 977 A.D., is the oldest institution of its kind in the world.

PROFILE

Area & Population: Roughly rectangular, with a triangular appendage at its right-hand corner, the Arab Republic of Egypt measures 385,230 square miles. Its estimated population in 1992 was 57,215,000.

Cities: With a population of 6,663,000, Cairo, the capital, is also the largest city. Next in size are Alexandria 3,295,000, Giza 2,242,000, Shubra al Khaima 843,000, and Mahalla al Kubra 491,000.

Constitution: The 1971 constitution, approved by a referendum, was amended in 1980. It describes Egypt as an Arab republic with a democratic, socialist system. It prescribes Islam as the state religion, and the Sharia, Islamic law, as the "principal source" of legislation. The state ensures equality of men and women in accordance with the Sharia, safeguards the public sector, and protects the assets of co-operative societies and trade unions. The constitution bans propagation of atheism and attacks on "divine religions." The sole presidential candidate, endorsed by at least two-thirds of the parliamentary deputies, is offered to the voters for approval. He has a six-year tenure, and can be elected for "other terms." He exercises executive authority , and appoints or dismisses vice-presidents and ministers, including the premier. He also nominates 10 members to the parliament, called the National Assembly, which consists of at least 350 elected members, with terms of five years. It has the power to force a minister to resign. In the case of the prime minister, it has the right to submit an adversarial report to the president. If the president rejects the report, the matter is put to a referendum. If the voters accept the report, the full cabinet must resign; if the voters reject it, the president must dissolve the Assembly. Following amendments to the 1971 constitution in May 1980, a 210-member Consultative Council with a three-year term was established to preserve the principles of the 1952 republican revolution and the 1971 "correctionist" revolution by President Anwar Sadat. One-third of its members are appointed by the president. Since the first three elections were boycotted by the opposition, the ruling National Democratic Party (NDP) filled all the elected seats. The opposition participated in the 1989 election, but failed to win a single seat.

Economy: At the national Gross Domestic product of $41.8 billion, the per capita GDP was $731.

Education: Literacy in the population aged 15 and above (1990) was 48.8 percent (female 33.8 percent, male 62.9 percent)

Ethnic Composition: Arabs 99.5 percent, others 0.5 percent.

Geography: Only 4 percent of the land of African Egypt is arable; the rest is desert. The agricultural area is in the Nile Valley and the Suez Canal zone. The Nile Valley consists of Lower (or northern) Egypt, with its apex at Cairo and its base along the Mediterranean coast between Alexandria and Port Said, and Upper (or southern) Egypt, a 20-mile-wide strip along the Nile. There is also an arable strip along the 106-mile Suez Canal. A roughly triangular peninsula, the Sinai, measuring 23,500 square miles, has Mount Sinai to its south. The rest of the peninsula is a plateau sloping towards the Mediterranean Sea.

Governmental System: Egypt is a republic, with a president elected by parliament and then endorsed by voters.

Military: Egypt's total armed forces number 440,000 actives and 254,000 reserves. Military expenditure as percent of GDP is 5 percent.

Mineral Resources: Egypt's mineral resources include gypsum, iron ore, phosphate rock, and salt. At 6.3 billion barrels, Egypt's oil reserves amount to 0.6 percent of the global aggregate; and at 400 billion cubic meters, its gas deposits are 0.3 percent of the world total. At the production rate of 900,000 barrels/day, its petroleum reserves will last until 2012; and at the extraction rate of 31 million cubic meters/day, its gas deposits will be exhausted by 2032.

Religious Composition: Muslim 94.4 percent, Christian 5.6 percent. Almost all Muslims are Sunni. Unofficial estimates put the Christian population at 10 percent. Due to common Christian and Muslim names, it is easy for Christians to declare themselves Muslim to census-takers.

HISTORY BEFORE 1952

The adoption of the Egyptian calendar in 4241 B.C. is the starting point of recorded human history in Egypt. About 3400 B.C., Menes united two earlier kingdoms to create a centralized Egyptian state, with its capital at Memphis. Thirty royal dynasties headed by kings bearing the biblical title of pharaoh ruled Egypt over the next 34 centuries. During the 4th Dynasty, around 2900 B.C., the Egyptians constructed the first pyramid. Then each monarch built his own pyramid to preserve his mummified body. The Great Pyramid of Cheops (Khufu to Egyptians) at Giza, built in 2640 B.C., is the largest monument of its kind, with a square base of 768 feet. During the 46 centuries of its existence, it has lost only 30 feet of its original height of 482 feet. The pyramids were only part of the colossal monuments that the pharaohs built. These monuments and the civilization that spawned them became known far and wide.

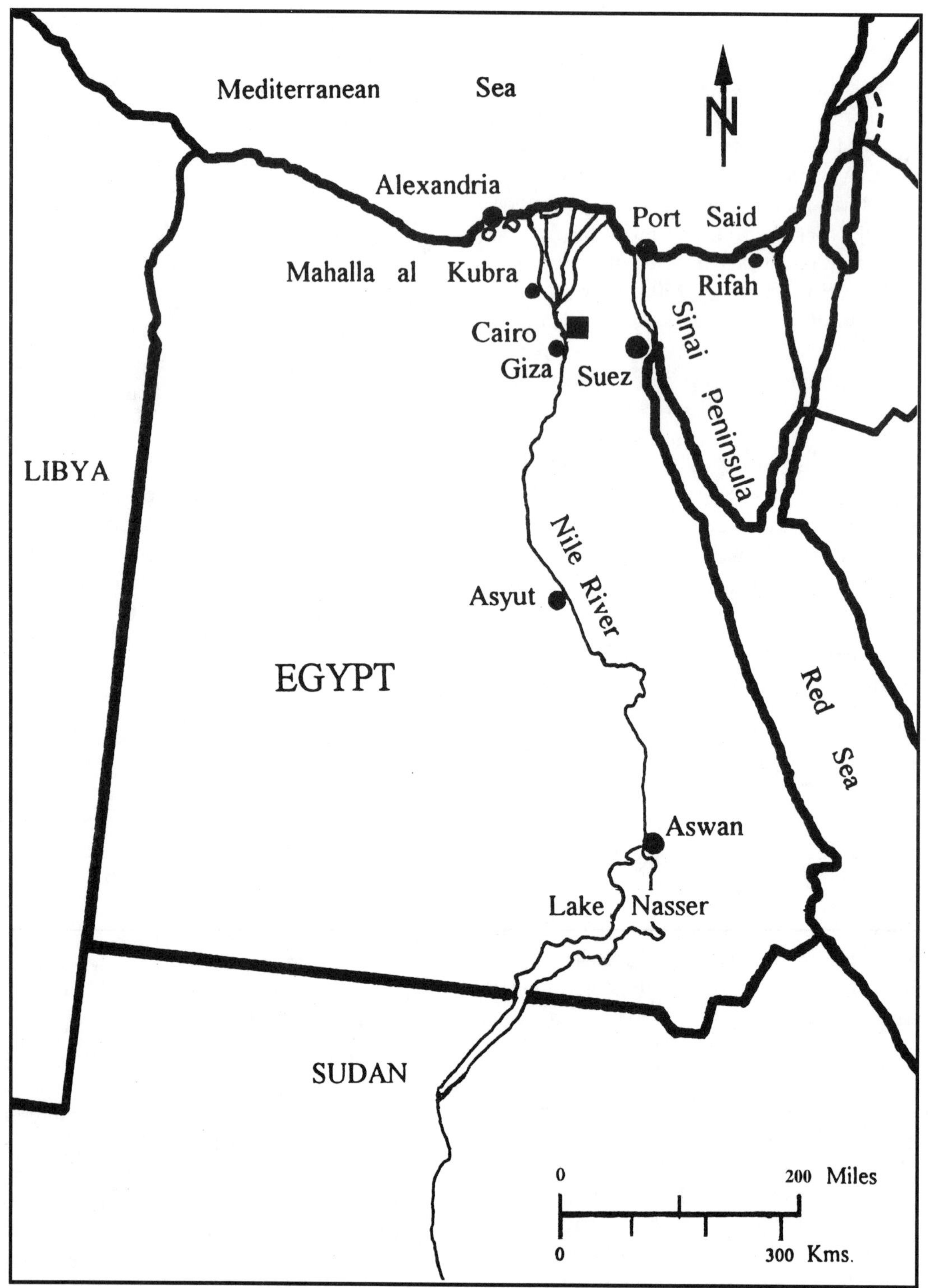
Mediterranean Sea
N
Alexandria
Port Said
Mahalla al Kubra
Rifah
Cairo
Giza
Suez
Sinai Peninsula
LIBYA
Nile River
Asyut
EGYPT
Red Sea
Aswan
Lake Nasser
SUDAN
0
200 Miles
0
300 Kms.

Egypt

Inevitably, the Egyptian state and society began to decay. The pharaohs of the 27th through the 30th dynasties occupied their thrones under the tutelage of the Persians (525–332 B.C.). In 332 B.C., Alexander the Great conquered the land. He founded a Greek empire in Egypt. For the next three centuries, successive Ptolemaic kings, descended from Alexander's general Ptolemy Soter, held their Graeco-Egyptian courts in Alexandria. Their reign ended with the deaths of Cleopatra and Mark Antony in 30 B.C., when Egypt became a province of the Roman Empire. When the empire split between east and west 400 years later, Egypt became part of the Eastern Roman or Byzantine Empire. In 640 A.D., the Muslim Arab conquest ended Byzantine rule, and turned Egypt into a province of the Umayyad Empire, based in Damascus.

After a period of semi-independence under the nominal rule of the Abbasids (751 A.D.–1258), Egypt became the center of the Fatimid dynasty in 969 A.D. It then fell to Salah al Din Ayubi (known as Saladin in the West) in 1171. After nearly a century under the Ayubids, it fell into the hands of a series of military oligarchies, called the Mamlukes (1260–1517). They combined military success with artistic achievement.

However, under Ottoman tutelage, the Mamluke governors turned into despots. Napoleon Bonaparte briefly interrupted Ottoman rule between 1798 and 1801. Muhammad Ali, an Albanian soldier, who arrived in Egypt with the Ottoman forces sent to eject the French, remained in the province. He overpowered the Mamlukes, and won the recognition of the Ottoman sultan as viceroy, or khedive, of Egypt in 1805. Before his death in 1849, he won the sultan's confirmation of the viceroyalty of Egypt and Sudan for his successors. He was followed by his grandson Abbas (1849–1854), and then by the latter's son Said (1854–1863).

Khedive Said gave permission to Ferdinand de Lesseps, a French engineer, to connect the Mediterranean Sea with the Gulf of Suez, and thus with the Red Sea, by a canal. The result was the Suez Canal, built by the Paris-based Universal Suez Maritime Canal Company (USMCC), and completed in 1869 during the reign of Said's nephew, Khedive Ismail (1863–1879).

Ismail's financial incompetence turned Egypt into a heavily indebted country. To stay solvent, he had to sell his own 44 percent share of the USMCC to the British government in 1875. Four years later, at the instigation of London and Paris, the Ottoman sultan forced Ismail to abdicate in favor of his son Tawfiq. This humiliating foreign interference in their country's internal affairs enraged the Egyptians, and paved the way for a nationalist uprising headed by army officers under Colonel Ahmad Arabi Pasha in 1882. Great Britain intervened directly, quelled the uprising, and occupied Egypt. Oddly enough, this occupation did not alter Egypt's position as a nominal viceroyalty of the Ottoman Empire, an anomalous situation that continued until the outbreak of World War I, when Great Britain declared Egypt to be its protectorate.

After the war, talks between Great Britain and the nationalist Wafd Party proved sterile. It was only after the Egyptian masses had rioted and demonstrated on a large scale that London conceded some form of independence in 1922. It recognized Egypt as a sovereign state under King Ahmad Fuad (1922–1936), but maintained its military occupation. An anti-imperialist movement, spearheaded by the Wafd Party, resulted in the Anglo-Egyptian Treaty of 1936.

The treaty preserved many British privileges, including its military presence in the Suez Canal zone. The poor performance of Egyptian troops in the 1948–1949 Arab-Israeli War encouraged pan-Arab nationalist officers, organized as the Free Officers, to plan a coup. On 22 July 1952, they seized power from King Farouq (1936–1952), who went into exile in Italy. The officers formed an 18-member Revolutionary Command Council (RCC).

The Pyramids, Giza, Egypt. Photo © Cherif Cordahi.

REPUBLICAN EGYPT SINCE 1952

Although Egypt was not declared a republic until June 1953, for all practical purposes monarchy had ended with the officers' coup a year earlier. And even though the nominal head of the ruling RCC was General Muhammad Neguib (1901–1984), the leader who really mattered was Gamal Abdul Nasser.

The Nasser Era

Born into the family of a postal clerk in Bani Mor village in Asyut province, Nasser was a graduate of the Royal Military Academy, Cairo. He participated in the 1948–1949 Arab-Israeli War as a major in the Egyptian army. Promoted to colonel in 1950, he was appointed lecturer at the military academy. After the 1952 coup, he emerged as the number two, with Neguib as the republic's president. The power struggle between Nasser and Neguib intensified after the RCC, at Nasser's behest, banned the Muslim Brotherhood in early 1954. A compromise between the two ended in November when the RCC removed Neguib as president and put him under house arrest. Nasser's subsequent presidency of the republic lasted until his death.

Starting out as a non-ideological officer, committed merely to ridding Egyptian public life of corruption and decadence, Nasser turned increasingly ideological and radical as conservatives at home and the Western powers abroad tried to smother his Arab nationalist regime. He succeeded in stopping the expansion of the Western-sponsored Baghdad Pact. Denied weapons by the U.S., he accepted an arms sales offer from Czechoslovakia. When Washington reacted by withdrawing its offer of aid for the Aswan High Dam project, and getting the World

Bank to do the same, Nasser nationalized the Suez Canal, and accepted economic and technical assistance from the Soviet Union. The resulting aggression by an alliance of Great Britain, France, and Israel against Egypt, leading to the Suez War in October-November 1956, further radicalized Nasser. He became the leading political demon in the West and Israel, and teams from the U.S., Great Britain, France, and Israel tried unsuccessfully to assassinate him. The withdrawal of the aggressors from Egypt by March 1957—with a United Nations Emergency Force (UNEF) posted in Sinai on the Egyptian side—raised Nasser's prestige at home and in the Arab world. It also strengthened his resolve to confront Israel on behalf of the Palestinians.

Following the merger of Egypt and Syria into the United Arab Republic (UAR) in early 1958, Nasser was elected president of the UAR. He visited the Soviet Union for the first time. He was now well established as a leader of the non-aligned movement. But he suffered a severe setback when Syria seceded from the UAR in September 1961, shattering his hopes of gradually uniting the Arab world under his stewardship.

When Syria took an increasingly radical line in domestic policies, an embittered Nasser quickened the pace of socio-economic reform in Egypt so as to seem no less militant than the Syrian regime. Land reform, launched a decade earlier, was consolidated, along with further nationalization of industries and services. In 1962, following a convention of the delegates drawn from the peasants, workers, and intellectuals, Nasser inaugurated the Arab Socialist Union (ASU). Later that year, Nasser sided with the republicans in the civil war in North Yemen. In 1964, he hosted a summit of the Organization of African Unity (OAU) in Cairo.

As the sole candidate, he was re-elected president in 1965 for a six-year term. With the ascendancy in early 1966 of radicals in the Syrian regime, who encouraged escalation of the Palestinian guerrilla campaign against Israel, Nasser once again found himself upstaged by Damascus. Later that year, he concluded a defense pact with Syria, specifying a joint command for Egyptian and Syrian forces in case of war.

With tension rising in the spring of 1967, Israel warned Syria against allowing Palestinian operations against Israel from its soil. In mid-May, stung by his critics' taunts that he was hiding behind the protection of the UNEF stationed in Sinai, Nasser called on the UN secretary-general to withdraw the force. Once this was done, Nasser closed the Straits of Tiran at the mouth of the Gulf of Aqaba to Israeli shipping. King Hussein of Jordan, who hitherto had been hostile to Nasser, now rushed to sign a mutual defense pact with Egypt on 30 May. This was the short-lived zenith of Nasser's power and prestige.

Once Israel realized that the international community would not force open the Straits of Tiran for it, it mounted devastating preemptive attacks on the air forces of Egypt, Syria, and Jordan on 5 June. The debacle of the June 1967 Arab-Israeli War, which resulted in Egypt's loss of Sinai, almost finished Nasser. For the time being, though, he contrived to turn defeat into victory. Taking responsibility for the defeat, he resigned, but popular demonstrations made him retract. His retraction covered the whole gamut of his domestic and foreign policies.

In November 1967, he accepted United Nations Security Council Resolution 242, which called for peaceful co-existence of Israel and the Arab states in return for an Israeli evacuation of the occupied Arab territories. However, to prevent Israel from consolidating its occupation of Sinai, Nasser initiated an undeclared, low-level war of attrition in 1968 after having re-equipped his military with Soviet weaponry. He compromised with his arch-enemy in the Arab world, the conservative Saudi King Faisal, and withdrew Egyptian troops from the North Yemeni civil war in December 1967. Yet, he remained the elder statesman of the progressive Arab world.

When conflict between the Palestine Liberation Organization (PLO) and Lebanon became explosive, both parties turned to

Nasser for mediation. The result was the November 1969 Cairo Agreement. After the fight between the PLO and the Jordanian army in mid-September 1970, the two sides approached Nasser for a rapprochement. The strain of these talks induced a fatal heart attack in Nasser. Thus ended the rule of a charismatic figure, the first Egyptian to govern Egypt for many centuries.

Anwar Sadat

Nasser was succeeded by his vice president, Anwar Sadat. Born into the family of a petty civil servant in Mit Abul Kom village in the Nile delta, Sadat grew up in Cairo. He graduated from the Cairo Military Academy in 1938. Found guilty of spying for the Germans, Captain Sadat was jailed in the summer of 1942. He escaped in 1944 and went underground until the detention order was lifted. He spent two years in jail, 1946–1948, as a suspect in the assassination of Ahmad Osman, a cabinet minister, but was acquitted. When his business venture failed, he rejoined the army in late 1949, regaining his rank of captain. He was posted to Rifah in the Sinai where he came into contact with Nasser.

Sadat participated in the 1952 coup and secured a seat on the ruling RCC. He edited *Al Gumhuriya* ("The Republic"), the regime's mouthpiece. From 1959 to 1969, he served as speaker of the parliament. In late 1969, Nasser, performing a rightward shift, appointed Sadat the sole vice-president. On his death, Sadat became acting president, and was later confirmed in his post in a referendum.

Sadat began to dilute many of Nasser's policies. In 1971, he promulgated a new constitution that played down the socialist guidelines of the earlier document. Yet the year also saw the completion of the Aswan High Dam, built with Soviet financial and technical aid. The High Dam had the capacity to hold back from the tail-end of the Nile's autumn flood some 5 billion cubic meters of water, and thus prevent flooding. Its hydro-electric plants produced 10,000 million kilowatt-hours of electricity, increasing the country's electric output five-fold.

Having signed a 15-year Treaty of Friendship and Cooperation with the Soviet Union in late may 1971, Sadat demanded in July 1972 that all Soviet military advisors, who had arrived after the June 1967 war, leave Egypt. Some 15,000 Soviet personnel departed, taking with them fighter aircraft, interceptors, and surface-to-air missiles. Sadat became prime minister, and began planning an invasion of the Israeli-occupied Arab territories. During the October 1973 Arab-Israeli War, Egyptian troops performed unprecedentedly well, capturing land in the Sinai from the Israelis, and retaining it. This showing enhanced Sadat's standing at home and in the region. But, instead of pursuing peace under the United Nations auspices, he opted for American mediation in his talks with Israel, and broke Arab ranks. After two interim disengagement agreements with Israel in 1974 and 1975, however, the peace process stalled.

On the economic front, the establishment of an oil ministry in 1973 increased the pace of exploration and extraction, with output reaching 420,000 barrels/day in 1977. But Sadat's economic liberalization, involving removal or reduction of subsidies on essentials, triggered countrywide bread riots in January 1977. They ceased only when he canceled the price increases. He appealed for aid to the U.S., which responded positively. After Moscow refused to reschedule the Egyptian debt of $10 billion, he unilaterally abrogated the Soviet Friendship Treaty.

In November 1977, in a dramatic move, Sadat traveled to Jerusalem to address the Israeli parliament and offered peace. This move made him something of a hero in the Western world. The U.S. began providing military aid to Egypt. Sadat signed accords—drafted at the American president's retreat in Camp David, Maryland—with Israeli Premier Menachem Begin at the White House in Washington on 18 September 1978 in the presence of President Jimmy Carter. The peace treaty concluded in March 1978 ended the state of war that had existed between the

The streets of modern Cairo, Egypt. Photo © Cherif Cordahi.

two states since the founding of Israel in May 1948 and provided for full Israeli withdrawal from Sinai for total peace by April 1982. Within a year, the signatories exchanged ambassadors, and Israel returned two-thirds of the occupied Sinai to Cairo. Egypt's unilateral peace treaty with Israel led to its suspension from the Arab League and the Islamic Conference Organization (ICO), and the severing of links by all Arab League members, except Oman.

To overcome Egypt's increasing isolation, Sadat assumed increased powers at home. He dissolved parliament two years ahead of its normal tenure, and rigged the first multi-party election in June 1979, with his National Democratic Party (NDP) securing 83 percent of the seats. Egypt became more dependent on the U.S. for economic survival.

In May 1980, Sadat appointed himself prime minister. By immediately holding a stage-managed referendum, he abrogated the constitutional provision that limited the presidency to one six-year term. His peace treaty with Israel, and the growing corruption and ostentatiousness of the new rich alienated the Islamic forces, especially the Muslim Brotherhood, whom he had courted in the early years of his regime. A ban on strikes and demonstrations, and the end of Nasser's pricing mechanism, which fueled inflation, caused hardship to the working and lower middle classes. Contemptuous of opposition, secular and religious, Sadat became increasingly intolerant and autocratic, indulging his fancy for imperial grandeur. His sweeping crackdown on dissidents in September 1981 resulted in some 2,000 arrests. The next month he was assassinated by Islamic militants during a military parade on the anniversary of the October 1973 war. In contrast to the mass grief demonstrated at the death of Nasser, Sadat's demise went unnoticed by most Egyptians. He was succeeded by his vice president, Hosni Mubarak (1928–).

Hosni Mubarak

Born into the family of a judicial court functionary in the Nile delta village of Kafr al

Musaliha, Mubarak graduated from the air force academy in 1950. After serving as a fighter pilot from 1940 to 1954, he taught at the air force academy, where he later became director-general. Appointed commander of the West Cairo airbase in 1961, he underwent courses at Soviet military academies. After Egypt's debacle in the June 1967 war, he was transferred to his earlier job of director-general of the air force academy. Two years later, he was appointed chief of staff of the air force. In the October 1973 Arab-Israeli War, the air force under his command performed well; he was promoted next year to air marshal. In April 1975, President Sadat appointed him vice-president. Mubarak uncritically followed Sadat's line in domestic and foreign affairs.

Following Sadat's assassination, Mubarak also took over the leadership of the NDP. After briefly moderating his stance toward Islamic fundamentalists, he resumed Sadat's hardline policy. While maintaining a close alliance with the U.S., he thawed Egypt's relations with the Soviet Union. He withdrew the Egyptian ambassador from Tel Aviv, in protest against Israel's invasion of Lebanon in June 1982, but rejected Arab demands for breaking diplomatic ties with the Jewish state. He continued Sadat's policy of militarily aiding Iraq in its war with Iran, hoping thus to erode the Arab League's boycott of Egypt. His success came in 1984 when Jordan, Iraq's close ally, resumed diplomatic ties with Cairo.

As the sole candidate, Mubarak was re-elected president in 1987. He led Egypt into the Arab Cooperation Council (ACC) in early 1989. The next year, Egypt was allowed to return to the Arab League. When Iraqi president Saddam Hussein occupied Kuwait in August 1990, Mubarak condemned his action. In the Arab League, he led the majority that demanded Iraq's immediate and unconditional withdrawal, an action that ended the ACC. In October, the Arab League headquarters was returned from Tunis, Tunisia, to Cairo. This formally re-established Egypt's leadership of the Arab world.

Mubarak sent Egyptian troops to Saudi Arabia to bolster Saudi defenses. As part of the U.S.-led coalition, the Egyptians participated in the Gulf War. After the conflict, Egypt and Syria offered to station troops in the region to provide protection for the oil-rich Gulf monarchies, but nothing came of the idea. Mubarak played an important role in bringing about an accord between Israel and the PLO in September 1993, and its subsequent implementation, but his efforts to bring about reconciliation between Israel and Syria failed.

At home, his government lost popularity. Almost all opposition groups boycotted the parliamentary election in late 1990, demanding the lifting of the state of emergency, which was refused. The return in the spring of 1992 of Egyptian fundamentalists who had participated in the victorious *jihad* against the Soviets and local leftist forces in Afghanistan gave a boost to Islamic militancy. This happened against the background of rising unemployment, official inefficiency and corruption, a widening chasm between rich and poor, and the government's drift toward dictatorship. Instead of formulating an integrated policy to solve socio-economic problems, curbing corruption and allowing greater freedom of expression, the Mubarak administration further restricted trade union and press activities and showed scant regard for human rights.

By getting himself re-elected in 1993, and failing to name a vice-president, Mubarak showed that he had no intention of loosening his grip on power. Two years later, having survived an assassination attempt by al Gamaat al Islamiya, he widened and deepened his campaign against Islamic groups. He targeted the moderate Muslim Brotherhood, which had been allowed to function quasi-legally for the past quarter century, and which was committed to achieving its aim of an Islamic state through parliamentary means. By so doing, Mubarak was in danger of alienating large sections of Egyptian society from his regime.

CHAPTER 18

Syria

Today's Arab Republic of Syria is part of Greater/Natural Syria. Known historically as *Bilad al Sham* (country on the left/north [of Mecca]), and measuring nearly 120,000 square miles, Natural Syria is enclosed by the Taurus Mountains to the north, the Mediterranean Sea to the west, the Arabian desert to the south, and the Euphrates River to the east. Besides present-day Syria, it includes Lebanon, Israel, the West Bank and Gaza Strip, Jordan, and the Alexandretta region of Turkey. From 1831 to 1840, during an interregnum in Ottoman rule, which originated in 1517, it was governed as a single entity by Khedive Ibrahim, the Egyptian viceroy. With the return of direct Ottoman rule, it was split into several provinces. Following the defeat of the Ottoman Empire in 1918, it was carved up by the Allies to create a Syria that was three-fifths the size of Natural Syria.

PROFILE

Area & Population: Roughly quadrilateral, Syria measures 71,500 square miles, including 454 square miles of the Golan Heights occupied by Israel since 1967. The estimated population in 1992 was 13,480,000.

Cities: With a population of 1,378,000, Damascus, the capital, is the largest city. Next in size are Aleppo 1,355,000, Homs 481,000, Hama 237,000, and Latakia 267,000.

Constitution: The 1973 constitution, approved in a referendum, describes Syria as a democratic, popular, socialist state, and requires that Islam be the religion of the head of state. Executive power is vested with the president, who is elected directly by voters for a seven-year term. He has the authority to appoint or dismiss vice-presidents, the prime minister, and individual ministers. He is also the commander-in-chief of the military. Legislative power lies with the popularly elected 250-member People's Assembly, where 84 seats are reserved for independent members.

Economy: At the national Gross Domestic Product of $23.7 billion, the per capita GDP is $1,758.

Education: Literacy in the population aged 15 and over (1990) was 64.5 percent (female 50.8 percent, male 78.3 percent).

Ethnic Composition: Arabs 89 percent, Kurds 6 percent, and others 5 percent.

Geography: Geographically, Syria and Lebanon are a single entity with four basic zones: the coastal plain, the north-south mountain ranges, the plains and plateaus, and the steppe and desert. A narrow, fertile coastal strip has a Mediterranean climate. The northern Ansariya Mountain range ends near Homs, and, after a gap extending to Tripoli, the Lebanon Mountain range rises and then slopes down into the hills of Galilee in Israel. Parallel to Mount Lebanon on its east, beyond the Beqaa Valley, lies the Anti-Lebanon Mountain range that merges with Mount Hermon. Further east, across the Hauran Valley, rise the Druze Mountains. East of these ranges lies a plateau that slopes in a southeastern direction. Those valleys and plains that receive good rainfall are fertile. Finally, the rocky Syrian Desert, occupying a third of the country and lying to the south and east of the fertile region, merges with the vast deserts of the Arabian Peninsula.

Governmental System: Syria is a republic, with a president elected directly by voters.

Military: Syria's total armed forces number 408,000 actives and 398,000 reserves. Military expenditure as percent of GDP is 9.3 percent.

Mineral Resources: Syria's mineral resources include natural asphalt, phosphates, and rock salt. At 3 billion barrels, its oil deposits amount to 0.3 percent of the global aggregate; and at 225 billion cubic meters, its gas reserves amount to 0.15 percent of the world total. At the production rate of 570,000 barrels/day, its oil deposits will last until 2008. Its gas extraction plans were not fully operational in 1995.

Religious Composition: Muslim 89.5 percent, with Sunni 67.5 percent, Alawi (Shia) 14 percent, Ismaili (Shia) 2 percent, and Druze 6 percent; Christian 9 percent; and others 1.5 percent.

HISTORY BEFORE 1946

Lying at the heart of the hinterland of the Mediterranean Sea, Greater/Natural Syria has been coveted by conquerors since ancient times. Recorded history shows the Egyptians, Babylonians, Hittites, Greeks, and Romans incorporating it into their empires. When Roman Emperor Constantine (306–337 A.D.) adopted Christianity as the state religion, Syria became a predominantly Christian land. In 636 A.D., its leading city, Damascus, fell to the invading Muslim Arabs. Later, Damascus became the capital of the Islamic caliphate under the Umayyads (661–750 A.D.). As the Islamic empire fractured, segments of Greater Syria fell to non-Muslim rulers. During the crusades, its coastal areas were seized by the Crusaders in 1110, who retained the territories until they were expelled by Salah al Din (Saladin) Ayubi in 1171. The Mamlukes, who followed the descendants of Ayubi, combined Greater Syria and Egypt into one state. The Ottoman Turks came in 1517 and ruled, with a brief break from 1831 to 1840, until the end of World War I. In 1918, Greater Syria was controlled by Allied troops, mainly British.

Under British occupation, there was a French military administration on the coast, and a civilian Arab government under Faisal ibn Hussein al Hashem in Damascus. The French wanted to legitimize their control of this strategic land. The Allied Council of Ten, meeting in Paris in February 1919, decided to apply the new form of trusteeship, called mandate, to the Arab part of the Ottoman Empire. With the withdrawal of British troops in late 1919, the situation reached a critical point. In March 1920, a representative Syrian National Congress, meeting in Damascus, proclaimed Faisal king of Greater Syria.

The next month, the Supreme Council of the League of Nations, meeting in San Remo, Italy, rejected this. It gave the mandate for the whole of Syria to France, and the man-

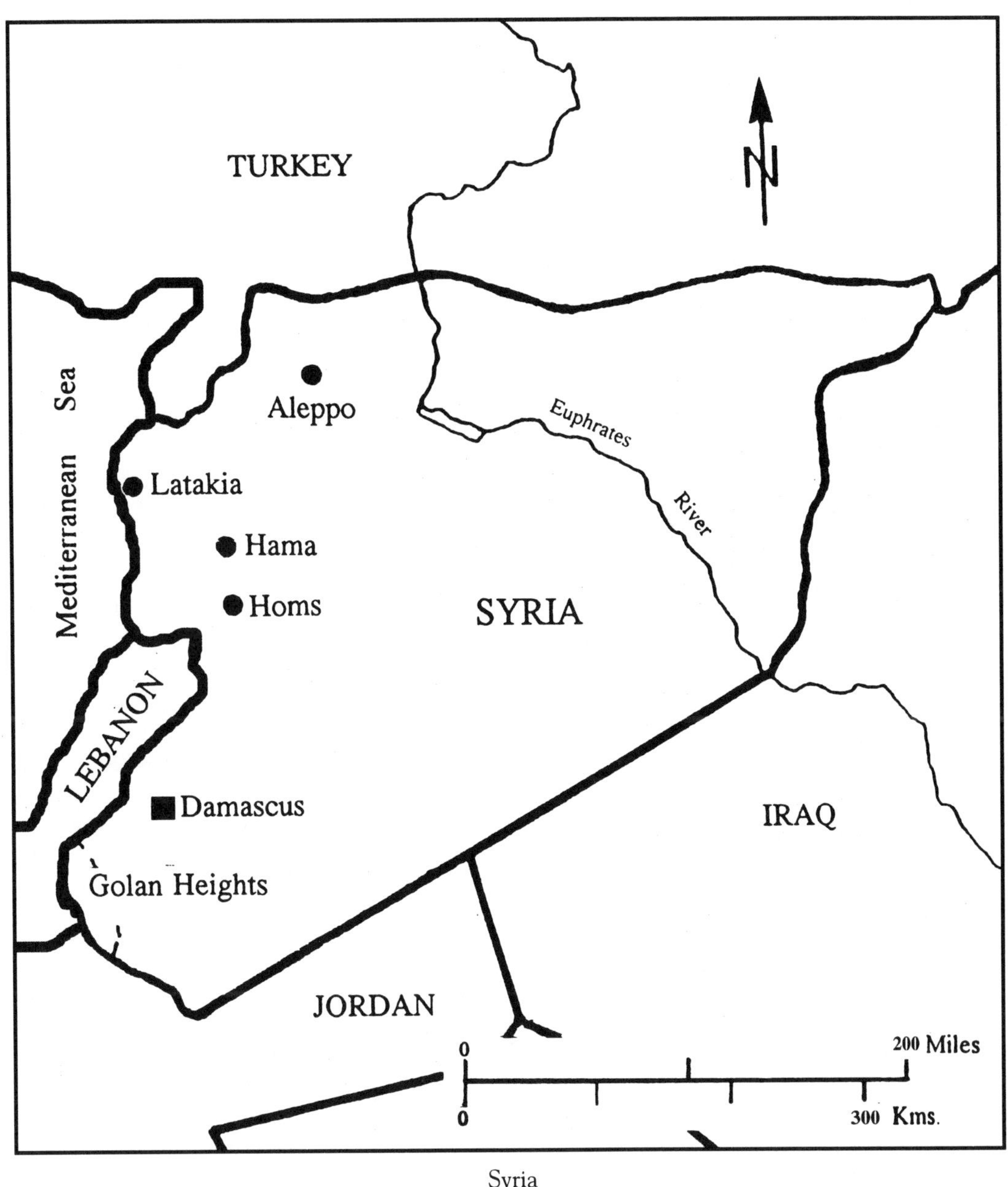

Syria

dates for Palestine and Mesopotamia (i.e., the Ottoman provinces of Baghdad and Basra) to Great Britain. When Faisal ignored the French ultimatum in June, Paris sent into action 90,000 troops (mainly of Senegalese and North African Arab origin). They defeated Faisal and occupied Damascus in late July 1920. Later that year, France rearranged the borders by allocating parts of Syria to the Emirate of Mount Lebanon to create Greater Lebanon. It surrendered a section of the Syrian province of Aleppo to Turkey in October 1921. France then divided the territory into the provinces of Latakia, Jebel Druze, Aleppo, and Damascus. While the League of Nations mandate was seen by Arabs as a guardianship of young nations to lead them to independence, France acted otherwise, and established a colonial regime that gave rise to popular resistance. France took two years to quell the armed rebellion that erupted in Jebel Druze and spread elsewhere in 1925. The subsequent talks resulted in the convening of an elected national assembly of Syrians in 1928.

Dominated by the nationalist National Bloc, the assembly adopted a constitution that refused to recognize the French mandate. Paris dissolved the parliament and imposed its own constitution in 1930. The parliament elected under this constitution reached an impasse with the French high commissioner on the terms of a treaty to replace the mandate, and was suspended.

Popular protest reached a peak in early 1936 and shut down public services and markets for two months. This unrest compelled the French to negotiate with the National Bloc. The accession of a leftist Popular Front government in Paris made these talks successful. According to the Franco-Syrian Treaty, initialed in September 1936 (but not ratified), Paris agreed to grant independence to Syria in three years in exchange for long-term military, political, and economic privileges. A National Bloc government, elected in November 1936, was in power on the eve of World War II, when France, suspending the 1930 constitution and the government, imposed martial law.

After the occupation of northern France by Nazi Germany in 1940, and the subsequent establishment of a pro-German regime in the central French town of Vichy, control of the overseas French territories passed to the Vichy regime. This regime was defeated in Syria (and Lebanon) by the British and Free French forces in June 1941, and Syria was granted nominal independence.

When a general election was called in 1943, the National Bloc won handsomely. In 1944, Syria secured the recognition of the U.S. and the Soviet Union. By declaring war against Germany in February 1945, it got invited to the founding conference of the United Nations. The next month, Syria also became one of the founder-members of the Arab League. After World War II, France tried a comeback in Syria, but failed. The French left in April 1946.

INDEPENDENT SYRIA SINCE 1946

Independent Syria's unsuccessful participation in the 1948–1949 Arab-Israeli War led to large scale rioting, and paved the way for an army coup in March 1949. Military rule lasted for five years under different soldiers, the last of whom was Adib Shishkali. His overthrow was followed by the restoration of parliamentary democracy.

The election of September 1954 was the first free election in the Middle East. All adults, male and female, were allowed to vote. The election led to the rise of radical groups, including the Arab Baath Socialist Party. When faced with a choice of aligning either with traditional parties, such as the National Bloc, or the radical ones, such as the Communists, the Baath chose a way out by proposing a union with Egypt. The resulting United Arab Republic (UAR) lasted from early 1958 to September 1961. Its breakup was a great setback for pan-Arabism.

The secret Military Committee of Baathist officers was the main force behind the coup in Damascus in March 1963. Among the reforms this regime carried out was the nationalization of the oil industry in 1964. It canceled the concessions given in the mid-1950s to a West German-led consortium and an American company, which had led to the discovery of petroleum, and the setting up of the Syrian Petroleum Company (SPC).

Factional infighting soon broke out within the Baath. The fighting was settled in favor of the hardliners, led by Salah Jadid, in early 1966. The new government, which included Hafiz Assad as defense minister, pursued radical socio-economic policies at home, and actively opposed the conservative Arab governments in the region.

Hafiz Assad

Born in a rural notable's family in the village of Qurdaha near Latakia, Hafiz Assad graduated as an air force pilot at the Homs military academy. The dissolution of al Syrian parties, including the Baath, of which Assad was a member, after the formation of the United Arab Republic in early 1958, left him disgruntled. In 1960, while serving in Egypt, he became one of the five founders of the clandestine Military Committee. After the secession of Syria from the UAR in 1961, the Military Committee became active.

Now, as defense minister, Assad developed an Arab nationalist perspective, which differed from the socialist perspective of his rival, Salah Jadid. Assad used his official position to consolidate his standing in the military. Although the Baathist regime successfully withstood its defeat in the June 1967 Arab-Israeli War, it became divided on apportioning blame. Assad's nationalist wing blamed Jadid's socialist faction. The clash between the two came in early 1969. Assad won ascendancy in the party high command and the government, but Jadid continued to dominate the party machine. The final clash came in November 1970 during the Baath National Congress in Damascus. Assad gained full control, and arrested his leading opponents. He assumed the additional offices of prime minister and secretary-general of the Baath. The new party high command nominated a 173-member People's Assembly to draft a constitution.

The draft constitution that emerged in January 1973 described Syria as a "democratic, popular, socialist state." An influential group of Muslim clerics attacked the document as "secular and atheistic," and demanded the insertion of an article declaring Islam the state religion. Assad compromised by amending the constitution to specify that the president had to be Muslim. The clergy did not think this sufficient and questioned the Muslim credentials of Assad, who was a member of the Alawi community, a Shia subsect. To appease them, Assad declared the October 1973 Arab-Israeli War a *jihad* against the enemies of Islam. The Syrian gains on the Golan Heights front during the initial phase of the conflict were lost later. In early 1974, Assad went on a short pilgrimage to Mecca, which established him as a true believer.

Assad was re-elected president in 1978, 1985, and 1992, being the only candidate. In 1995, he completed a quarter century of rule. Among other things, he put Syria on a firm institutional path, with elections to the people's Assembly held every four years. The Baath-led National Progressive Front has dominated the Assembly, but real power lies with the high command of the Baath, which is led by Assad. Complementing Baath rule is an intelligence network that permeates all important segments of society and government. The major opposition force, the Muslim Brotherhood, has been outlawed since the mid-1960s.

When Assad intervened in the Lebanese civil war in mid-1976 and sided with the Maronite Christians, support for the Muslim Brotherhood increased. The Brotherhood started a campaign of assassinations and terrorism, which escalated into near-insurrections in Aleppo and Hama in March 1980. It reached a peak with an assassination attempt on Assad in June. Assad crushed the Islamists temporarily, but the Brotherhood's violent activities resumed and culminated in an insurrection in Hama, the leading center of the Sunni religious establishment, in February 1982. Assad hit back with unprecedented force, and re-imposed control at the cost of 5,000 to 10,000 lives—including about 1,000 soldiers—and the destruction of about a quarter of the old city. Signs of fission within the ruling elite surfaced when Assad suffered a heart attack in November 1983. His younger brother, Rifaat, tried to grab power but failed.

Assad finally overcame this crisis, which threatened a civil war, in March 1984, the month he succeeded in aborting a Lebanese-Israeli peace treaty that Lebanon, cajoled by the U.S., had initialed 10 months earlier. Assad's involvement in the Lebanese civil war was based on his belief that there was a special relationship between Lebanon and Syria, and that defection of Lebanon to the American-Israeli camp would pose unbearable danger to his country's security.

Following the arrest and conviction in October 1986 of Nizar Hindawi—a Jordanian purportedly linked with the Syrian embassy in London—for attempting to plant a bomb on an Israeli airliner in London, Great Britain broke off diplomatic relations with Syria. The U.S. recalled its ambassador from Damascus, and placed Syria on the list of nations supporting international terrorism. A year later, the U.S. ambassador returned to Damascus, but Washington retained Syria's name on its list of terrorist nations.

Meanwhile, continuing his involvement in the Lebanese civil war, Assad successfully followed the strategy of creating dissension in the coalition of right-wing Christian forces fighting the pro-Damascus coalition. Finally, in October 1990, with the region in the grip of the crisis caused by Iraq's invasion of Kuwait, the pro-Syrian side won in Lebanon. He formalized a close relationship with Lebanon by concluding a Treaty of Brotherhood, Cooperation and Coordination that requires the two countries to coordinate their policies in foreign affairs, defense and security, and soci-economic affairs. Among other things, it legitimized the stationing of 30,000 Syrian troops in Lebanon.

He was far less successful in dealing with the Palestine Liberation Organization (PLO), led by Yasser Arafat. Following Egypt's defection from the Arab camp in 1979, Assad embarked upon a plan to achieve strategic parity with Israel, an ambitious proposition to be implemented with active Soviet backing. He tried to be a mentor of Arafat, but Arafat, intent on maintaining the PLO's independence, resisted him. The subsequent Assad-inspired rebellion within Arafat's party, Fatah, weakened Arafat, who then turned to moderate King Hussein of Jordan.

Because Assad sided with Iran in the Iran-Iraq War, relations between Damascus and Baghdad soured. After the conflict, Iraqi President Saddam Hussein tried to get even with Assad by helping his enemies in Lebanon.

With the rapid decline of the Soviet Union as a superpower after 1989, Assad had to moderate his strategy towards Israel. He took a realistic view of U.S. leadership in regional and international affairs. Following Saddam Hussein's invasion and occupation of Kuwait in August 1990, Assad tried to persuade the Iraqi leader to reverse his action. When that failed, he joined the anti-Iraq coalition led by the U.S. and sent troops to assist in Saudi Arabia's defense.

In October 1991, he agreed to Syria's participation in the Middle East peace conference, which was meant to lead to bilateral talks between Israel and its Arab enemies. He ensured that the conference was held on the basis of UN Security Council resolutions 242 and 338, calling on Israel to withdraw from the territories it occupied during the 1967 war. He disapproved of the 1993 Israeli-PLO Accord and the 1994 Israeli-Jordanian Peace Treaty, but refrained from undermining them.

He has insisted that Israel must state its willingness to vacate all the Golan Heights in return for total peace with Syria before details of any peace treaty could be fleshed out. Israel has failed to do so. Anxious to get the two sides to embark upon fruitful negotiations, the U.S. began playing an active role in the talks. President Bill Clinton twice met Assad, once in Damascus, but no Syrian-Israeli accord was in sight in 1995.

The Syrian leader has continued his strategic alliance with the Islamic Republic of Iran. This has enabled Tehran to arm Hizbollah, a militant Shia organization in Lebanon.

His long years in power have shown Assad to be consistent and tenacious. A distant and authoritarian personality, Assad has the ability to combine realism with a cool, calculating disposition. His successful involvement in the long, drawn-out civil conflict in Lebanon was a testimony to these qualities.

CHAPTER 19

Lebanon

Given the common history and geography of the Republic of Lebanon and the Arab Republic of Syria, it is hard to separate the two. Yet the socio-political make-up of independent Lebanon has evolved differently. The main feature that makes Lebanon exceptional in the Arab world is the comparatively high proportion of Christians in the population. It is the only Arab League member whose head of state is required by its constitution to be Christian. It also has the dubious distinction of having endured the longest civil war in the region, during which it was invaded twice by Israel. Yet its citizens, true to their Levantine origins, have showed themselves to be resilient and enterprising.

PROFILE

Area & Population: Roughly rectangular, Lebanon measures 4,036 square miles. Its estimated population in 1992 was 3,410,000, including about 400,000 Palestinian refugees in camps.

Cities: With a population of 1,500,000, Beirut, the capital, is the largest city. Next in size are Tripoli 180,000, Sidon 80,000, and Zahle 65,000.

Constitution: Promulgated by the French mandate in May 1926, the constitution was amended in 1927, 1929, and 1943 by France, and in 1947 and 1990 by the Lebanese parliament. The 1990 amendments resulted in changes to 31 articles. Lebanon is a multi-party, multi-religious republic; confessionalism has been built into the political-administrative system of the country since 1943. The constitution specifies that the president of the republic is to be a Maronite Christian (a sect founded by St. Maron in the fourth century and now affiliated with the Vatican), the prime minister a Sunni Muslim, and the parliamentary speaker a Shia Muslim. The 1990 amendments curtailed the power of the president, who is elected for a six-year term by parliament, and increased the authority of the cabinet, making it more autonomous. The president has the power to approve and implement the laws passed by the National Assembly, but his decisions must be co-signed by the prime minister. The president must appoint a prime minister in consultation with the Assembly's speaker and senior members. The cabinet ministers need not be Assembly members, but are responsible to it. The National Assembly is a unicameral house with 128 members, divided equally among Christians and Muslims, who are elected on universal suffrage for a four-year term. The Assembly has legislative and constitutional powers, and is also an electoral college for election of the president. If it fails to choose a president by a two-thirds majority on the first secret ballot, it makes its choice by a simple majority. In constitutional matters, a quorum of two-thirds is required, but decisions are taken by a simple majority. Following the outbreak of a civil war in April 1975, the Assembly, elected in 1972, periodically extended its life until September 1992, when a new election was held under the amended constitution which provided for a parliament of 128 seats. The new share of the 64 Muslim seats among these different sects, with the old share in parentheses, is Sunni 27 (20), Shia 27 (19), Druze 8 (6), and Alawi 2 (0). The new share of the 64 Christian seats among the sects is Maronite 34 (30), Greek Orthodox 14 (11), Greek Catholic 6 (6), Armenian Catholic and Armenian Orthodox 6 (5), and Protestant Christian and non-Muslim minorities 4 (2).

Economy: At the national Gross Domestic Product of $5.7 billion, the per capita GDP was $1,671.

Education: Literacy in the population aged 15 and above (1990) was 80.1 percent (female 73.1 percent, Male 87.8 percent).

Ethnic Composition: Arab 92.5 percent, with Lebanese 81 percent and Palestinian 11.5 percent; Armenian 2.5 percent; and others 5 percent.

Geography: The coastal strip along the Mediterranean Sea becomes the Lebanese Mountain range, which runs north to south. Parallel to and east of Mount Lebanon, beyond the Beqaa Valley, lies the Anti-Lebanon Mountain range which slopes into the plains of Syria.

Governmental System: Lebanon is a republic, with a president elected by parliament.

Military: Lebanon's total armed forces number 44,300 actives. Military expenditure as percent of GDP is 4.1 percent.

Mineral Resources: Lebanon lacks any mineral resources.

Religious Composition: Muslim 60-73 percent with Shia 31-39 percent, Sunni 21-26 percent, Druze 7 percent, and Alawi 1 percent; Christian 26-39 percent, with Maronite 16-25 percent, Greek Orthodox 5-6 percent, Greek Catholic 3-4 percent, and Armenian Catholic and Orthodox 2-3 percent; and others 1 percent.

HISTORY BEFORE 1946

The history of Greater/Natural Syria before 1918 includes that of Lebanon. After receiving a mandate for Greater Syria from the League of Nations in 1920, France enlarged the ex-Ottoman Emirate of Mount Lebanon by adding areas hitherto part of Syria to its north, west, and south, and calling the new entity Greater Lebanon. In 1926, France promulgated a republican constitution, with a parliament and president elected by parliament. The constitution named the country the Republic of Lebanon.

France suspended the constitution in 1932. A census held in that year produced figures for 16 recognized religious sects: Armenian, Assyrian, Chaldean, Greek, Maronite, Roman, and Syrian Catholic; Armenian, Greek, and Syrian Orthodox; Protestant Christian; Alawi, Druze, Shia and Sunni Muslim; Bahais; and Jews. In 1936, Paris reinstated the constitution. The Franco-Lebanese Treaty initialed (but not ratified) in September 1936 promised considerable autonomy to Lebanon.

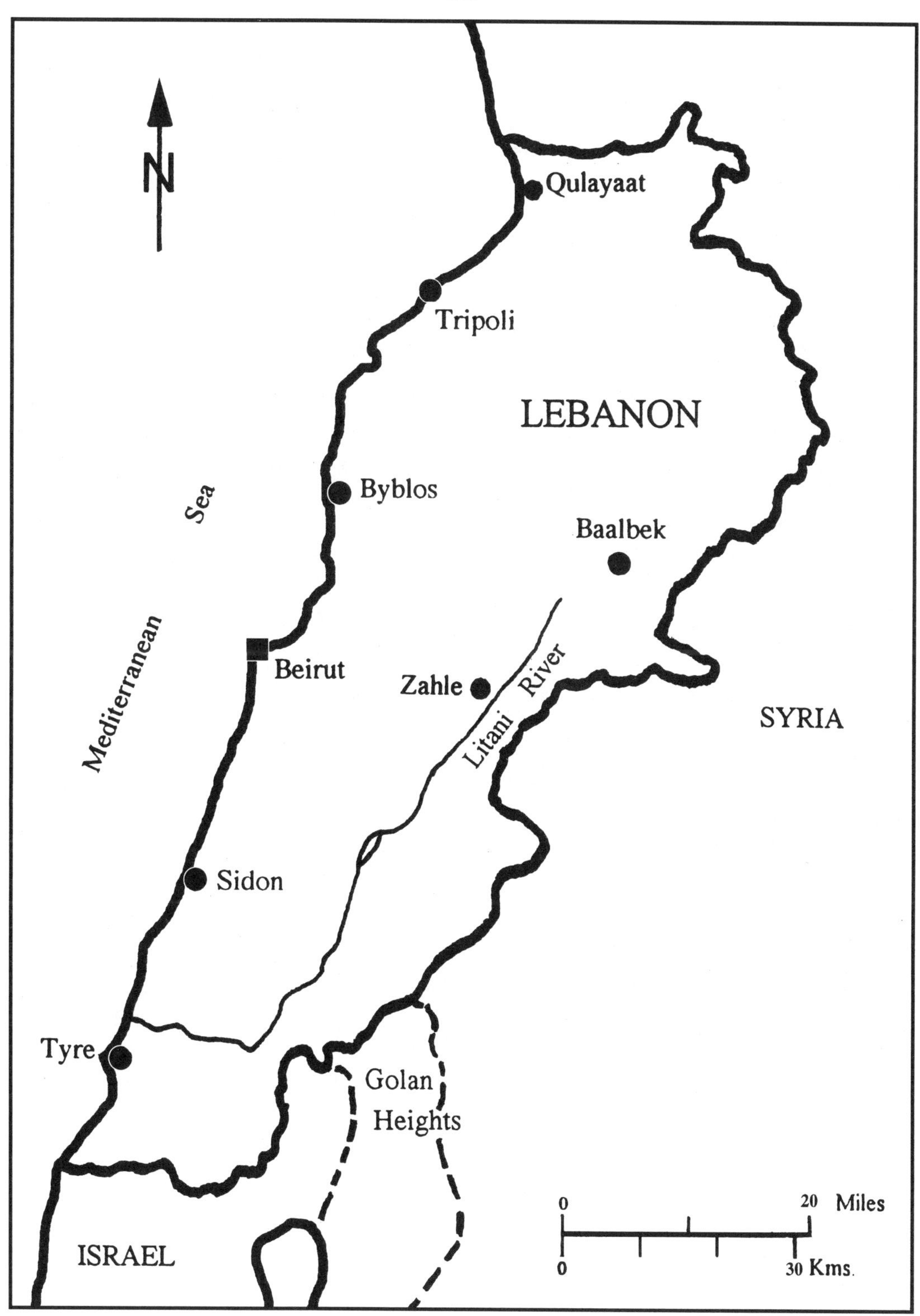
N
Qulayaat
Tripoli
LEBANON
Byblos
Sea
Baalbek
Mediterranean
Beirut
Zahle
Litani River
SYRIA
Sidon
Tyre
Golan Heights
ISRAEL
0
20 Miles
0
30 Kms.

Lebanon

After the outbreak of World War II in 1939, France's pro-German Vichy government took over French overseas territories, including Lebanon, in 1940. Vichy forces were defeated in Lebanon by the British and Free French forces in June 1941, and Lebanon was given nominal independence. The National Pact of March 1943, devised by the British, provided a formula of 6 Christian to 5 Muslim parliamentarians. In September, Bishara Khouri (1890-1964) was elected president. In 1945, Lebanon was one of the founder-members of the Arab League. With the departure of the French in December 1946, it became fully independent.

INDEPENDENT LEBANON SINCE 1946

Lebanon participated in the Arab-Israeli War of 1948–1949, and signed a truce with Israel in March 1949. Khouri was re-elected president later that year, but was forced to resign in 1952 following charges of corruption. Camille Chamoun (1900–1987) succeeded him as president.

Disregarding the program of his supporters to concentrate on domestic reform, Chamoun focused on foreign affairs. Despite pressure from Muslim politicians, he did not break links with Great Britain and France during the latter's aggression against Egypt in October 1956 in the Suez War. His open alignment with the West, coupled with his rigging of the 1957 general election and repression of the opposition, angered the pan-Arab camp, led by Kamal Jumblat.

The gap between president Chamoun and the opposition widened after the formation of the union of Egypt and Syria into the United Arab Republic (UAR) in February 1958. On 8 May, Nasib Metni, a Christian newspaper publisher who had just served a jail sentence for criticizing the president, was killed. His murder led to anti-government rioting in Tripoli, which left 35 dead. The opposition staged countrywide strikes, and Chamoun declared a state of emergency.

The civil war that erupted on 12 May 1958 was between the Chamoun partisans—the gendarmarie and the Maronite militia—and the Jumblat supporters, with the army staying neutral. When fighting between the two sides intensified, the 8,000-man army intervened to end it. In mid-July, when the Jumblat camp controlled about a third of Lebanon, the pro-Western Iraqi monarch, Faisal II ibn Ghazi, was overthrown by republican army officers.

Deprived of his only strong ally in the region, Chamoun requested military aid from U.S. President Dwight Eisenhower, who had earlier promised assistance to any Middle East country menaced by "international communism." Soon 14,500, U.S. marines and airborne ground troops arrived and were backed up by the 76-ship U.S. Sixth Fleet. The arrival of U.S. forces intensified the civil conflict. To expedite the departure of foreign troops, opposition parliamentarians agreed in September to elect as president General Fuad Chehab, the army commander who had remained neutral in the war. The conflict killed between 1,400 and 4,000 Lebanese. The U.S. troop withdrawal was completed by 25 October.

With bipartisan backing, Chehab maintained stability. He did so by aligning his external policies with those of the Arab hinterland, and by co-opting the leaders of urban Muslims into ruling the country. At home, supported by military officers and technocrats, he tried to modernize a political-administrative machine steeped in feudal and sectarian values. His public works program, including road building in rural areas, accelerated migration into cities from the countryside. In the course of their residence in cities, the rural migrants became politically aware and began supporting radical parties, thus radicalizing Lebanese politics. After stepping down in 1964, Chehab continued to wield influence.

The pace of reform slowed during the presidency of Charles Helou (1912–). Lebanon stayed out of the June 1967 Arab-Israeli War.

The growing presence of armed Palestinians led to clashes between them and the Lebanese army. However, a working arrangement was hammered out between Lebanon and the Palestine Liberation Organization (PLO) in 1969 with the assistance of Egyptian President Nasser.

In his bid for the presidency in August 1970, Suleiman Franjieh received the support of Chamoun and Pierre Gemayel, and defeated Elias Sarkis by one vote. Franjieh's adoption of an anti-Palestinian stand, advocated by right-wing Maronites, made him unpopular with the pan-Arab Muslims, who actively backed the PLO, which set up its headquarters in Beirut in 1972. Franjieh kept Lebanon out of the 1973 Arab-Israeli War.

The Lebanese Civil War

An attack on the Palestinians by a Maronite militia in predominantly Christian East Beirut on 13 April 1975 heralded the start of a civil war, which lasted until 13 October 1990. The conflict was between reformist, left-wing Lebanese factions—gathered under the umbrella of the Lebanese National Movement (LNM) led by Kamal Jumblat—and right-wing Christian forces, collectively called the Lebanese Front, headed by Camille Chamoun, with its militia, the Lebanese Forces, commanded by Bashir Gemayel. The PLO allied with the LNM.

The civil war sucked in Syria and Israel, as well as, briefly, the U.S., France, Great Britain, and Italy. The role of Syria was crucial, and in the end, Syrian interests prevailed. During the conflict, Israel invaded Lebanon twice, in 1978 and 1982. The second invasion affected Israeli domestic politics, leading, among other things, to the resignation of Prime Minister Menachem Begin.

During the First Phase of the civil war, April 1975 to May 1976, the reformist alliance was ascendant. Violence spread throughout Lebanon. The LNM demanded reform of the political system to make it equitable to Muslims, now a majority. The Lebanese Front insisted on the expulsion of the armed Palestinians from Lebanon before discussing political-constitutional reform. Intense, countrywide fighting in January 1976 destroyed vital state institutions and public buildings, and caused the break-up of the Lebanese army.

By early April 1976, the LNM-PLO alliance controlled two-thirds of Lebanon. In desperation, the Lebanese Front turned to Syria through President Franjieh. At the behest of Syrian President Hafiz Assad, Franjieh issued a Constitutional Reform Document that changed the 6:5 Christian-Muslim ratio in parliament to parity. But reform was stillborn. However, Assad was equally concerned about the impact of events on regional politics. He reckoned that a radical government in Lebanon would give the PLO a wide berth in implementing its strategy of an intensified guerrilla campaign against Israel, which in turn would provoke Israel into direct military intervention in the Lebanese civil conflict. Therefore, in order to spike the emergence of a radical Lebanon, Assad decided to aid the Maronite-dominated Lebanese Front. The capital, Beirut, was divided into the Christian East and the predominantly Muslim West.

The Second Phase, June 1976 to February 1978, was marked by Syria's dominance. Its military intervention saved the Lebanese Front from total defeat. A ceasefire prepared the ground for the election of a new president. Elias Sarkis (1924–1985), a Syrian nominee, won and took office in September 1976. Within two months, the country was pacified, except in the south, where the PLO's activities against Israel were being hampered by an Israeli-backed Christian militia. After the assassination of Kamal Jumblat in March 1977, his son, Walid, succeeded him.

Following a Palestinian guerrilla attack on Israel on 11 March 1978, the Israelis invaded South Lebanon to end the presence there of some 5,000 Palestinian guerrillas and their infrastructure. The invasion aimed to create a six-mile wide buffer along the 62-mile border. Finding the Palestinians on the run, the

Israelis captured half of South Lebanon, about 10 percent of the country.

By the time the Israelis accepted United Nations Security Council Resolution 425, calling for a ceasefire, on 21 March, they had destroyed 82 villages, killed 1,000 people, and displaced 160,000. The Israeli pullback, which started in mid-April, took two months to complete. The Israelis put the Lebanese border zone, two to six miles wide and 50 miles long, under an Israeli-controlled Christian militia, called the South Lebanon Army (SLA). In the rest of the evacuated territory, the United Nations Interim Force in Lebanon (Unifil) took over from the departing troops.

During the next phase, November 1978 to May 1982, the mini-state set up by the Christians consolidated itself. The Maronite militias forged strong ties with Israel, but their attempts in 1981 to extend their sway to Zahle, a largely Greek Orthodox city in the Beqaa valley, were frustrated by Syria. Syria now maintained 30,000 peacekeeping troops in Lebanon under the aegis of the Arab League and backed the LNM. Once the hawkish Ariel Sharon became defense minister of Israel in 1981, he increased arms shipments to the Maronite militias, and began planning a second invasion of Lebanon.

The next phase of the war, June 1982 to February 1984, consisted of the second Israeli invasion and its aftermath. In early June 1982, following a failed Arab attempt to assassinate the Israeli ambassador in London, Israel invaded Lebanon. Within a week, Israeli forces occupied two-fifths of the country, including Beirut, and expelled President Sarkis from his official palace in Baabda, a Beirut suburb. Israel was then instrumental in getting Bashir Gemayel elected president. Its invasion ended on 1 September after 11,644 PLO fighters and 2,700 Syrian troops had left West Beirut.

On 13 September 1982, President-elect Bashir Gemayel was killed in an explosion that destroyed the headquarters of his Phalange Party. Israeli units occupied Beirut to maintain order and prevent retaliatory violence. But between 16 and 18 September, some 2,000 Palestinian refugees were massacred by the Phalange militia in Beirut's Sabra and Shatila camps. On 20 September, the deployment of a Western Multi-National Force (MNF), consisting of American, British, French, and Italian units, began. The next day, Bashir's elder brother, Amin Gemayel, was elected president by parliament. On 29 September, the Israelis left Beirut.

Under American pressure, Amin Gemayel initialed a draft peace treaty with the Jewish state. Israel signed the document after the Lebanese parliament adopted it by an overwhelming majority on 17 May 1983, but President Gemayel withheld his signature.

Following the Israeli withdrawal from the Shouf region near Beirut in early September 1983, their positions were taken up by the Phalange militia and the Christian-commanded Lebanese army. This led to fighting between them and the Druze-PLO alliance. The U.S. and France intervened with warplanes and warships on the side of the Lebanese army. A ceasefire was mediated by Saudi Arabia in late September, but the U.S. continued its reconnaissance missions over west-central Lebanon from its aircraft carriers. The Muslim camp resented American intervention on behalf of the Lebanese Christians.

On 23 October 1983, the truck-bombing of U.S. and French military headquarters killed 241 Americans (the largest number of American troops killed in a single incident since the Vietnam War) and 59 French troops. The assaults were carried out by militant Shias in retaliation for the American and French bombing of Lebanese Muslim targets.

Meanwhile, efforts were afoot to reconcile the warring Lebanese camps. The First National Reconciliation Conference was held in Geneva in early November 1983. But any gains made there were lost three months later when the Lebanese army disintegrated following the defection of its Muslim soldiers. The U.S. withdrew its troops from Beirut, and other members of the Western MNF followed suit. This withdrawal was an indirect admission by the West, especially the U.S., that Lebanese politics were too convoluted to warrant determined Western intervention.

Among those who fell victim to the conflict in 1984 was Dr. Malcolm Kerr, president of the American University of Beirut (AUB). Founded as the Syrian Protestant College by the American Protestant Mission of New York in 1866, it was a non-sectarian institution. Following the French mandate over Lebanon after World War I, the trustees changed the name to the American University in Beirut. The education in the arts and sciences imparted by it to the student body, drawn from all over the Arab world, had helped create a class of Arab intellectuals with a wide perspective. The AUB had thus become a significant factor in stimulating political and intellectual activity in the region. The university and its affiliated hospital continued to function during the conflict.

During Phase Six of the civil war, March 1984 to January 1986, there was a return of Syrian dominance on the heels of setbacks for Israel. Facing strong hostility to the draft Israeli-Lebanese Peace Treaty at home and from Syria, President Gemayel decided to abrogate it. The Lebanese parliament endorsed his decision in March 1984. That month, following the Second National Reconciliation Conference in Lausanne, Switzerland, a national reconciliation government was formed. In June 1985, Israel handed over its positions in South Lebanon to the South Lebanon Army, a Christian militia it controlled.

The next phase, February 1986 to September 1988, witnessed Syria consolidating its position. Its troops returned to West Beirut. Having failed to sideline Syria, American secretary of state George Shultz decided to coordinate U.S. policy on Lebanese political reform with Damascus.

When Lebanon's parliament failed to elect a new president, outgoing President Gemayel instructed his chief of staff, General Michel Aoun, in September 1988, to form a temporary military government. Of the five other officers he appointed to his cabinet, the three Muslim members refused to join. During the next year, Aoun launched his "war of liberation" against Syria. Damascus imposed land and sea blockades on the Christian enclave under Aoun's control. In August 1989, 14 Lebanese groups formed an anti-Aoun front.

During the last phase of the war, October 1989 to October 1990, a consensus grew around the accord devised by Lebanese parliamentarians in Taif, Saudi Arabia. In October 1989, 58 of the 62 surviving Lebanese law-makers debated and adopted the National Reconciliation Charter, which outlined political reform. Aoun rejected it but the Christian Lebanese Front accepted it. After endorsing the Taif Accord in the northern Lebanese town of Qulayaat in November, Lebanon's parliament elected Rene Muawad president. He was assassinated a few weeks later. The parliament then elected Elias Hrawi president.

From January to March 1990, there was intense fighting between Aoun loyalists and the Maronite militia, known as the Lebanese Forces (LF). As a result, Aoun ended up with only a third of the Christian enclave. The LF declared allegiance to Hrawi. In August, the parliament decided to overhaul the constitution as outlined in the Taif Accord. A month later, Hrawi's decision to impose a land blockade on Aoun's enclave was backed by the LF. By now, in the midst of the crisis created by Iraq's invasion and occupation of Kuwait, Syria had joined the U.S.-led coalition against Iraq. On 13 October 1990, in a joint air and ground campaign, Lebanese and Syrian troops defeated Aoun and brought the civil war to an end.

Fatalities during the 15½ years of war—including the almost 19,000, mainly civilians, killed in the 1982 Israeli invasion—were put at 150,000. During the first half of the conflict, the direct annual cost of war was put at $900 million.

Lebanon Since 1990

After the conflict, a national unity government disarmed the various militias and ended the division of the capital into East and West

Beirut. In May 1991, the parliament passed a law giving Muslims and Christians parity in the chamber. Later that month, Presidents Hrawi and Assad signed the Treaty of Brotherhood, Cooperation and Coordination between Lebanon and Syria. It required the two neighbors to coordinate their policies in foreign affairs, defense, and the economy. It specified the formation of joint agencies at different levels to implement the treaty—from the Higher Council, consisting of the presidents, prime ministers, deputy prime ministers, and parliamentary speakers, to the committees on defense and security, foreign affairs, and socio-economic affairs.

Elections to the enlarged parliament were held between August and October 1992. Due to a boycott by the Maronite-dominated parties, the new chamber and the consequent government were strongly pro-Syrian. Unlike right-wing Maronites, Suleiman Franjieh's party participated in the election and won half the seats reserved for Maronites.

Lebanon participated in the Middle East peace process inaugurated by the Madrid conference in October 1991. But, mirroring the impasse between Syria and Israel, its bilateral talks with Israel made little progress. The government called on Israel to vacate south Lebanon unconditionally as demanded by the 1978 United Nations Security Council Resolution 425. It also allowed the militant Shia organization, Hizbollah, to function as a counterforce to the Israeli-run South Lebanon Army, based in Israeli-occupied Lebanese territory.

CHAPTER

Palestine and the Palestinians

Palestine does not exist now, but Palestinians do. The term comes from a Greek derivative of the Hebrew word for "Land of the Philistines." It is impossible to write about the Palestinians without dealing with Palestine. Also known as the Holy Land because it is sacred to Jews, Christians, and Muslims, Palestine has a long, checkered history. It ceased to exist in 1948 when a large part of it was conquered by the Zionists, who established Israel. The rest, composed of the West Bank and the Gaza Strip, and inhabited by Arab Palestinians, came under the control, respectively, of Jordan and Egypt. Jordanian and Egyptian rule ended in 1967 when Israel captured the West Bank and the Gaza Strip. Following an accord between Israel and the Palestine Liberation Organization (PLO) in 1993, a Palestinian entity, administered by the Palestinian Authority, began to rise. Whether it will graduate to an independent sovereign state in the near future remains unclear.

PROFILE

Area & Population: Roughly rectangular, the Gaza Strip measures 146 square miles, the kidney-shaped West Bank measures 2,270 square miles, and East Jerusalem is 27 square miles. The estimated population of the territories in 1992 was Gaza Strip 850,000, excluding 3,000 Jewish settlers; the West Bank 1.2 million, excluding 130,000 Jewish settlers; and East Jerusalem 160,000, excluding 140,000 Jewish settlers.

Cities: In the Gaza Strip, the capital, Gaza City, with a population of 250,000, is the largest city. In the West Bank, East Jerusalem, at 300,000, is followed by Nablus at 180,000 and Hebron at 100,000.

Economy: The per capita Gross Domestic Product of the Gaza Strip was $739, and that of the West Bank $1,438.

Education: Literacy in the population aged 15 and above (1993) was 82.4 percent in the Gaza Strip (female 75.2 percent, male 89.7

percent) and 82.3 percent in the West Bank (female 73.6 percent, male 91.2 percent).

Geography: The narrow Gaza Strip along the Mediterranean Sea next to the Egyptian border is about 28 miles long and five miles wide. It is flat except for the two shallow valleys that run across it. The West Bank is part of the limestone plateau that lies to the west of the valley of the Jordan River. Fertile in the north, it becomes increasingly barren in the south. It consists of three major sections: the Mount Hebron massif, lying between Hebron and Bethlehem, with a peak of 3,050 feet; the Jerusalem hills, which touch the northernmost point of the Mountain Hebron massif; and the Mount Samaria hills in the northern half of the territory, with its central section around Nablus reaching a summit of 2,800 feet before sloping down northwards to the Jenin hills, with a peak of 1,200 feet.

Governmental System: According to the interim 1993 Israeli-PLO Accord, administrative authority is being transferred from Israel, the occupying power since 1967, to the Palestinian Authority formed by the Palestine Liberation Organization.

Legislature: The 88-member Palestinian Council, elected in January 1996 under the 1993 Israeli-PLO Accord, was authorized to legislate only in socio-economic affairs.

Religious Composition: The Gaza Strip: Muslim 99 percent, and Christian 1 percent. The West Bank: Muslim 90-92 percent, and Christian 8-10 percent.

HISTORY SINCE 1918

Under the Ottomans (1517–1918), whose empire included Greater Syria, there was no single administrative unit called Palestine. What was to emerge as Palestine under the British mandate in 1922 was divided into three sections during the Ottoman period. The declaration by Great Britain's foreign secretary, Arthur (later Lord) Balfour, in November 1917 referred to the "establishment in Palestine of a National Home for the Jewish people."

During World War I, the failed Ottoman offensive in Palestine in 1915 made London realize the strategic importance of Palestine as a buffer to safeguard Egypt and the Suez Canal, Great Britain's lifeline to its empire in India. Great Britain therefore insisted on, and acquired, a mandate over Palestine at the meeting of the Supreme Council of the League of Nations in San Remo, Italy, in April 1920. Approved by the League in July 1922, the mandate went into effect in September 1923.

Arab Palestinians resisted both the British mandate and Jewish immigration. This culminated in the Arab Revolt of 1936-1939. Tensions eased during World War II. After the war, Great Britain turned over the Palestine problem to the United Nations, the successor to the League of Nations.

The UN's 1947 Partition Plan was superseded by the armed conflict between Israel and its Arab neighbors in May 1948. The borders of the Jewish state were temporarily defined by the armistice agreements that Israel signed with Egypt, Jordan, Syria, and Lebanon in 1949. These truces left Israel controlling 75 percent of Palestine. Of the two areas retained by the Arab side, the Gaza Strip was administered by Egypt, and the West Bank was annexed by Jordan, subject to "a final settlement."

During the invasion in October 1956 of Egypt by Israel, in conjunction with Great Britain and France, Israel occupied the Gaza Strip. But it was forced to vacate it in March 1957 under pressure chiefly by the United Nations and the United States.

In 1964, an Arab League summit decided to set up an umbrella body, the Palestine Liberation Organization, to enable the Palestinians to play their part in liberating Palestine and determining their own future. The PLO held its first congress in East Jerusalem, then under Jordanian control. The congress adopted the Palestine National Charter, which called for the founding of a democratic and secular state in a Palestine as constituted un-

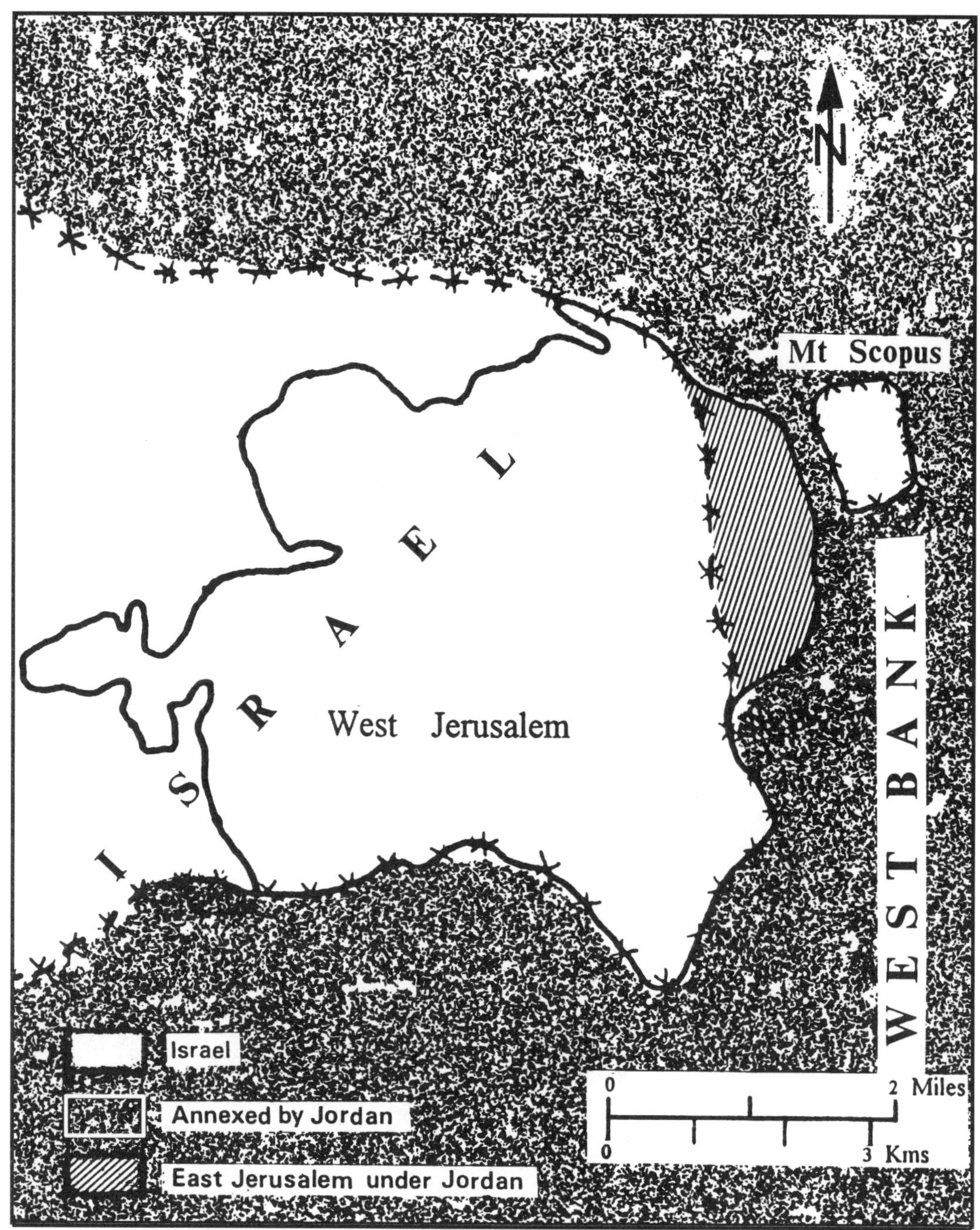

Jerusalem in 1949

der the British mandate. Each of the affiliated bodies were represented on the Palestine National Council (PNC), which elected a central council and an executive committee.

The 1967 War and After

During the June 1967 Arab-Israeli War, Israel occupied the West Bank and the Gaza Strip, as well as Egypt's Sinai Peninsula and Syria's Golan Heights. The PLO's importance rose in the aftermath of the Arab defeat. The change in its charter in 1968, which declared armed struggle to be the only way to literate Palestine, paved the way for the affiliation of radical groups. One of these was Fatah (meaning victory), led by Yasser Arafat.

Born in 1929 in Cairo during his Palestinian father's brief stay there, Yasser Arafat and his parents found themselves in the Gaza Strip during the 1948-1949 Arab-Israeli War. He graduated as a civil engineer in 1955 from a university in Cairo, where he was chairman of the local Palestinian Students' Union, based in the Egyptian-administered Gaza Strip. Then he took up a civil engineering job in Kuwait. Along with Salah Khalaf and Khalil Wazir, fellow-Palestinians from the Gaza Strip, Arafat formed a secret group, called Fatah, in 1958. Five years later, Fatah was allowed to open an office in Algiers, Algeria, to train commandos. This was in line with the Fatah strategy of employing revolutionary violence to liberate the Palestinian homeland. In 1964 in Damascus, Fatah, guided by Arafat, decided on guerrilla actions against Israel from Syria. It mounted its first such operation on 1 January 1965.

After the June 1967 Arab-Israeli War, Arafat met Egyptian President Gamal Abdul Nasser, who pledged support. In March 1968, after Fatah commandos had engaged the Israelis in a battle in the Jordanian border town of Karameh, the popularity of Fatah and Arafat rose. In July 1968, Fatah delegates attended the fifth session of the Palestine National Council in Cairo. Fatah emerged as the PLO's largest constituent, and the PNC elected Arafat chairman of the PLO's executive committee. Arafat stuck to two basic positions: No single Arab regime should be allowed to dominate or co-opt the PLO; and all political ideologies committed to the liberation of Palestine must be accommodated. The Soviet Union backed the PLO's guerrilla activities as a legitimate expression of the Palestinian right to self-defense in the face of continued Israeli military occupation.

Following the expulsion of the PLO from Amman, Jordan, in the wake of Palestinian fighting with Jordanian forces in 1970-1971, the PLO moved its headquarters to Beirut. Here, financed by private and governmental contributions channeled through the Palestine National Fund, the PLO emerged as a state-within-state.

The 1973 War and After

In the wake of the October 1973 Arab-Israeli War, the PNC adopted, in June 1974, the idea of a Palestinian state in the occupied territories as a transient stage for the liberation of all Palestine. Four months later, the Arab League summit recognized the PLO as the sole representative of the Palestinian people, and granted it membership in the League. In mid-November, Arafat addressed the UN General Assembly during its debate on the Palestinian issue. On 22 November, UN General Assembly Resolution 3236, describing the PLO as "the representative of the Palestinian people," reaffirmed the Palestinian right to self-determination and national independence, and the right of the Palestinian refugees to return to their homes and property. The PLO was given observer status at the UN. Its representative, Zehdi Terzi, was invited to a UN Security Council session on the Palestinian issue in December 1974 to participate in the debate. On 22 January 1975, the UN Security Council endorsed the General Assembly stand by adopting a resolution affirming the Palestinian right to establish an independent state. But the American admin-

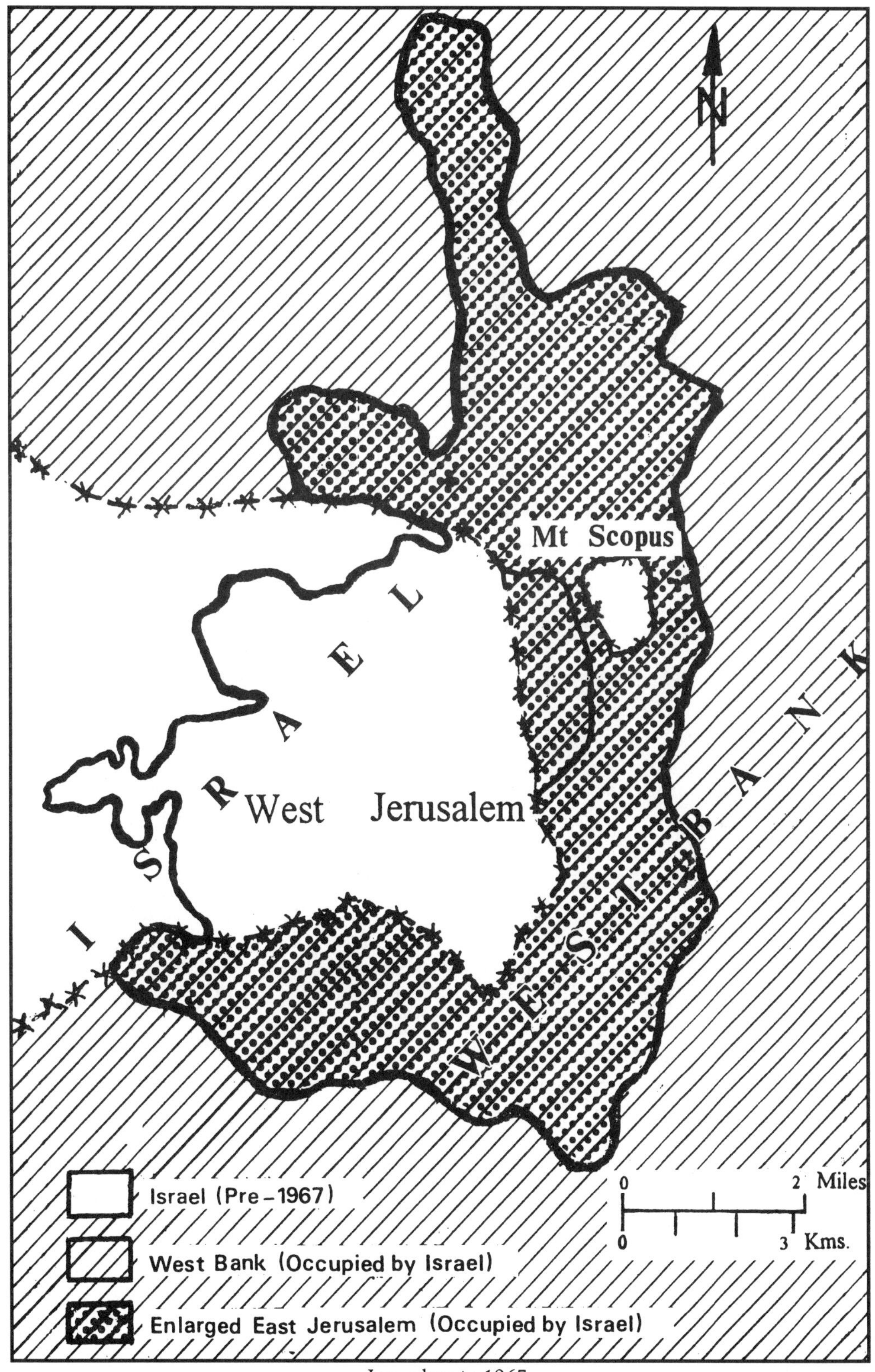

Jerusalem in 1967

istration of President Gerald Ford (1913–) vetoed the resolution.

In the Lebanese civil war, which erupted in April 1975, Arafat, along with other Palestinian leaders, sided with the leftist Lebanese National Movement to fight the right-wing Lebanese Forces. Arafat's opposition to Egypt's American-inspired effort to reach unilateral peace with Israel in 1977–1979 turned him leftwards. Fatah's fourth congress in May 1980 decided to intensify the armed struggle against the Jewish state. Israel reciprocated.

By the late 1970s, the PLO had won the recognition of over 100 countries, far more than recognized Israel. Its annual budget of $500 million consisted of $350 million in grants by oil-rich Arab states, and $150 million in indirect Palestine taxes collected by some Arab states, all of which were paid into the Palestine National Fund. The PLO commanded some 23,000 armed guerrillas, and almost 10,000 troops of the Palestine Liberation Army (PLA). Groups affiliated with the PLO included the Arab Liberation Front, the Democratic Front for the Liberation of Palestine, Fatah, the Palestine Communist Party, the Popular Front for the Liberation of Palestine, the Popular Front for the Liberation of Palestine-General Command, the Popular Struggle Front, and Saiqa. The PLO's affiliates also included 14 organizations for students, workers, women, journalists, lawyers, and doctors.

Following its invasion of Lebanon, which culminated in the siege of Beirut, Israel compelled Arafat in August 1982 to remove the PLO headquarters and troops from the city. He moved the PLO administrative staff to Tunis, and dispersed the Palestinian fighters to several Arab states. In Tunis, the PLO became progressively more moderate. Following a series of meetings with King Hussein of Jordan, Arafat agreed in early 1985 to joint Palestinian-Jordanian moves towards a peace settlement with Israel. But this change of policy by the PLO had no impact on Israel. On 1 October, the Israelis bombed the PLO headquarters in Tunis, killing 71 people, but missed their main target, Arafat. Following this raid, Arafat had difficulty winning the approval of the majority of the PLO's constituents for his new position. Indeed, the Palestine National Council, meeting in April 1987, annulled Arafat's agreement with King Hussein.

The main sufferers of the Israeli military occupation were the inhabitants of the West Bank and the Gaza Strip. After having waited, in vain, for two decades for outsiders to end the Israeli rule, they decided to act on their own. The result was the eruption of the *intifada* in the Gaza Strip in December 1987. A grass roots movement, it spread rapidly to the West Bank. It stemmed from 20 years of collective and individual frustrations and humiliations endured by the Palestinians in their dealings with Jewish Israelis and the Israeli authorities, military and civilian. Soon the PLO backed the *intifada* as did the locally based Hamas and Islamic Jihad organizations. They and the local adherents of the PLO in the occupied territories formed coordinating committees under the United National Leadership of the Uprising (UNLU) to direct the movement.

Many of those involved were young educated Palestinians, fluent in Hebrew and familiar with Israeli norms. They took over the leadership from the older generation of Arab notables, who professed peaceful co-existence with the Israelis. UNLU urged the Palestinians to resign from all posts of the government, stop using public services, withdraw money from Israeli banks, boycott Israeli products, cease paying taxes, and join the strikes being called. UNLU committees issued circulars containing instructions in these matters, and urged all Palestinians to share the sacrifices required by the *intifada*. The Palestinians used charity funds to support the large number of families whose husbands or brothers were jailed. Repressive actions by the Israeli security forces, involving firings, curfews, harassment, arrests, house searches, and demolitions became commonplace.

In November 1988, the PNC declared the independence and establishment of the State of Palestine, "on our Palestinian land," on the basis of the UN General Assembly's Partition Resolution 181 of November 1947. It named Yasser Arafat president of the State of Palestine. He renounced the use or threats of force or violence or terrorism to achieve the PLO's aims, and declared that the State of Palestine—consisting of the Gaza Strip, West Bank, and East Jerusalem—would co-exist peacefully with Israel. The next month, he addressed the UN General Assembly, specially convened in Geneva, reiterating the new PLO position. Of the 103 countries that had recognized the PLO, 70 now accorded it full diplomatic status. The U.S. established open contacts with the PLO, albeit at a low level. There was no change in the policy of Israel, which was then experiencing a rising tide of Jewish immigration from the Soviet Union. This immigration pushed the number of Jewish immigrants to Israel from 13,300 in 1988 to 199,500 in 1990.

When Arafat failed to condemn an unsuccessful raid by a Palestinian group affiliated with the PLO against an Israeli military target (which according to the PNC statement was still legitimate), the U.S. suspended its talks with the PLO in June 1990. This episode and the rising immigration of Soviet Jews into Israel led Arafat to ally himself with Iraq's President Saddam Hussein. Arafat sided with the Iraqi leader in the latter's conflict with the UN following Baghdad's invasion of Kuwait in August 1990. He did so after Saddam Hussein had linked an Iraqi withdrawal from Kuwait with an Israeli evacuation of the occupied Arab territories. Arafat's stance had the backing of most Palestinians in the West Bank and Gaza. This position angered the oil-rich Gulf states, which stopped funding the PLO, a near fatal blow to its finances. It also estranged Arafat from the Egyptian and Syrian presidents, who joined the U.S.-led anti-Iraq coalition to reverse the Iraqi aggression.

The Peace Process in the 1990s

After Baghdad's defeat in February 1991, Arafat tried to regain his lost popularity with the Arab leaders, an uphill task. Deprived of the advice and friendship of his long-time comrades, Khalil Wazir (assassinated in April 1988) and Salah Khalaf (assassinated in January 1991), he felt increasingly isolated. But the *intifada* in the West Bank and the Gaza Strip continued. During its first four years, it claimed the lives of 1,413 Palestinians. Most of them were killed by the Israeli security forces, and the rest by fellow-Palestinians for being Israeli agents. More than 90,000 Palestinians, about one-sixth of the male population above 15, were arrested. (When the Israeli-PLO Accord was signed in September 1993, there were more than 12,000 Palestinians in jail for their participation in the *intifada*.)

During the preliminary talks leading up to a Middle East peace conference under joint U.S.-Soviet auspices in October 1991, Arafat agreed to the Israeli demand of a Jordanian delegation divided equally between Jordanians and Palestinians (who were acceptable to Israel). The subsequent bilateral talks between the Israeli and Jordanian-Palestinian (later functioning separately) delegations made little progress. But once the right-wing Likud government in Israel was replaced by a left-wing Labour administration after the June 1992 election, the situation altered. The new government removed the ban on contacts with the PLO in early 1993. This set the scene for clandestine talks between the two sides. These took place in Norway.

Meanwhile, the campaign against Israeli agents in the occupied territories intensified in the early 1990s. It destroyed the Israeli Security Service's (Shin Beth) intelligence network among the Palestinians. Deprived of this highly effective instrument, the Israeli authorities found it hard to re-impose full control, and restore law and order. This development made them amenable to compromise.

The Dome of the Rock, Jerusalem.

The resulting accord, based on the mutual recognition of Israel and the PLO (as the representative of the Palestinian people), was made public in August 1993. The PLO's recognition came only after Arafat had stated in his letter to Israeli Premier Yitzhak Rabin that those articles in the Palestine National Charter denying Israel's right to exist and contradicting the PLO's commitment to renounce terrorism and other acts of violence were henceforth "inoperative and no longer valid."

The Israeli-PLO Accord was signed by Mahmoud Abbas, the second most senior PLO official, and Shimon Peres (1923–), Israel's foreign minister, on the White House lawn in Washington, DC. They did so in the presence of Arafat, Israeli Premier Yitzhak Rabin, and U.S. President Bill Clinton. The Accord required Israel to vacate the Gaza Strip and the West Bank town of Jericho as a first step towards granting Palestinians autonomy in the occupied territories, which was to be exercised by a popularly elected Palestinian Council. By May 1996, the two parties were to enter into negotiations on the final status of the occupied territories, including Jerusalem and the Jewish settlements set up in these territories.

Of the 10 groups affiliated to the PLO—the Arab Liberation Front, the Democratic Front for the Liberation of Palestine, the Democratic Palestinian Union (DPU), Fatah, the Palestine People's Party (PPP), the Palestine Liberation Front, the Popular Front for the Liberation of Palestine, the Popular Front for the Liberation of Palestine-General Command, the Popular Struggle Front (PSF), and Saiqa—only the DPU, Fatah, the PPP, and the PSF accepted the deal. The rejectionists argued that Israel had not conceded the right of Palestinians to self-determination and the establishment of an independent state. Also, Israel had not even described itself as the occupying power, something many UN Security Council resolutions had done—a vital point in international law. These groups therefore vowed to continue resisting Israel's military occupation by any means necessary, including attacks on Israeli targets in the occupied territories as well as in pre-1967 Israel. This position was also held by such religious-political organizations as Hamas and the Islamic Jihad, which were not affiliated with the PLO.

Such opposition did not sway Israel and the PLO from transforming the agreement on principles into a working document, and signing it in Cairo in May 1994. Among other things, it gave rise to the Palestinian Authority under the chairmanship of Arafat. He left Tunis in July to administer the Gaza Strip and Jericho from Gaza City. The PLO maintained offices in Tunis and Amman. Later that year, Arafat shared the Nobel Prize for Peace with Yitzhak Rabin and Shimon Peres.

On the eve of the PLO-Israeli Accord, nearly a third of the Gaza Strip was taken up by Jewish settlements or out-of-bounds military zones. The Accord put a further 10 percent of the Strip under joint Israeli-Palestinian control. The Palestinian Authority's administration covered only three-fifths of the tiny Strip, where nearly a million Palestinians lived.

The West Bank had 128 Jewish settlements and more than 130,000 settlers. In addition, there were 140,000 Jewish settlers in Greater East Jerusalem, which occupied 13 times the area East Jerusalem did under the Jordanians. After their victory in the June 1967 war, the Israelis attached large areas of the West Bank to Jordanian East Jerusalem, and then combined the Greater East Jerusalem with West Jerusalem. The Jewish colonization of the West Bank had begun within a year of the 1967 war in Hebron under a Labour administration. These settlements were in contravention of the Fourth Geneva Convention on War (1949). According to the UN Security Council, Israel was the occupying military power in the areas it had seized in the 1967 war, and was required to respect the provisions of the convention and not confiscate Palestinian land or interfere with the local demography.

In August 1973, the ruling Labour Party formally reversed its policy of merely holding on to the Arab territories until the Arab states were ready to negotiate peace with it directly. It allowed Jewish individuals and public bodies to purchase land in the occupied Arab territories. It also permitted the government to supplement the hitherto privately funded settlement program. This action angered the Palestinians. In the local elections of April 1976, they expressed their opposition to Israel's actions. Most of the 24 elected mayors were supporters in varying degrees of the Palestine National Front, a front organization of the PLO, which was banned. But there was no slowdown in Jewish colonization of the West Bank. By the time Labour was replaced by Likud as the leading governing coalition partner, there were 34 Jewish colonies.

The Camp David Accords between Israel and Egypt in September 1978 included an agreement for autonomy for the Palestinians in the West Bank and the Gaza Strip. The autonomy applied only to people, not to land or water. The plan was scheduled to be implemented by May 1980. Since the PLO was not party to these talks and wanted nothing less than a Palestinian state, this agreement was still-born.

Israel postponed the local elections of April 1980 indefinitely. The Jewish colonies continued to increase, with the existing ones getting more populous. The Palestinian *intifada*, originating in the Gaza Strip in December 1987, quickly spread to the West Bank. In July 1988, Jordan cut all its constitutional and administrative links with the territory, thus underscoring the principle that only the Palestinian inhabitants of the occupied territories had the right to decide their own future.

In contravention of the Fourth Geneva Convention on War (1949) and various UN Security Council resolutions, Israel continued to confiscate Palestinian land and interfere with the territory's demography. By the time the Israeli-PLO Accord was signed in September 1993, more than half the land in the West Bank had passed into Jewish hands.

The enforcement of the Accord was tardy. There was a delay of five months in the implementation of the first phase. The second phase—the removal of Israeli troops from West Bank urban centers and the holding of elections to the Palestinian Council—was behind schedule by more than a year.

On the other hand, the Palestinian Authority began to take shape. It recruited more than 18,000 policemen and paramilitary forces to maintain law and order in the Gaza Strip and Jericho. It began to cooperate with the Israeli authorities to curb the terrorist activities of the armed wings of Hamas and the Islamic Jihad. This cooperation helped to reduce, though not eliminate, such actions. The degree of popular support for the Palestinian Authority could only be ascertained through elections to the Palestinian Council. These took place in January 1996, and were boycotted by the Palestinian opposition, religious and secular.

Of the over one million Palestinian electors, 75 percent voted. In the 88-member Palestinian Council, 50 belonged to Fatah, another 15 were pro-Fatah, and the rest independent, likely to form an opposition bloc. In the contest for the presidency of the Palestinian Authority, Arafat, opposed by Samiha Khalil, a woman social worker, won 88 percent of the vote.

Following his victory, Arafat once again described the present stage in the peace process as a step towards the establishment of an independent State of Palestine. But since Israel was by far the stronger party in the ongoing negotiations, more depended on what its leaders said or did than what the PLO and Arafat said or did.

CHAPTER 21

Israel

The ancient name of Israel is today borne by a young nation. Often described as the Jewish state, Israel is a predominantly immigrant country. Although established in 1948, Israel has yet to acquire internationally recognized, permanent borders. Lacking a fully fledged constitution, it is run according to the Transition Law, adopted by its Constituent Assembly in 1949.

PROFILE

Area & Population: The pre-1967 Israel measures 7,820 square miles. Its estimated population in 1992 was 4,930,000, including Jewish settlers in East Jerusalem, the Gaza Strip, Golan Heights, and West Bank.

Cities: Jerusalem, with a population of 544,000, is the self-declared capital. Tel Aviv-Jaffa, with a population of 353,000, is the internationally recognized capital. Next in size are Haifa 251,000; Holon 162,000; and Petah Tikwa 149,000.

Constitution: The Constituent Assembly, elected in January 1949, adopted a Transition Law in February. It declared Israel to be a republic, headed by a president elected for a five-year term by a simple majority of the Knesset, a single-chamber parliament of 120 members. The Knesset was to be elected by adult franchise under the system of proportional representation, with the election threshold at 1 percent; the leader of the largest group in the Knesset was to be invited by the president to become the prime minister and form the government. The Constituent Assembly then transformed itself into the First Knesset. Following a debate on a report on the question of a written constitution by the Knesset's Committee on Constitution, Law and Justice, the house decided in June 1950 to assign the task of preparing a draft constitution to the Committee on Constitution, Law and Justice "chapter by chapter . . . [with] each chapter submitted to the Knesset" and "all the chapters [after the Committee had finished its work] shall be incorporated into the Constitution." Between 1950 and 1964, four such "chapters" have been adopted by the Knesset. These four Basic Laws fixed the Knesset term at years (1958), created the National Land Authority (1959), and required the president to be an Israeli citizen resident in the country (1964). The Knesset deals with legislation, general policy matters, budgets, and international treaties. It has the right to dismiss the state president for misdemeanor by a simple majority.

Economy: At the annual Gross Domestic product of $64.67 billion, the percapita GDP was $13,118.

Education: Literacy in the population aged 15 and over (1993) was 94.4 percent (female 93.1 percent, male 97.4 percent).

Ethnic Composition: Jews 82 percent, Arabs 18 percent.

Geography: The northern part of the narrow coastal plain is called the Plain of Sharon. Its extension, known as the Vale of Esdraelon/ Jezreel, runs inland from the Mediterranean plain to the Jordan Valley. To its south, lie the fertile highlands of Galilee. Bounded by Lake Tiberias and the Jordan Valley to the east, they slope down to the hills of Samaria and Judea to the south. Further south lies the Negev Desert. Occupying three-fifths of Israel, the Negev stretches from the southern edge of the Judean plateau to the Gulf of Aqaba.

Governmental System: Israel is a republic, with a president elected by parliament to act as head of state. The executive authority rests with the prime minister.

Military: Israel's total armed forces number 173,000 actives and 430,000 reserves. There have been unconfirmed reports of biological and chemical weapons research. In 1993, it was officially acknowledged that Marcus Klinberg, a germ warfare specialist, had been convicted a decade earlier of spying for the Soviet Union and sentenced to life imprisonment, a stiffer sentence than the one imposed in late 1986 on Mordecai Vanunu for leaking nuclear arms secrets. The Israeli military's nuclear program got going at Dimona near Beersheba, in the Negev Desert, in September 1957 following a secret agreement with France for the construction of a building and supply of a nuclear reactor capable of producing two low-yield weapons annually. A reprocessing plant to transform uranium into weapons-grade plutonium was completed in 1962. The French presence in Dimona continued until 1966. In early 1968, the Dimona plant began producing four to five nuclear arms annually, and there were more than 25 such weapons by the time of the October 1973 Arab-Israeli War. According to the account by Mordecai Vanunu, a technician at the reprocessing plant, Israel possessed about 200 nuclear weapons. In addition to this nuclear reactor and the reprocessing plant, there are six other reprocessing plants. Furthermore, since 1984 Israel had manufactured neutron bombs—two-stage thermonuclear devices that kill all living things within a given range. An analysis of photographs taken by Vanunu led experts to conclude that Israel had the capacity to produce a low-yield neutron bomb. During the 1991 Gulf War, following Iraqi missile attacks on Israel, Premier Yitzhak Shamir put Israel on full-scale nuclear alert, and (according to American satellite pictures) ordered Israeli mobile missile launchers armed with nuclear warheads deployed in the open facing Iraq. Military expenditure as percent of GDP was 14.1 percent.

Mineral Resources: Israel's mineral resources include phosphate rock and potash. Its current oil output of 6,000 barrels/day is less than five percent of its needs. The production of natural gas was 23.3 million cubic meters/day in 1992.

Religious Composition: Jew 82 percent; Muslim 15.5 percent, with Sunni 14 percent and Druze 1.5 percent; and Christian 2.5 percent.

HISTORY SINCE 1948

Israel was established on 14 May 1948 at the end of the British mandate over Palestine, which dated back to 1922. An immediate war with its Arab neighbors ended in January 1949, with Israel acquiring 21 percent more

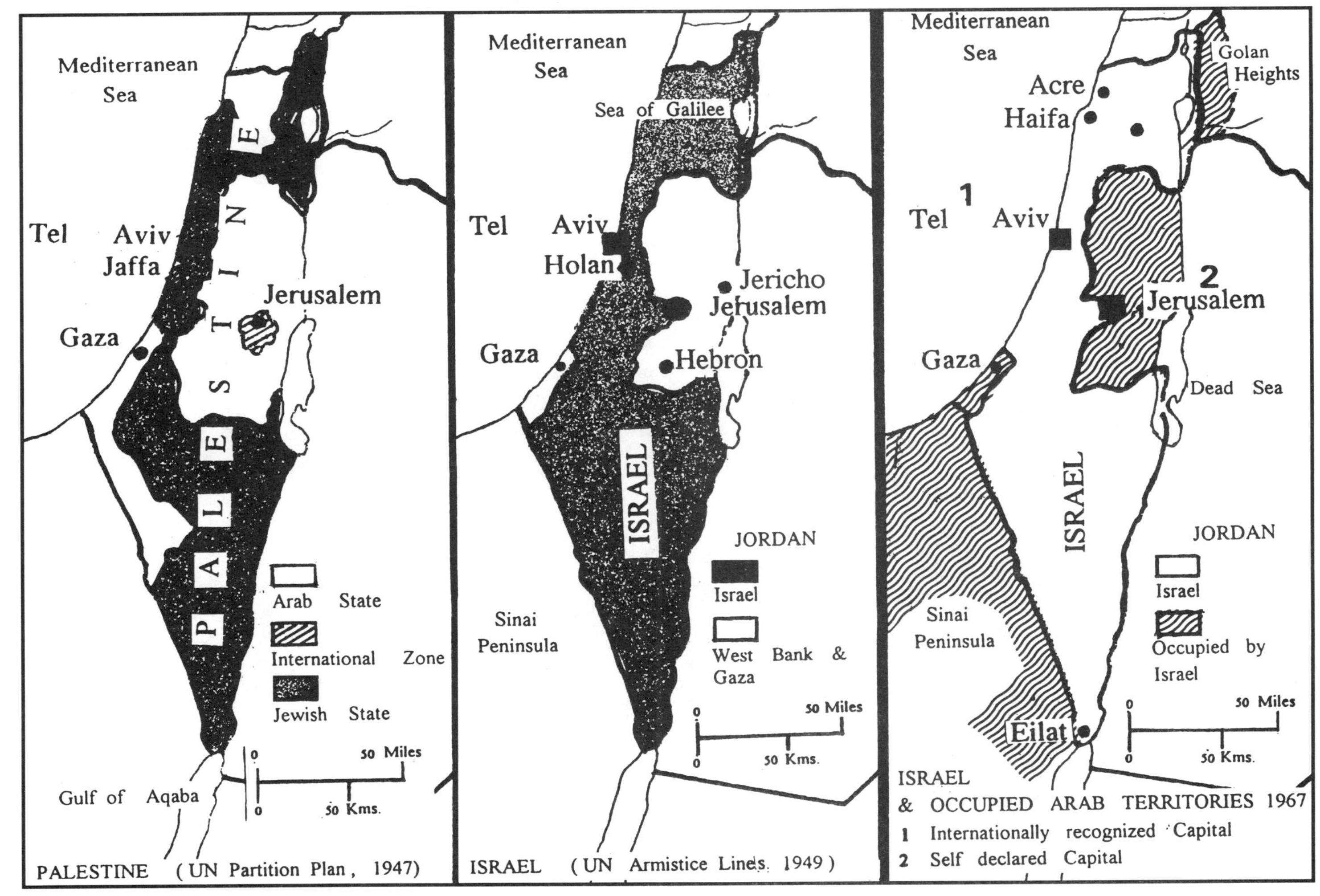

Palestine, 1947 Israel, 1949 Israel, 1967

area than the 54 percent allocated to it by the United Nations partition plan of 1947. The human losses in the first Arab-Israeli war, including the preceding five months of civil conflict in Palestine, amounted to 18,500 Arabs, including 16,000 Arab Palestinians, and 6,000 Jews.

A Constituent Assembly, elected in January 1949, passed a Transition Law next month, and then transformed itself into a parliament, the Knesset. As leader of Mapai (Hebrew acronym for the Israel Workers Party), the largest group in the Knesset, David Ben-Gurion (1886-1973) became prime minister. His life summed up well Zionist history before and after the founding of Israel.

David Ben-Gurion

Born David Green in Plonsk, Poland, into a lawyer's family, David Ben-Gurion went to Warsaw University in 1904, and joined the Poale Zion ("Workers of Zion"). Two yeas later, he left for Palestine where he became a farm hand. In 1912, he enrolled at the University of Istanbul to study law. The outbreak of World War I brought him back to Palestine. In 1915, following deportation as a troublemaker, he sailed for New York. Trained in Canada, Ben-Gurion arrived in Egypt as a member of the British 40th Royal Fusiliers.

After the war, he became involved in setting up an umbrella organization called Histadrut to encompass all labor-pioneer parties of Zionist persuasion. He played a leading role in the establishment of Mapai in 1930, and was elected its head in 1933. Two years later, he became the leader of the executive committee of the Jewish Agency for Palestine, which was recognized by the British mandate as the official representative of the Jews in Palestine.

During World War II, he encouraged fellow Jews to join the British Africa Corps. In 1942, he was the main instigator behind a resolution of the American Zionist Organization that declared the founding of a Jewish state in Palestine to be the paramount objective of Zionism.

Following the war, backed by Jewish Agency funds, Ben-Gurion, in his role of Histadrut chief, began purchasing arms in Europe. His appointment as head of the World Zionist Organization's defense department in December 1946 enabled him to bring various Jewish armed organizations in Palestine under a single command. By the time the UN adopted the partition plan in November 1947, the Jewish community in Palestine, called the Yishuv, had a large professional army, backed by 79,000 reserves, armed police, and home guards. By the following spring, at Ben-Gurion's behest, the Jewish Agency had transferred its executive powers to the people's administrative committee of the Yishuv assembly's national council. This committee of 13, headed by Ben-Gurion, and functioning as the provisional government, declared the establishment of the State of Israel on 14 May 1948 in Tel Aviv.

Twelve days later, it established the Israel Defense Forces (IDF) consisting of 60,000 troops, with Ben-Gurion as the defense minister. The IDF performed well in the First Arab-Israeli War, known as the War of Independence among Israelis.

Ben-Gurion welcomed the Tripartite (Anglo-American-French) Declaration of May 1950, which opposed any attempt to change the armistice boundaries of Israel set in January 1949, and promised to supply arms to Arabs and Israelis only to the extent that such supplies did not create "imbalance." In the Second Knesset, Mapai won 45 seats. Having played a leading role in shaping the basic outline of Israeli's internal and external policies, Ben-Gurion resigned as prime minister in December 1953, and retired to his kibbutz (commune) in the Negev Desert.

But his retirement was brief. He was appointed defense minister in early 1955. By the autumn of 1956, he involved Israel in invading and occupying the Sinai Peninsula in collusion with Great Britain and France in the Suez War. Pressured by the U.S., the Soviet Union, and the United Nations, he withdrew Israeli troops from the Sinai in March 1957.

In this conflict, Egypt lost 1,650 lives, Israel 190, Great Britain 16, and France 10.

Ben-Gurion headed the coalition government formed after the August 1961 election, but found that he lacked the kind of authority he had exercised before. He resigned from the government in 1963, and then began campaigning against his successor, Levi Eshkol (1895-1969). He formed his own group, Rafi (Hebrew acronym for Israel Workers List), in 1965.

The Eshkol, Meir, and Rabin Governments

Levi Eshkol withstood the challenge posed by Ben-Gurion's group, which won only 10 seats (versus Mapai's 45) at the general election later that year, and led the governing coalition. On the eve of the 1967 Arab-Israeli war, Eshkol came under increased public pressure to broaden his administration. He set up a government of national unity by including the right-wing Likud in his cabinet. He gave up the defense ministry in favor of Moshe Dayan.

Born in Palestine, Moshe Dayan became an active Zionist in his youth. In 1941, he led a British reconnaissance unit into Vichy-controlled Syria. He was wounded and lost his left eye. During and after the First Arab-Israeli War, he became a protégé of Premier Ben Gurion, who was also defense minister. In 1953, he was promoted to chief of staff. His military leadership reached its apogee during the Suez War when Israel mounted its lightning Sinai campaign. After retiring from the military in 1958, he turned into a Mapai politician and was elected to parliament.

During the build-up to the June 1967 war, Israel told its American ally that it would go to war if one or more of the following events occurred: departure of the United Nations Emergency Force from Egypt, blockade of the Tiran Straits by Egypt or Jordan, signing of a Jordanian-Egyptian defense pact, and dispatch of Iraqi troops to Jordan. By the end of May, all but one of these eventualities had come to pass. The Israeli military under Moshe Dayan was ready to strike.

Early on 5 June, Israel mounted preemptive air and ground assaults on Egypt, Jordan, and Syria. It captured the Gaza and Sinai from Egypt, the West Bank from Jordan, and the Golan Heights from Syria. In the naval battles, the Israelis captured Sharm al Shaikh, thus ending the blockade of the Tiran Straits. By 10 June, the war was over and Dayan's prestige rose sharply.

The war cost 14,200 Arab lives and 778 Israeli lives. Of the Arab casualties, 11,000 were Egyptians, many of whom died of thirst in the Sinai Peninsula, 2,000 were Jordanians, and 700 were Syrians.

Following the sudden death of Eshkol in February 1969, Golda Meir (1898–1978) was elected head of the ruling Labour Party (formed in 1968 by the amalgamation of Mapai with smaller left-of-center groups) to stave off a power struggle between Moshe Dayan and Yigal Allon. Born in Kiev, Ukraine, she had grown up in Milwaukee in the U.S. After marriage to Morris Meyerson, she and her husband migrated to Palestine in 1921. She became the first head of the Israeli legation in Moscow in June 1948. She served briefly before getting elected to the Constituent Assembly/Knesset in early 1949. She became foreign minister in 1956 and held that job for 10 years.

As premier, Meir followed hardline policies in regional affairs. She spurned the chance of reaching accommodation with Egyptian President Anwar Sadat even after he had shown his antipathy toward Moscow by summarily expelling thousands of Soviet military personnel in mid-1972. She thus left him and Syrian President Hafiz Assad no option but to open hostilities to recover their lands lost in 1967. Both she and her defense minister, Dayan, ignored intelligence reports that Cairo and Damascus were preparing for war.

The surprise Egyptian-Syrian attack on the Israeli-occupied Arab territories on 6 October 1973, Yom Kippur, the Jewish Day of Atonement, shattered the invincible image of Israel and Dayan. Although Dayan recovered

The Women's Section, the Wailing Wall, Jerusalem.

from the initial shock, and the Israeli military performed well later, the label of failure stuck to him. Meir provided strong leadership, including purportedly ordering the mounting of the entire stock of 23 atomic bombs on specially adapted bombers.

In terms of casualties and loss of military hardware, the October 1973 Arab-Israeli War was the bloodiest. The U.S. and the Soviet Union were involved in urgently supplying arms to their respective proxies during the conflict. Washington airlifted 20,000 tons of weapons to Israel, plus 40 Phantom bombers, 48 A4 Skyhawk ground attack jets, and 12 C-130 transporters. Moscow's arms shipments by air to Egypt and Syria amounted to 15,000 tons. Nine Arab states dispatched 50,000 troops and air units to Egypt and Syria.

The war claimed a total of 15,052 lives: 9,000 Egyptians, 3,500 Syrians, and 2,552 Israelis.

Despite its breach of the UN-mediated truce on 21 October 1973 to regain lost territory, Israel had failed to recapture the lost Egyptian territory. Cairo managed to hold on to the Suez Canal and the strip along its eastern bank that it had gained during the early phase of the war. Most Israelis attributed their failures in the war to Dayan. Resisting popular pressure, Dayan refused to resign as defense minister, even though Prime Minister Meir wanted him to. The only way she could bring this about was to offer the resignation of the whole cabinet, including herself, which she did in April 1974.

Following Meir's resignation, Yitzhak Rabin challenged Shimon Peres for the leadership of the ruling Labour party. He won by 298 to 254 votes. Born into a middle class Jewish family in Jerusalem, Rabin graduated from an agricultural college in 1940. During World War II, he participated in the Allied campaign in 1941 in Syria, then under a pro-Nazi French government. In the 1948–1949 Arab-Israeli War, he commanded a brigade that saw combat on the Jerusalem and Negev fronts. He became chief of staff in 1964. Under his command, the Israeli armed forces performed brilliantly in the June 1967 war. After serving as ambassador in Washington from

1968 to 1973, he returned home, and was elected a Labour member of parliament in the December 1973 election. He was appointed minister of labor in the cabinet formed by Golda Meir in March 1974.

Rabin performed poorly as prime minister. His party became increasingly divided on the issue of colonizing the occupied Arab territories. Should there be official colonization or not? Also, a series of financial scandals involving Labour leaders surfaced. In March 1977, it was revealed that during his ambassadorship in the U.S. Rabin's wife, Leah, maintained an active bank account in Washington, an illegal act. The next month he resigned as the Labour leader. Shimon Peres became his successor.

The Begin Government

Peres lost the general election in May 1977 to Likud, led by Menachem Begin (1913-1992), largely because of the defection of the Jews from the Arab countries, called Mizrachi, a geographical term, or Sephardim, a sectarian label. The dominance of the Ashkenazi or European Jews, a feature of Israel at its inception, lessened as large numbers of Jews arrived from the Middle East and North Africa in the 1950s. Raised in Arab countries, and speaking Arabic, these Mizachi Jews suffered discrimination in a country that had been colonized and established by European Jews. Initially, they had no choice but to attach themselves to the ruling Mapai (later Labour) Party in order to survive in a new land. But as years went by and they gained confidence, they started to protest. Due to a high birth rate, they became a majority in Israel in the mid-1960s. With right-wing groups slowly but surely gaining ground, more and more of the Mizrachi Jews began to drift away from Labour. The October 1973 war dented the image of Israel and its Labour leadership. However, the December 1973 election was too near the event to cause large-scale defection from Labour. Yet the trend was definitely against Labour, and the traditional left-of-center governing party lost power in the next general election in 1977 to the right-wing Likud Party.

For Begin, who had been shunned by the Labour establishment for many years, becoming prime minister was quite an achievement. Born in Brest-Litovsk (then in Poland, later in Russia), Begin obtained a law degree at the University of Warsaw, where he was an active Zionist. On the eve of the Nazi invasion of Poland in 1939, Begin fled to Vilnius, Lithuania, then under Soviet occupation. In 1940, he was sentenced to eight years' hard labor in a Siberian camp. But after the Soviet Union joined World War II in mid-1941 on the Allied side, he was released and drafted into the Free Polish army. He arrived in Palestine in 1942 as a soldier of that force. After being demobilized in 1943, he became commander of the underground Irgun Zvai Leumi (National Military Organization), popularly called Irgun. It declared an armed struggle against the British mandate in January 1944. Irgun's terroristic actions led the British to declare an award of £10,000 ($40,000) for Begin's arrest. In July 1946, the Irgun bombed the British government offices in the King David Hotel in Jerusalem, killing 91 British, Arab, and Jewish officials and staff.

Begin was one of the chief planners of the attack on 10 April 1948 on the Arab village of Deir Yassin near Jerusalem, which resulted in the massacre of 254 men, women, and children—an event that caused the intended massive exodus of Arabs from Palestine. Led by Begin, Irgun ranks participated in the First Arab-Israeli War as a separate entity. This continued until late June when Ben Gurion, clashing with Begin on the question of delivery of arms and volunteers to Irgun from a freighter anchored off Tel Aviv, ordered his forces to destroy the ship. In September, Begin disbanded Irgun. However, former Irgun members and right-wing Zionists soon re-emerged as the Herut Party led by Begin.

In 1949, Begin was elected to the Knesset, and maintained his membership until 1984. In the first five general elections, his party won about 12 percent of the vote, emerging as the largest opposition faction in the parliament. In 1965, at his behest, Herut joined the Liberal party to form the Gahal Party, which won 21 percent of the seats in that year's general election. On the eve of the June 1967 Arab-Israeli War, Begin joined the national unity government headed by Eshkol. He stayed in the cabinet until July 1970 when, protesting against the majority decision to accept an American peace plan that envisaged Israel's withdrawal from the Sinai, he resigned and resumed his opposition role. In 1973, when the Likud bloc, containing all secular right-wing factions, was formed, Begin was elected its leader.

Begin's premiership lasted six years. He signed the Camp David Accords with Egyptian President Anwar Sadat in September 1978, which in turn led to the conclusion of a peace treaty between Israel and Egypt. He and Sadat shared the Nobel Peace Prize.

Begin invaded and occupied Lebanon twice—in March 1978 and June 1982. The first occupation, limited to southern Lebanon, ended shortly. But the second invasion, when the Israelis advanced to Beirut and began dictating the politics of Lebanon, proved controversial in Israel. The growing public criticism, fueled by the rising Israeli death toll in Lebanon, combined with inflation at 400 percent a year to make Begin an unpopular leader. He resigned as prime minister in August 1983 and was followed by Yitzhak Shamir.

The Shamir and Peres Governments

Born Yitzhak Yzernitzky in a religious family in Poland, Shamir moved to Palestine in 1935, and two yeas later joined Irgun Zvai Leumi. When Irgun split in 1940, with Avraham Stern forming Lehi, Shamir opted for the new group. Following Stern's assassination in 1942, he became one of the three commanders of Lehi in charge of organization and operations, which included the assassination in 1944 of Lord Moyne, the British resident minister in the Middle East. Arrested by the British in 1946, Shamir was dispatched to a detention camp in Eritrea, East Africa. He escaped after four months, and found his way to Paris, where he lived until the founding of Israel in May 1948. After his arrival in Israel, Shamir became active with the political wing of Lehi, the Fighters Party. He joined the Israeli intelligence agency, Mossad, in 1955, and served in various senior positions until 1965. After running a mattress factory for five years, he re-entered politics by joining the Herut Party. Three years later, he became chairman of the Herut executive; in the December 1973 election, he won a seat in the Knesset. He served as speaker from 1977 to 1980, and then as foreign minister.

After the stalemated election of 1984, Shamir reached a rotation accord with Labour leader Peres in a national unity government. He served as deputy premier and foreign minister until 1986 and then became the prime minister. During Peres's premiership, Israeli troops carried out the final withdrawal from Lebanon in June 1985, giving control of the strip of Lebanon along the Israeli border to the Israeli-run South Lebanon Army. The situation in the occupied West Bank and Gaza deteriorated, and in late 1987 the Palestinians began the *intifada*.

Following the 1988 elections, Shamir continued as premier leading a national unity coalition with Labour. In March 1990, disagreeing with Shamir's policy on pursuing peace with Arab neighbors, Labour withdrew from the national unity administration in an unsuccessful bid to bring down the Likud government. Likud co-opted ultra-nationalist groups into the government and finished its term two years later. Unfettered by Labour's presence in the cabinet, the Shamir government accelerated Jewish colonization of the West Bank. During the Gulf War, two Israeli cities were hit by long-range Iraqi ground-to-ground missiles, causing the deaths of 12 Israelis. Washington reckoned that if Israel hit back and became directly involved in the conflict with Baghdad, the Arab and Muslim members of the anti-Iraq coalition would break away because they could not possibly be part of a military alliance that included Israel. The U.S. therefore urged Israel to stay its hand. It did, and was generously rewarded by the U.S. and Germany, with grants totaling about $1.2 billion.

In October 1991, Shamir participated in the Middle East peace conference in Madrid while insisting on expanding Jewish settlements in the occupied Arab territories. The bilateral talks between Israel and its Arab neighbors made no progress mainly because, as Shamir revealed after his defeat in the June 1992 election, his government had planned on dragging them out for 10 years.

Rabin and the Peace Process

The installation of a Labour government led by Yitzhak Rabin had little impact on the Palestinian *intifada*. The uprising, and the growing strength of Hamas at the expense of the secular PLO, led the Rabin government to open secret talks with the PLO in Norway. The subsequent Israeli-PLO Accord of September 1993 paved the way for the formation of the Palestinian Authority in the Gaza Strip and the West Bank town of Jericho as a first step towards autonomy for the occupied Palestinian territories.

Opinion polls showed nearly two-thirds of Israelis supporting the Israeli-PLO Accord. But Likud and other right-wing groups bitterly opposed the agreement. They argued that the West Bank was part of the land promised to Jews by God in his covenant to Abraham, and there was no question of Israel foregoing its sovereignty over it. But, recognizing that Arab Palestinians now lived there, they were prepared to concede municipal powers to them as people while retaining sovereignty over land and water. This was the position Menachem Begin had taken in 1978–1979 in his talks with Anwar Sadat. Benjamin Netanyahu, elected leader of Likud in 1993, pledged to scrap the Israeli-PLO Accord if returned to power. He had the enthusiastic support of the Jewish settlers in the West Bank and the Gaza Strip. Their vow to expand their settlements raised tensions in the occupied territories. Sporadic violence involving Jewish colonizers and Palestinians continued.

On 25 February 1994, Dr. Baruch Goldstein, a U.S.-born resident of the Kiryat Arab settlement, adjacent to Hebron, shot dead 29 Palestinians at prayer during the Muslim holy month of Ramadan in the Ibrahimi Mosque, the Mosque of Abraham. Called the Tomb of the Patriarchs by Jews, the mosque stands on the burial sites of Abraham and Sarah, Isaac and Rebecca, and Jacob and Leah. (These prophets and their wives are revered by both Jews and Muslims.) The killings shocked not only Palestinians but also the Israeli government. It immediately banned the Kach Hai, the extremist Jewish group to which Goldstein belonged. The PLO suspended talks on implementing the Israeli-PLO Accord. Hamas and the Islamic Jihad threatened to mount retaliatory attacks on Israeli targets. After some weeks, the PLO resumed negotiations, which culminated in an agreement in May.

Before the end of 1994, members of the armed wings of Hamas and the Islamic Jihad carried out four suicide bombings in Israel and one in the Gaza Strip, killing themselves and 38 Israelis. These terroristic actions by the Palestinians reduced popular support for the peace process in Israel. The Israeli government pressured the Palestinian Authority to curb the activities of Hamas and the Islamic Jihad in the Gaza Strip. The Authority did so by arresting scores of Hamas and Islamic Jihad members. There was increasing cooperation between the Israeli and Palestinian authorities on countering terrorism. As a result, after a double suicide bombing by Islamic Jihad activists near an Israeli seaside resort in January 1995, no major attack occurred in Israel for six months.

But when Israel and the PLO failed to meet the 1 July 1995 deadline to reach an agreement on the redeployment of Israeli troops in the West Bank as a prelude to holding elections to the Palestinian Council, tensions rose again. A Palestinian suicide bomber blew himself up in a Tel Aviv suburb in late July, killing five Israelis.

Opinion polls showed Israelis evenly divided between those who wanted to continue the peace talks and those who wanted to stop. Those who backed the negotiations argued that if they ceased PLO supporters would join the rejectionists and escalate the violence. The best way to reduce terrorist activities was by reducing the popular base on which such activities thrived. Opponents of the talks questioned the authority of the Rabin administration which, they said, enjoyed only minority support among Jewish voters. The hard core among them, the Jewish settlers in the West Bank, began a civil disobedience movement to bring down the Labour-led government.

The Rabin administration emphasized the diplomatic and other gains Israel had made as a result of the 1993 Israeli-PLO Accord. The number of countries recognizing Israel had risen to 150-plus. Two Arab countries, Morocco and Tunisia, had opened liaison offices in Tel Aviv. Most importantly, Jordan had concluded a peace treaty with Israel. This meant that two of the four Arab states sharing borders with Israel had made peace with it.

On the other hand, the Jewish state's negotiations with Syria were stalled. Syrian President Assad wanted a total Israeli withdrawal from the Golan Heights, just as Egyptian President Sadat had earlier received total Israeli evacuation of the Sinai Peninsula for total peace. Rabin seemed to have agreed to this principle, but the major sticking point was an early warning system for Israel. When Rabin proposed installing an early warning facility on the Golan Heights after Israeli evacuation, Assad demanded a similar system for Syria in northern Israel. This was unacceptable to Rabin, and even the active involvement of the U.S. in these talks failed to break the deadlock. The chances of a breakthrough improved only slightly when, following Yitzhak Rabin's assassination in November 1995, Peres became the prime minister. Peres was aware that if he were seen to be rushing to make peace with Assad, he would be vulnerable to his opponents' accusation that he was "soft" on the security of Israel. This would hurt the prospects of his Labour Party at the next parliamentary election to be held by October 1996. (The polling date was later advanced to May 1996.)

Since the Golan Heights were only 0.7 percent of Syria, Assad was not overly concerned. He was aware that the longer these talks dragged on the nearer he would be to the negotiations between Israel and the PLO on the future of Jerusalem, scheduled to start no later than May 1996. Since Jerusalem was sacred to all Muslim Palestinians, Assad counted on affecting these negotiations and raising his stature in the rest of the Arab world.

As it was, in the Israeli-Jordanian peace treaty, Israel had accepted the Hashemite dynasty as the guardians of the Haram al Sharif, the site of the third holiest shrine of Islam, consisting of the al Aqsa Mosque and the Dome of the Rock.

CHAPTER 22

Jordan

The Hashemite Kingdom of Jordan, also known as the East Bank (of the Jordan River), is a southern part of historical Greater/Natural Syria. It came into being as Transjordan in 1922 following a compromise offered to the al Hashem dynasty by Great Britain after the collapse of the Ottoman Empire in 1918. Besides it geographical position, the Transjordan was distinguished from the territory west of the Jordan River by being exempted from Great Britain's 1917 Balfour Declaration on the creation of a Jewish homeland.

PROFILE

Area & Population: Shaped roughly as a pistol, Jordan measures 34,442 square miles. Its estimated population in 1992 was 3,983,000, including about 250,000 Palestinian refugees in camps.

Cities: With a population of 1,010,000, Amman, the capital, is also the largest city. Next in size are Zarqa 345,000, Irbid 178,000, Ruseifa 79,000, and Salt 51,000.

Constitution: The present constitution of Jordan, approved by King Talal ibn Abdullah al Hashemi (1951–1952), was promulgated in 1952. It prescribes monarchical government with a parliament. Executive power rests with the king who exercises it through his ministers. He appoints, dismisses, or accepts the resignation of the prime minister, upon whose recommendation the king appoints, dismisses, or accepts the resignation of other ministers. The king also appoints the members and speaker of the 20-member Senate, the upper house of the parliament, which is called the National Assembly. The cabinet manages all state affairs. If the parliament's lower chamber, the popularly elected 80-member House of Representatives with a four-year tenure, withdraws its confidence from the cabinet or any minister, the latter must resign. The king is the supreme commander of the military.

Economy: At the national Gross Domestic Product of $4.71 billion, the per capital GDP was $1,182.

Education: Literacy in the population aged 15 and above (1990) was 80.1 percent (female 70.3 percent, male 89.3 percent).

Ethnic Composition: Arabs 99 percent, of which more than half are of Palestinian origin; others 1 percent.

Geography: Jordan consists of three geographical regions: the desert, the highlands, and two large valleys. The Transjordanian plateau, running north to south, with a peak of 5,000 feet, slopes eastwards into the desert uplands of Syria, Iraq, and Saudi Arabia. Much of the Jordan Valley lies below sea level between Lake Tiberias and the Dead Sea. The sandy Araba Valley runs southwards from the Dead Sea to the Gulf of Aqaba.

Governmental System: Jordan is a monarchy, with the king as head of state and chief executive.

Military: Jordan's total armed forces number 100,600 actives and 35,000 reserves. Military expenditure as a percent of GDP is 10.9 percent.

Mineral Resources: Jordan's mineral resources include natural gas, phosphate rock, and potash. The extraction rate of gas in 1993 was 1.3 million cubic meters/day.

Religious Composition: Muslim 93 percent, Christian 5 percent, and others 2 percent.

HISTORY SINCE 1916

During the governorship of his father, Hussein ibn Ali al Hashem, in Hijaz, Abdullah ibn Hussein al Hashem represented Mecca in the Ottoman parliament from 1912 to 1914. Two years later, he participated in the Arab revolt his father led against the Ottomans. The collapse of the Ottoman Empire in 1918 strengthened the hands of Hussein ibn Ali and his sons. However, the decision of the Syrian National Congress in Damascus in March 1920 to crown Faisal ibn Hussein, a younger brother of Abdullah, as king of Greater Syria was rejected by the Supreme Council of the League of Nations at the behest of Great Britain and France. In July, French troops captured Damascus and put Faisal to flight. Abdullah assembled an army to expel the French from Syria. He entered the British-mandated territory east of the Jordan River, called Transjordan, in January 1921 and set up a government in Amman two months later. In July, London offered to recognize Abdullah's rule in Transjordan if he accepted the British mandate over it and Palestine, as decreed by the League of Nations, and renounce his plant to capture Syria. Abdullah consented provided the clauses of the mandate about the founding of a national home for the Jews were not applied to the Emirate of Transjordan. This was agreed by Great Britain, and endorsed by the League of Nations.

In April 1923, Great Britain announced that it would recognize Transjordan as an autonomous emirate under Emir Abdullah's rule if a constitutional regime were established there and a preferential treaty with London signed. Abdullah consented, and declared Transjordan "independent." But it was not until 1928 that he proclaimed a constitution, which stipulated that legal and administrative powers rested with the ruler through a legislative council. The resulting nominated council was powerless until 1939, when the council was transformed into a cabinet and given some authority. Tied to London and its subsidy, Abdullah remained loyal to Great Britain.

When London recognized the independence of Transjordan in May 1946, Abdullah changed its name to the Hashemite Kingdom of Jordan, and called himself king. This necessitated revising the 1923 Anglo-Transjordanian Treaty, which was done in March 1948. To extend his realm across the Jordan River to Palestine, then being colonized by Zionists, Abdullah reached a clandestine, unwritten understanding with Zionist leaders. He would not oppose the partition of Palestine and the emergence of a Jewish state if they let him take over the Arab part of Pal-

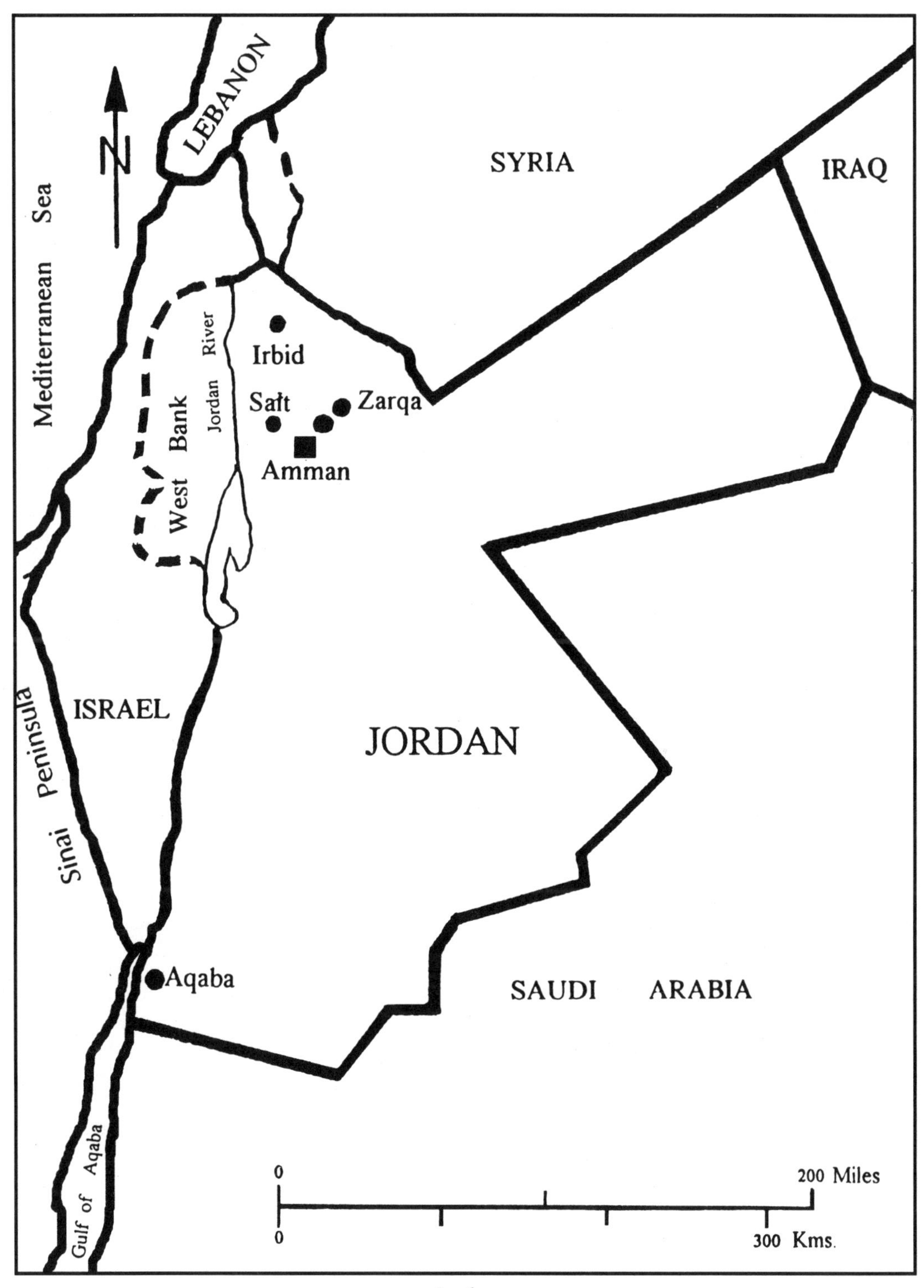
LEBANON
SYRIA
IRAQ
Mediterranean Sea
N
Irbid
Jordan River
West Bank
Salt
Zarqa
Amman
ISRAEL
JORDAN
Sinai Peninsula
Aqaba
SAUDI ARABIA
Gulf of Aqaba
0
200 Miles
0
300 Kms.

Jordan

estine. When the secret leaked, other members of the Arab League resolved to foil the plan. In his clandestine meetings with Golda Meir, a Zionist leader, in November 1947 and early May 1948, Abdullah reportedly explained his inability to stick to his agreement. The change also coincided with London's advice to him to gain control of the Arab segment of Palestine in cooperation with other Arab countries rather than through a deal with the Zionist leaders.

After the Arab League's decision to dispatch troops to capture Palestine on the eve of the British departure on 14 May 1948, Abdullah become commander-in-chief of the forces from Egypt, Iraq, Jordan, Lebanon, and Syria. His own Arab Legion captured substantial parts of Arab Palestine but did not attack the zones allocated to the Jews in the United Nations partition plan of November 1947. In Jerusalem, earmarked for international control, the Legion seized the eastern part.

In December 1948, some 2,000 Arab Palestinian delegates meeting in Jericho acclaimed Abdullah as "King of all Palestine," which meant most of what could be saved from the Israelis and now called the West Bank. But this arrangement was made without prejudice to the final, internationally agreed settlement of the Palestinian problem.

Formal annexation followed in April 1949, and changed the character of Abdullah's realm. West Bankers were given full Jordanian citizenship, and equal parliamentary representation with East Bankers (30 each). After a general election in early 1950, the new parliament declared the East and West Banks united in the Hashemite Kingdom of Jordan.

The kingdom now contained a large body of politicized Palestinians who felt betrayed. Most of them considered Abdullah a traitor, a lackey of the British, who had made underhand deals with the Zionists at the expense of Arab interests. In July 1951, a young Palestinian, named Shukri Ashu, assassinated Abdullah as he entered al Aqsa mosque in East Jerusalem for Friday prayers.

The Rule of King Hussein

His son Talal ibn Abdullah ascended the throne. But, because of mental illness, he abdicated in August 1952 in favor of his son, Hussein ibn Talal (1952–). Before abdication, however, King Talal promulgated a constitution that provided for a multi-party, two-chamber parliament consisting of a nominated Senate and an elected House of Representatives. Power was exercised by a regency council until May 1953, when Hussein turned 18.

Because Hussein rigged the general election held in the autumn of 1954, the opposition demonstrated against electoral malpractices. Bowing to popular pressure, the king ordered new elections. Held in 1956, these were free and fair. A national-leftist government under Suleiman Nabulsi (1956–1957) assumed office. It abrogated the 1948 treaty with Great Britain that entitled the British to maintain military bases in Jordan. King Hussein acquiesced. But after crushing an incipient coup by his newly appointed chief of staff in April 1957, he dismissed the Nabulsi government and dissolved parliament and political parties. The U.S. backed his actions and provided him with aid under the Eisenhower doctrine. The foreign policy doctrine of President Dwight Eisenhower, adopted by the U.S. Congress in March 1957, pledged military and economic aid on request to any Middle Eastern country that felt threatened by any nation "controlled by international communism." The last phrase included Egypt, then ruled by President Abdul Gamal Nasser, who was seen by the U.S. as being under Soviet control.

King Hussein felt threatened when his cousin Faisal II was deposed and assassinated by the republican Free Officers in Iraq in July 1958. Despite several attempts, inspired by Egypt or Syria, to overthrow him, Hussein survived, partly because he allowed American intelligence agencies to operate freely in his kingdom in return for a financial retainer.

He held new elections in July 1963 and April 1967 without lifting the ban on political parties. In the charged atmosphere of June 1967, he joined the Egyptian-Syrian defense pact. The subsequent loss of the West Bank resulted in 250,000 Palestinian refugees pouring into Jordan. A rise in the number of refugees from the West Bank, and growing militancy among the Palestinians already in Jordan, led to fighting between Palestinian commandos and the Jordanian army in September 1970, in which the latter won. About 4,000 Palestinians were killed. A major offensive by the Jordanian army in July 1971 pushed the last of the Palestinian commandos out of the kingdom.

During the October 1973 Arab-Israeli war, Hussein rejected calls by Egypt, Syria, and Saudi Arabia to open a third front against Israel, and accepted Washington's advice to stay out of the conflict. With enhanced U.S. military and diplomatic backing, Hussein felt confident enough to resume face-to-face talks with Israeli leaders, which had begun before the 1967 war. He continued to press for Israel's evacuation of the West Bank until a summit conference of the Arab League in late October 1974 recognized the Palestine Liberation Organization (PLO) as the sole and legitimate representative of the Palestinian people, and supported the right of the Palestinian people to establish an independent national authority on any liberated territory of Palestine. Hussein reluctantly accepted the Arab League resolution.

Dismissing West Bank members of the parliament who had been elected in April 1967, he suspended the chamber in early 1975. He advocated a comprehensive peace settlement through a UN-sponsored conference. He refused to join the peace process initiated by the Camp David Accords between Egypt and Israel in September 1978. He now strengthened Jordan's ties with the Soviet Union, which he had first visited in 1967. Hussein concluded an arms deal with Moscow in 1981 and backed the call of Soviet leader Leonid Brezhnev for an international conference on the Middle East crisis.

King Hussein sided with Iraq in the Iran-Iraq War of the 1980s, thus accelerating Jordan's economic integration with Iraq. Emulating Iraqi President Saddam Hussein's example of giving his regime a parliamentary veneer, the Jordanian monarch revived the suspended House of Representatives in January 1984. A year later he concluded an agreement with PLO chairman Yasser Arafat on a future confederation of a Palestinian state and Jordan, and a joint approach to a Middle East peace settlement. But this deal was rejected by the Palestine National Council (PNC) in April 1987. Hussein responded by severing all Jordan's legal and administrative links with the West Bank in July 1988. He also dissolved the House of Representatives.

A free and fair election in November 1989 to the 80-seat lower house of parliament, now representing only the East Bank, resulted in the Islamic Action Front (IAF) and independent Islamists winning a total of 32 seats. During the Kuwait crisis and the Gulf War, the Islamic bloc of deputies favored Saddam Hussein, especially after the Iraqi leader had linked Iraq's withdrawal from Kuwait with Israel's evacuation of the occupied Arab territories.

King Hussein worked hard to find an Arab solution for the Kuwait crisis, but failed. He blamed the U.S., Egypt, and Saudi Arabia for his failure and the subsequent escalation of the crisis into a full-scale war. Reflecting public opinion at home, Hussein combined his critical stance towards Washington with a pro-Baghdad tilt that cost him dearly in Western capitals.

After the end of the 1991 Gulf War, he tried to repair the damage by distancing himself from Saddam Hussein. He participated in the talks that preceded the holding of the Middle East peace conference in Madrid in October 1991, and agreed to a joint Jordanian-Palestinian delegation, as proposed by Israel. However, in August 1993, when the secret Israeli-PLO Accord became public, Hussein denounced it. It contradicted the agreed policy of the four Arab parties to pursue a joint strategy in their bilateral talks with Israel. But after a meeting with Arafat, he moderated his stance.

Following the legalization of political parties in September 1992, nine parties were licensed. The first proper multi-party election since October 1956 was held in November 1993. A majority of seats went to independents, including six pro-Islamists. The IAF, winning 16 seats, was the only party to win more than one seat. However, King Hussein was satisfied to see the total Islamist strength decline by 10 to 22, and said so.

When he found the Israeli-PLO Accord actually being implemented, the Jordanian monarch resumed bilateral talks with Israel without consulting Syria and Lebanon as he had done so far. In July 1994, he concluded an agreement with Israeli Premier Yitzhak Rabin in Washington ending the state of belligerency between their countries. This agreement led to the signing of a peace treaty between Israel and Jordan on 26 October 1994 at a site along their common border in the Araba Valley. Jordan thus followed the example of Egypt.

This treaty encountered popular and parliamentary opposition. In the House of Representatives about a third of the deputies voted against it. The monarch allowed a token opposition to be expressed in the street. By so doing, he pacified those people at home and abroad who wanted to see democracy progress in Jordan. This was the last in a long list of maneuvers that King Hussein had performed since becoming the monarch of Jordan in 1952. Despite numerous attempts on his life, and cataclysmic changes in the Middle East over four event-filled decades, he has survived. Indeed, he has emerged as the longest serving ruler in the most volatile region of the world.

GLOSSARY

Alawi: The word means "follower of Ali," and is also spelled Alavi (mainly in Turkey, where the alphabet lacks "w"). Alawis are an offshoot of Shias, sharing their belief that Iman Ali, cousin and son-in-law of Muhammad, was the Prophet's legitimate heir but was deprived of his status by the first three caliphs. Alawis portray Ali as a bearer of divine essence and hold him in higher esteem than any of the earlier prophets mentioned in the Koran. *See also* Shia, Sunni.

Arab Cooperation Council (ACC) (1989–1990): This regional Arab organization consisted of Egypt, Iraq, Jordan, and North Yemen. The ACC was formed in February 1989 to cooperate on economic and non-military matters. The Iraqi invasion of Kuwait in August 1990 led to its disintegration as Egypt allied with the U.S. to forge an anti-Iraq alliance.

Arab League: This collective of independent Arab states is officially titled the League of Arab States. It was formed in March 1945 by Egypt, Iraq, Lebanon, North Yemen, Saudi Arabia, Syria, and Transjordan (later Jordan) in Cairo. In March 1990 its other members (with year of affiliation) were Libya (1953), Sudan (1956), Morocco (1958), Tunisia (1958) Kuwait (1961), Algeria (1962), South Yemen (1967), Bahrain (1971), Oman (1971), Qatar (1971), the United Arab Emirates (1971), Mauritania (1973), Somalia (1974), the Palestine Liberation Organization (1974), and Djbouti (1977). In May 1990, its membership declined by one when North and South Yemen were unified into the Republic of Yemen.

Armenian Catholic: Affiliated to the Roman Catholic church, but performing an Eastern rite, the Armenian Catholic Church was established in 1742 by Abraham Artzivian, the Armenian bishop of Aleppo.

Armenian Orthodox: The Armenian Orthodox Church split from the Eastern Orthodox Church in the fourth century A.D., and in 506 A.D. adopted the Monophysite doctrine, which holds that Christ had only one divine nature, not two natures, human and divine, united in one person.

Ashkenazim: Askenazim is the plural of Ashkenaz, a derivative of Ashk'naz, meaning Germany. From the ninth century onward the term was applied to German Jews and their descendants, including those who had left German lands. Nowadays the term means Jews of European origin, living outside Asia and Africa. *See also* Sephardim.

Druze: Druzes are members of a movement within Islam called al Daraziyya, derived from Muhammad al Darazi (d. 1019), who became an adviser to Fatimid Caliph atl Hakim (996-1021) in Cairo in 1017. Darazi regarded the inner truth and its representative superior to the outer truth and its representative. He attributed to al Hakim, who later disappeared, supernatural powers. Druzes do not feel bound by two of the five leading injunctions of Islam: fasting during the holy month of Ramadan and making a pilgrimage to Mecca.

Eisenhower Doctrine: In January 1957, U.S. President Dwight Eisenhower unveiled a strategy to counter Soviet influence in the Middle East. It included a provision for safeguarding the independence and territorial integrity of individual countries requesting American aid against overt aggression from any nation "controlled by international communism." This phrase included Egypt under president Gamal Abdual Nasser, who was seen by the U.S. as under Soviet control. In March, the U.S. Congress adopted the Eisenhower doctrine.

European Community (EC): *See* European Union.

European Economic Community (ECC): *See* European Union.

European Union (EU): Founded in 1957 as an economic union called the Common Market by the six West European nations of Belgium, France, Italy, Luxembourg, Netherlands, and West Germany, the group expanded to 12 by 1993, including Denmark, Great Britain, Greece, Ireland, Portugal, and Spain. The Common Market changed its name first to the European Economic Community (EEC), and then to the European Community (EC). In 1993, after planning further economic and political integration, it changed its name to the European Union (EU). In 1995, its membership of 15 included Austria, Finland, and Sweden. Its secretariat is in Brussels, Belgium.

Greek Catholic: In 1724, a section of the Greek Orthodox church was reconciled with the Roman Catholic Church and called itself Greek Catholic. It was allowed to conduct its Byzantine liturgy in Arabic. *See also* Greek Orthodox.

Greek Orthodox: The Greek Orthodox Church is part of the Eastern Orthodox Church. Because Greek colonizers predominated in its congregations in Syria and Egypt, the church came to be known as Greek Orthodox.

Gross Domestic Product (GDP): GDP refers to the total market value of a country's goods and services produced in a year. The figures used in this book have been obtained by dividing the amount in local currency by its exchange value in U.S. dollars. This calculation can be misleading, especially in states that are self-sufficient in food grains. In such countries as Turkey, Lebanon, Syria, Egypt, and Iran, the purchasing power of a U.S. dollar is two to three times higher than in the U.S.

Gulf Cooperation Council (GCC): This regional body consists of Bahrain, Kuwait, Oman, Qatar, Saudi Arabia, and the United Arab Emirates. The GCC was formed in May 1981 in Abu Dhabi. Its primary objectives are to coordinate the internal security policies and practices and the national economies of the member-states. Its secondary objectives are to settle border disputes and coordinate the member-states' purchase of foreign weapons.

Hadith: The Hadith contains the sayings and doings of Prophet Muhammad. Some 2,700 acts and sayings of Prophet Muhammad were collected and published in six canonical works called *Al Hadith*. The first compiler was

Muhammad al Bukhari (d. 870 A.D.). *See also* Sharia.

Imam: The word means "one whose leadership or example is to be followed." An imam is an Islamic religious leader. The word is used as both a noun and a title. The leader of prayers at any mosque is called an imam. Shias use this title for the religious leader at the highest level, such as for Ali, the cousin and son-in-law of Prophet Muhammad.

Islamic Conference Organization (ICO): The ICO is a pan-Islamic institution of intergovernmental cooperation. The ICO was formed in Rabat, Morocco, in September 1969 by the official representatives of 24 Muslim-majority countries. Its aims are to increase social, cultural, and economic cooperation among members; safeguard Islamic holy places; and assist the Palestinian struggle for national rights. Funded largely by Saudi Arabia, the ICO has its secretariat in Jiddah. In 1994, it had 49 members, including the Palestine Liberation Organization.

Ismailis: A Shia Muslim group, the Ismailis are distinguished from other sub-sects—such as Zaidis and Twelvers—by the number of revered figures they regard as Imams. They share the first six Imams with Twelvers, the last one being Jaafar al Sadiq. Then they revere Ismail, the older, militant son of al Sadiq who died before his father. Ismailis are also known as Seveners. *See also* Twelver Shias; Zaidis.

Jihad: Literally, jihad means effort or struggle, which is waged in various forms and degrees, the most extreme being war. Historically, the term has been used for armed struggle by Muslims against unbelievers in their mission to advance Islam or counter danger to it.

Maronite Church: Affiliated to the Roman Catholic Church, the Maronite Church is allowed to practice its own Eastern rites and customs. Its adherents, called Maronites, are the followers of St. Maron/Maro, a Christian hermit who lived in northeast Syria in the late fourth and early fifth centuries.

Marxism: Marxism is a socio-economic ideology named after Karl Marx (1818-1883). It is also known as scientific socialism. Karl Marx and Friedrich Engels outlined its basic assumptions in the *Communist Manifesto* in 1848.

Non-Aligned Movement: More than 50 nations of Asia, Africa, and Latin America met in Bandung, Indonesia, in 1955 on a platform of non-alignment with either the capitalist or socialist bloc, and thus formally established the Non-Aligned Movement (NAM). With the collapse of the Soviet Union in 1991, the two-bloc system disappeared, but the NAM, with a membership of over 100 nations, continues to exist.

Organization for Economic Cooperation and Development (OECD): In 1961, the Organization for Economic Cooperation and Development (OECD) superseded the Organization for European Economic Cooperation (OEEC), formed in 1947 to encourage intra-European cooperation in economic matters. In 1995, its members included Austria, Belgium, Canada, the Czech Republic, Denmark, Finland, France, Germany, Great Britain, Greece, Iceland, Ireland, Italy, Japan, Luxembourg, Mexico, the Netherlands, Norway, Portugal, Spain, Sweden, Switzerland, Turkey, the United States, and Yugoslavia. Its secratariat is in Paris, France.

Organization of Arab Petroleum Exporting Countries (OAPEC): Consisting of Algeria, Iraq, Kuwait, Libya, and Saudi Arabia, the Organization of Arab Petroleum Exporting Countries (OAPEC) was formed in January 1968 in Kuwait City to safeguard the interests of its members. Later, Bahrain, Egypt, Qatar, Syria, and the United Arab Emirates joined. During the October 1973 Arab-Israeli war, its members decided to impose an oil embargo on those countries, including the U.S., which directly aided Israel. This embargo was to continue until Israel had withdrawn from the occupied Arab territories and the Palestinians had won their legitimate rights, but OAPEC lifted the embargo in March 1974 even though neither of its conditions had been met. *See also* Organization of Petroleum Exporting Countries.

Organization of Petroleum Exporting Countries (OPEC): OPEC is an international body that coordinates the oil policies of its members. Consisting of Iran, Iraq, Kuwait, Saudi Arabia, and Venezuela, the Organization of Petroleum Exporting Countries was inaugurated in Geneva in January 1961. Its subsequent members were Qatar (1961); Indonesia and Libya (1962); Abu Dhabi (1967), whose membership was transferred to the United Arab Emirates (1974); Algeria (1969); Nigeria (1971); Ecuador (1973); and Gabon (1975). OPEC made little impact until the October 1973 Arab-Israeli War and the oil embargo imposed by the Organization of Arab Petroleum Exporting Countries (OAPEC). In 1992, Ecuador left OPEC because it failed to get a higher output quota. However, OPEC lacks authority to see that its members adhere to the quotas it decides every three months. *See also* Organization of Arab Petroleum Exporting Countries.

Sephardim: Sephardim is the plural of Sephardi, a derivative of Sepharad, meaning Spain. In the Middle Ages, the term Sephardi was applied to the Jews of Spain. When expelled from Spain in 1492, and then from Portugal, most Sephardi Jews settled along the shores of the Mediterranean. From the sixteenth century onward, differences between Sephardim and Ashkenazim became sharper in synagogue architecture and rites, social customs, and pronunciation of Hebrew. *See also* Ashkenazim.

Shafii: Within Sharia, Islamic Law, there are different legal codes, each named after its founder. Those Sunni Muslims who follow the Shafii Code, named after Muhammad ibn Idris al Shafii (767-820 A.D.), are called Shafiis. Al Shafi greatly influenced the legal-administrative apparatus of the Abbasid Empire (751 A.D.–1251). Shafii is one of the four leading Sunni Codes, the others being Hanafi, Maliki, and Hanbali.

Shaikh: This Arabic word meaning "old man," is a title used for a man of wisdom or power.

Shaikha: This Arabic word meaning "old woman," is a title used for a woman of wisdom or power.

Sharia: The Sharia is the Arabic term for Islamic Law. Consisting of divine revelation in the form of the Koran, and the prophetic practice, Sunna, as recorded in the Hadith, the Sharia governs the individual and social life of the believer. The Koran provides the principles, and the Hadith the details of their application. The Sharia is the basis for judging actions as good or evil. *See also* Hadith; Sunna.

Shia: An Islamic sect. Shia is a derivative of Shiat Ali, meaning partisans of Ali, cousin and son-in-law of Prophet Muhammad. Of the first caliphs—Abu Bakr, Omar, Othman, and Ali—Shias regard only Ali as legitimate. Shias differ from Sunnis in doctrine, ritual, law, theology, and religious organization. Today Shias are a minority, being 12 to 15 percent of the world Muslim population. *See also* Alawi; Sunni; Twelver Shia; Zaidi.

Sufism: Sufism is mystical philosophy in Islam. Subscribing to the general theory of mysticism that direct knowledge of God is attainable through intuition or insight, sufism is based on doctrines and methods derived from the Koran.

Sunna: In pre-Islamic times, the term sunna applied to social practices based on ancestral precedents. After the rise of Islam, early converts took their cue either from the behavior of the Prophet's companions or the residents of Medina, the capital of the Islamic Realm. *See also* Sunni.

Sunni: An Islamic sect. Sunni is a derivative of the Persian term Ahl al Sunna, "People of the Path" [of Prophet Muhammad]. Sunnis regard the first four caliphs—Abu Bakr, Omar, Othman, and Ali—as "Rightly Guided," and belong to one of the four schools of jurisprudence: Hanafi, Maliki, Shafii, or Hanbali.

Sunnis differ from Shias in doctrine, ritual, law, theology, and religious organization. Today Sunnis are more than 85 percent of the world Muslim population. *See also* Shafii; Shia; sunna.

Twelver Shia: The predominant category among Shias, Twelvers or Twelver Shias are so called because they believe in 12 Imams, the last of whom disappeared in 874 A.D. *See also* Alawi, Ismaili, Shia; Zaidi.

Ulema: Ulema is the term used collectively for religious-legal scholars of Islam.

Wahhabism: Wahhabism refers to an Islamic sect following a doctrine developed by Muhammad ibn Abdul Wahhab (1703-1792) within the Hanbali Code.

Waqf: In Islamic law, waqf, the term popularly used for a religious trust or endowment, means to "prevent a thing from becoming the property of a third person."

World Zionist Organization (WZO): In 1960, the Zionist Organization changed its name to the World Zionist Organization. *See also* Zionist Organization.

Zaidi: A Shia Muslim group. Zaidis share the first four Imams of Twelver Shias, the last one being Zain al Abidin, and then follow a different line with Zaid, son of Muhammad ibn al Hanafiya. *See also* Ismailis; Twelver Shia.

Zionism: Zionism refers to a Jewish ideology and movement. The term Zionism, named after Zion, the hill in ancient Jerusalem on which stood the royal palace of King David, was coined by Nathan Birnbaum in 1893. It applied to the Jewish nationalist movement aiming to create a Jewish state or national center in Ottoman Palestine, the historic homeland of Jews.

Zionist Organization: The first Zionist Congress was convened by Theodor Herzl in Basle, Switzerland, in 1897. The Congress established the Zionist Organization, which stated the following: "Zionism strives to create for the Jewish people a home in Palestine secured by public law." In 1951, the Zionist Organization moved its headquarters from London to Jerusalem. Following the adoption of a new constitution in 1960, the Zionist Organization became the World Zionist Organization. *See also* World Zionist Organization.

Zoroastrianism: Zoroastrianism is an ancient religion named after its founder, Zoraster of Zarathustra (c. 628–551 B.C.). It arose in ancient Persia, where society was divided into three castes: priests, warriors, and agriculturists. It became the state religion during the Sassanian period (224-637 A.D.). Recognized as a religious minority in Iran today, some 50,000 Zoroastrians are entitled to elect one parliamentary deputy.

ADDITIONAL READING

Abu-Amr, Ziad. *Islamic Fundamentalism in the West Bank and Gaza.* Bloomington, IN: Indiana University Press, 1994.

Akhavi, Shahrough. *Religion and Politics in Contemporary Iran.* Albany, NY: State University of New York Press, 1980.

Ansari, Hamied. *Egypt: The Stalled Society.* Albany, NY: State University of New York Press, 1986.

Bakhash, Shaul. *Reign of the Ayatollahs: Iran and the Islamic Revolution.* New York: Basic Books, 1985/London: I.B. Tauris, 1985.

Bulloch, John, and Morris, Harvey. *Saddam's War: The Origins of the Kuwait Crisis and the International Response.* Winchester, MA/London: Faber & Faber, 1991.

Chubin, Shahram, and Tripp, Charles. *Iran and Iraq at War.* New York/London: I.B. Tauris, 1988.

Deeb, Maurice. *The Lebanese Civil War.* New York: Praeger, 1980.

Dekmejian, R. Hrair. *Islam in Revolution: Fundamentalism in the Arab World.* Syracuse, NY: Syracuse University Press, 1985.

Dickson, H.R.P. *Kuwait and Her Neighbours.* London: Allen & Unwin, 1956.

Esposito, John L. *Islam and Politics.* Syracuse, NY: Syracuse University Press, 1980.

———. *The Islamic Threat: Myth or Reality?* New York/Oxford: Oxford University Press, 1992.

Eveland, Wilber Crane. *Ropes of Sand: America's Failure in the Middle East.* New York/London: W.W. Norton, 1980.

Fisk, Robert. *Pity the Nation: Lebanon at War.* London: Andre Deutsch, 1990/New York: Oxford University Press, 1991.

Farouk-Sluglett, Marion, and Sluglett, Peter. *Iraq Since 1958: From Revolution to Dictatorship.* New York/London: I.B. Tauris, 1990.

Ghareeb, Edmund. *The Kurdish Question in Iraq.* Syracuse, NY: Syracuse University Press, 1981.

Graz, Leisl. *The Turbulent Gulf.* New York/London: I.B. Tauris, 1990.

Hale, William. *The Political and Economic Development of Turkey.* New York: St. Martin's Press, 1981/London: Croom Helm, 1981.

Harris, George. *Turkey: Coping with Crisis.* Boulder, CO: Westview Press, 1985/London: Croom Helm, 1985.

Heikal, Mohamed. *The Road to Ramadan.* London: Collins, 1975.

———. *Secret Channels: The Inside Story of Arab-Israeli Peace Negotiations.* London: Harper Collins, 1996.

Henderson, Simon. *Instant Empire: Saddam's Ambitions for Iraq*. San Francisco: Mercury House, 1991.

Helms, Christine Moss. *Iraq: Eastern Flank of the Arab World*. Washington, DC: The Brookings Institution, 1984.

Hersh, Seymour M. *The Samson Option: Israel's Nuclear Arsenal and America's Foreign Policy*. New York: Random House, 1991/London: Faber & Faber, 1992.

Hiro, Dilip. *Inside the Middle East*. New York: McGraw-Hill, 1982/London: Routledge & Kegan Paul, 1982.

———. *Iran Under the Ayatollahs*. New York/London: Routledge & Kegan Paul, 1985.

———. *Holy Wars: The Rise of Islamic Fundamentalism*. New York: Routledge, 1989/London: Paladin Books, 1988.

———. *The Longest War: Iran-Iraq Military Conflict*. London: Grafton Books, 1989/New York: Routledge, 1991.

———. *Desert Shield to Desert Storm: The Second Gulf War*. New York: Routledge, 1992/ London: HarperCollins, 1992.

———. *Lebanon, Fire and Embers: A History of the Lebanese Civil War*. New York: St. Martin's Press, 1993/London: Weidenfeld & Nicolson, 1993.

———. *Dictionary of the Middle East*. New York: St. Martin's Press, 1996/London: Macmillan, 1996.

Hirst, David. *The Gun and the Olive Branch*. Winchester, MA/London: Faber & Faber, 1978.

Holden, David, and Johns, Richard. *The House of Saud*. London: Sidgwick & Jackson, 1981.

Hudson, Michael. *Arab Conflict: The Search for Legitimacy*. New Haven, CT/ London: Yale University Press, 1977.

Keddie, Nikki R. *Roots of Revolution: An Interpretive History of Modern Iran*. New Haven, CT/ London: Yale University Press, 1981.

Khadduri, Majid. *Republican Iraq: A Study of Iraqi Politics since the Revolution of 1958*. New York/ Oxford: Oxford University Press, 1969.

———. *Socialist Iraq: A Study in Iraqi Politics since 1968*. Washington, DC: The Middle East Institute, 1978.

Lucas, Noah. *The Modern History of Israel*. London: Weidenfeld & Nicolson, 1975.

Mackey, Sandra. *Lebanon: Death of a Nation*. New York: Congdon & Weed, 1989.

Mansfield, Peter. *The Arabs*. New York/ Harmondsworth, England: Penguin Books, 1988.

Marr, Phebe. *Modern History of Iraq*. Boulder, CO: Westview Press, 1985/London: Longman, 1985.

McDermott, Anthony. *Egypt from Nasser to Mubarak: A Flawed Revolution*. New York/London: Croom Helm, 1988.

Melman, Yossi. *The New Israelis: An Intimate View of a Changing People*. New York: Birch Lane Press, 1992.

Miller, Judith, and Mylorie, Laurie. *Saddam Hussein and Crisis in the Gulf*. New York: Times Books, 1990.

Mortimer, Edward. *Faith and Power: The Politics of Islam*. New York: Holt, Rinehart, 1982/London: Faber & Faber, 1982.

Pappe, Ilan. *The Making of the Arab-Israeli Conflict, 1947-1951*. New York/London: I.B. Tauris, 1992.

Peretz, Don. *The Government and Politics of Israel*. Boulder, CO: Westview Press, 1979.

Petran, Tabitha. *Syria: A Modern History*. London: Ernest Benn, 1978.

Porter, Jadranka. *Under Siege in Kuwait: A Survivor's Story*. Boston: Houghton Mifflin, 1991.

Randall, Jonathan. *Going All the Way: Christian Warlords, Israeli Adventurers and American Bunglers*. New York: Viking Press, 1983.

Rodinson, Maxime. *Israel and the Arabs*. Harmondsworth, England: Penguin Books, 1988.

Rubinstein, Danny. *The People of Nowhere: The Palestinian Vision of Home*. New York: Times Books, 1991.

Ruthven, Malise. *Islam in the World*. New York/ Harmondsworth, England: Penguin Books, 1985.

Safran, Nadav. *Israel: The Embattled Ally*. Cambridge, MA/London: Belknap Press of Harvard University Press, 1978.

Said, Edward. *The Question of Palestine*. London: Routledge & Kegan Paul, 1980/New York: Pantheon Books, 1981.

Sayigh, Rosemary. *Palestinians: From Peasants to Revolutionaries*. Atlantic Heights, NJ/London: Zed Press, 1979.

Seale, Patrick. *Asad: The Struggle for the Middle East*. London: I.B. Tauris, 1988/Berkeley: University of California, 1989.

Shaw, Ralph. *Kuwait*. London: Macmillan, 1976.

Shipler, David K. *Arab and Jew: Wounded Spirits in a Promised Land*. New York: Times Books, 1986.

Sifri, Micah, and Cerf, Christopher, eds. *The Gulf War Reader: History, Documents, Opinions*. New York: Times Books, 1991.

Stookey, Robert. *America and the Arab States: An Uneasy Encounter*. New York: John Wiley, 1975.

Tachau, Frank. *Turkey: The Politics of Authority, Democracy and Development*. New York: Praeger, 1984.

Taheri, Amir. *Newst of Spies: America's Journey to Disaster in Iran*. London: Century Hutchinson, 1988/ New York: Pantheon Books, 1989.

US News & World Report. *Triumph Without Victory: The Unreported History of the Persian Gulf War*. New York: Times Books, 1992.

Woodward, Bob. *The Commanders*. New York/London: Simon & Schuster, 1991.

Wright, Robin. *Sacred Rage: The Wrath of Militant Islam*. New York: Simon & Schuster, 1985/London: Andre Deutsch, 1986.

———. *In the Name of God: The Khomeini Decade*. New York: Simon & Schuster, 1990/London: Bloomsbury, 1990.

Yergin, Daniel. *Prize: The Epic Quest for Oil, Money & Power*. New York/London: Simon & Schuster, 1991.

INDEX

by Kay Banning